# More Praise for
## *Coaching Into Greatness*

"Kim George does a masterful job shattering the illusions that keep us from becoming our best selves. This smart, practical book will help you move from struggling with scarcity to living a life of abundance."

*—Daniel H. Pink*
*Author of A Whole New Mind*

"Einstein said that 'Things should be made as simple as possible, not simpler.' In this delightful book Kim George helps us bring clarity, wisdom, and optimal simplicity to our complex lives."

*—Michael J. Gelb*
*Author of Discover Your Genius and How to Think Like Leonardo Davinci*

"This is a wise and inspiring book full of wonderful stories and practical lessons you can apply as a coach—or to your own life."

*—Anita Sharpe, Co-Founding Editor and Chairman*
*Worthwhile Magazine, www.worthwhilemag.com*

"I love this book! Coaching into Greatness breaks new ground with the concept of Abundance Intelligence™. For the first time, we have a system that pinpoints where and how we're living in scarcity. By redefining abundance in tangible, practical terms, Kim George gives us a powerful roadmap for claiming the greatness that is already ours."

*—Dr. Joe Vitale*
*Author of way too many books to list here, including The Attractor Factor*
*www.mrfire.com*

"Amazing! This is what was missing in my coaching and in my life. Long before reading the final chapter, I was using the concepts with my clients and achieving incredible results."

*—Garry Schleifer, CPCC, President*
*ICF Toronto*

"Coaching into Greatness is a must-read for any business professional seeking to improve performance. In my experience, the most critical issue that sabotages entrepreneurs is having a 'scarcity' mindset instead of an 'abundance' mindset. With her clear examples and straightforward style, Kim George will help business professionals position themselves for success in an ever-changing world."

—*Mike Garrison, VP*
*The Referral Institute*®

"Business owners and leaders need Coaching into Greatness. If your team is not focused on the impact of scarcity on the bottom line, you are losing money, performance, productivity, and leadership. Coaching into Greatness is a must-read for all leaders and managers. Practical and doable, it will bring the concept of abundance alive within your business."

—*Jay Fulcher, CEO*
*Agile Software*

"Kim George challenges us to be our great selves, and sets forth a realistic path to that goal. What I found most useful was the distinction between conditioned patterns (that keep us bound to scarcity) and conscious patterns (that free us to move towards abundance)—these are powerful models to reframe how you see (and act upon) your life."

—*Michael Bungay Stanier*
*Author of Get Unstuck & Get Going . . . On the Stuff That Matters, and 2006*
*Canadian Coach of the Year*

"I love this book! Not only does Coaching into Greatness offer a new paradigm for the future of the coaching industry, it will teach any professional who's responsible for the success of a team how to lead it to greatness. Prepare yourself for some rather startling and marvelous results."

—*Michael Port*
*Author of Book Yourself Solid, The Fastest, Easiest, and Most Reliable System*
*for Getting More Clients Than You Can Handle*

"Kim George has created the ultimate guide to stripping away our illusions and maximizing our potential. Coaching into Greatness does a great job of helping us truly live our joy."

—*Suzanne Falter-Barns*
*Author of Living Your Joy*

"This book works for coaches and at the same time it coaches all of us with step-by-step ways to contact our immense greatness. I was especially impressed with how Kim gave practical recommendations for dealing with issues like control, caretaking, and finding ways to 'flow.' In doing so, she is giving us a handbook for our personal and spiritual evolution."

*—David Richo*
*Author of The Five Things We Cannot Change: And The Happiness We Find by Embracing Them*

"Kim George's four-step process is one of true greatness. Her simple and easy approach produces amazing results. Whether you're a coach, consultant, client, or manager, Coaching into Greatness gives you the tools to create abundance every day. Who wouldn't want that?"

*—Michelle Payne, Executive VP*
*Beyond Point B Consulting Group*

"This book is a jewel! Coaching into Greatness teaches how to break through all the illusions that have kept us bound from stepping into our greatness."

*—Yasmin Davidds*
*Author of Take Back Your Power: How to Reclaim It, Keep It, and Use It to Get What You Deserve*

"Today's smart clients want results they can measure. Coaching into Greatness will give you all the tools you need to serve your clients. Read this book and absorb its message. It gives you the pragmatic and real world insight you must have to bring your client's highest visions to life."

*—Richard l. Reardon, President*
*Re3R Business Development*

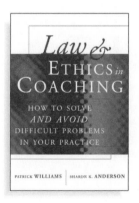

# Must-Have Resources
## for Coaches

**Getting Started in Personal
and Executive Coaching: How to Create
a Thriving Coaching Practice**
STEPHEN G. FAIRLEY AND CHRIS E. STOUT
0-471-42624-5 • $24.95

Packed with hundreds of proven strategies and techniques, *Getting Started in Personal and Executive Coaching* is a nuts-and-bolts guide covering all aspects of the coaching business with step-by-step instructions and real-world illustrations that prepare you for every phase of starting your own coaching practice.

**Foundations of Coaching: The Science
Behind the New Art of Coaching**
DAVID ROCK
0-471-74585-5 • $55.00

*Foundations of Coaching* integrates discussion of neuroscience, psychology, anthropology, organizational theory, and more into a fully realized, sophisticated understanding of what coaching is—while also creating a practical, hands-on template for real-world coaching practice.

**Evidence Based Coaching Handbook:
Putting Best Practices to Work for Your Clients**
DIANNE R. STOBER AND ANTHONY M. GRANT
0-471-72086-0 • $44.95

Drawn from the realms of psychology, business, and other disciplines, this practical handbook enables you to understand and apply established and proven behavioral theories. *Evidence Based Coaching Handbook* provides new ways to help your client as well as an understanding of how behavioral science applies to coaching as a change process.

**Coach U's Essential Coaching Tools:
Your Complete Practice Resource**
COACH U, INC.
0-471-71172-1 • $50.00

*Coach U's Essential Coaching Tools* is a handy book and CD package that includes both self- and client-assessment tools and worksheets/exercises to aid you in working effectively with your clients, as well as proven marketing and business development materials.

### WILEY
Now you know.

To order, call 1-877-762-2974 or online at www.wiley.com/psychology.
Also available from amazon.com, bn.com, and other fine booksellers.

# COACHING INTO
# GREATNESS

## 4 STEPS TO SUCCESS IN
## BUSINESS AND LIFE

**Kim George, B.S.**

**WILEY**

John Wiley & Sons, Inc.

Published by John Wiley & Sons, Inc., Hoboken, New Jersey.

Published simultaneously in Canada.

For general information on our other products and services or for technical support, please contact our Customer Care Department within the United States at (800) 762–2974, outside the United States at (317) 572–3993 or fax (317) 572–4002.

Wiley also publishes its books in a variety of electronic formats. Some content that appears in print may not be available in electronic books. For more information about Wiley products, visit our web site at www.wiley.com.

This book has been manufactured from a high-yield thermomechanical pulp, using fewer trees per ton of paper than traditional chemical pulping methods, resulting in a lighter stock that wields a better bulk/weight ratio. A totally chlorine-free process using oxygen and hydrogen-peroxide is applied to whiten the paper.

*Library of Congress Cataloging-in-Publication Data:*

George, Kim.
   Coaching into greatness : 4 steps to success in business and life / by
Kim George.
      p. cm.
   ISBN-13: 978-0-471-78533-0 (cloth)
   ISBN-10: 0-471-78533-4 (cloth)
  1. Success—Psychological aspects. 2. Success in business. I. Title.
   BF637.S8G395 2006
   158—dc22                                       2005037204

Printed in the United States of America.

10 9 8 7 6 5 4 3 2 1

# Contents

*Foreword*                                          *xi*

*Acknowledgments*                                   *xv*

*Introduction*                                       *1*

1. A New Way of Being                               13

2. Why Greatness?                                   29

3. Forgetting Who You Are                           39

4. Remembering Who You Are                          49

5. The Illusion of Not Enough                       59

6. The Illusion of Comparisons                      83

7. The Illusion of Struggle                        109

8. The Illusion of Control                         135

9. The Illusion of Time                            161

10. The Illusion of Hope                           185

11. The Illusion of Certainty                      211

12. Creating Abundance Intelligence™               235

*Appendix: The AQ System at a Glance*              245

*Recommended Reading*                              247

# CONTENTS

*Glossary*                                                              249

*About the Author*                                                      257

*Interested in Learning More about Abundance Intelligence^{TM}?*        259

*Index*                                                                 261

# Foreword

Kim George brings the whole of her passionate self to these pages on your behalf. She speaks with the voice of an abundant heart. In doing so, she is modeling the lessons she wishes to teach—and formidable and timely lessons they are.

Our illusions of separateness have resulted in our long history of self-interest, which in turn has produced the karma we are experiencing today. As a result, in many places and through many people, our world demonstrates daily the triumph of the personality over the soul. The personality is naturally guided by scarcity, and consequently, for the personality, there is never enough. The soul, on the other hand, is guided by abundance, and consequently, the soul can never give enough. Think of the people you know—they probably fall into two categories: personalities who keep taking because they are gripped by scarcity, on the one hand, and souls who are truly free, in the way which Kim has described, on the other, because they are firmly rooted in a generosity of spirit—an abundance mentality. Sometimes it seems the need of the personality to take (because there is never enough for the scarcity-minded personality) has eclipsed the desire of the soul to give. This has long been the general pattern of what I have referred to elsewhere as "the old story" of unenlightened business, political, religious, family, and community relationships. In our Western culture, we are encouraged from our earliest years to see the glass as half-empty.

There is a Middle Eastern legend that tells of a merchant's servant in Baghdad who came to his master one day in great consternation.

"Master," he cried, "Someone bumped into me in the crowded market place this morning. When I turned around I saw it was Death. I caught his eye and he gave me such a strange and terrifying look that I am now in fear of my life. Master, please lend me your horse so that I may flee . . . with your help I can be far away in Samarra by nightfall."

The merchant was a generous man, and, leading the servant to one of his fine horses, he sent him away. Later, the merchant was strolling through the market place where he noticed Death standing in the crowd.

"Why did you frighten my servant this morning and give him such a threatening stare?"

"I did not threaten him," said Death. "It was a look of surprise . . . I was astounded to see a man this morning in Baghdad when I have an appointment with him tonight in Samarra."

What we get is often what we expect, so it makes sense to reframe our expectations in order to set the intentionality for better outcomes. Reframing how we view life will not be easy for most of us—we have a long history of scarcity thinking ingrained in our hearts and minds. Indeed, our entire Western culture is built on such thinking—from consumerism, marketing, business, politics, religion, healthcare, education, and even our friendships and partnerships.

But we are intelligent beings, capable of changing—*if we want to*—and that is the hard part. It's like dieting: We know exactly what to do—no lessons are required. We just can't bring ourselves to *actually do it*.

But what kind of world might we create and embrace if we became soulful ambassadors of abundance, sharing this generosity of spirit and service within every one of our communities? This means contributing something much bigger than money or material things, of course. It means contributing something much more valuable: our time, energy, will, intellect, love, collaboration, and spirit. This commitment must rest on partnership, not competition, on a philosophy of abundance, not scarcity. It must be built on the principle of circulation, allowing the spiritual, intellectual, material, and financial resources to circulate freely between our hearts and those of others.

The Chinese conception of illness—or wellness and health, as they would prefer to describe it—is an imbalance of energy—too much in one place and not enough in another—and it is a perfect example of what happens when we reframe this way. The Western outlook based on scarcity produces inferior wellness rates in our respective societies. Is there a "Sick Kids Hospital" in your town? Or is it called a Children's Wellness Center? We are suffering from too much negative energy (scarcity thinking) within our communities in general and our corporate world in particular. Wellness (a word that originates from the root *wholeness*) flows from abundance — exactly what we need in our lives to become and remain well and whole.

And Kim George has created a path, brilliantly lit, that can guide us to abundance.

*Lance Secretan*
Author of *ONE: The Art and Practice of Conscious Leadership*

# Acknowledgments

*Each person represents a world in us, a world possibly not born until they arrive, and it is only by this meeting that a new world is born.*

ANAIS NIN

To Sid Smith, working with you has made such a difference in my experience of creating this book. You have my complete admiration and appreciation! To my agent, Paul Bassis, your support and guidance have meant the world to me. To my editor, David Bernstein, thank you for helping me bring the concept of AQ to the world. Your amazing ability to create a vision for this work and to really see me for who I am is very special.

To all the amazing abundant minds featured in this book: Susan Annunzio, Yasmin Davidds, Korrahn Droku, Keith Ferrazzi, Mike Garrison, Julia Butterfly Hill, Mike Macedonio, Dr. Ivan Misner, Richard Reardon, Eric Rice, and Joe Vitale. The world is a better place because of who you all are, and I am a better person for knowing you.

To Lance Secretan—you are an inspiration, a true leader, and a visionary. I am honored to call you my friend. To my dear friend Stephen Fairley—without your persistent (and sometimes annoying!) question, "Kim, when are you going to write a book?" this dream would not be a reality. Thanks for kicking my butt when I needed it most!

To Elizabeth Tull, you have been my cheerleader, my friend, and my sounding board. You have so much to give the world. To Garry Schleifer, Jennifer Quade, and Carol Zimmerman, thank you for your confidence, unwavering support, and your many contributions. I am honored to have you be the AQ Pioneers! To Brandi, Jule, and Pawn, thank you for being the first to work with the Living into Greatness material. By trusting me and fully embracing uncertainty, you have shown up abundantly and brought this work further than where it could have gone without you.

To Andrea Shea Hudson, you are my champion and my confidant, my best friend. To Dave Buck, Bea Fields, Linda Hanan, Jane Johnson, Ellie Pope, Marta Reily, and Gail Stone—the original branding team! We have grown and evolved together. I am blessed to know you. You have given me so much, not just in your friendship, but in your creativity, encouragement, and by living your personal examples. To Mary Gallagher and Colleen Schaefgen—the two of you are beautiful expressions of abundance. Thank you for your wisdom, your insight, and for helping me to be who I am. To MaryAnn, you have taught me so much. Through your eyes I see the beauty of life. To Ruth Ann Harnisch, thank you for your insight, for who you are being in the world, and for sharing my love of trees. To Kimberly Fulcher, you are a force of nature! Thank you for being a spiritual change agent in my life. To the other members of the Bottom Line Visionaries, Carol Kauffman, Donna Steinhorn, Dianne Stober, and Niki Vettel, thank you for supporting me and believing in my greatness. To Dovid Grossman, you've always made my heart smile—I just wish I could hug you! And to Chris Hutchinson, you are such a special person. I love your sensitivity and openness and cherish our friendship.

To all my clients, past and present, thank you for your trust, for your honesty, and for the honor of being your coach. You are an integral part of this book. To the members of the Springfield BNI chapter, you have been essential to my success as a coach. You are my extended family. To all the members of my R&D team, you have been with me from the beginning. Your feedback, suggestions, and probing questions have brought this material so much farther than anything I could have accomplished on my own.

To Earl, Newton, Crisco, Mr. Kitty, Spanky, Horshack, Mr. Bird, and Heidi: You have been my true companions. Thank you for reminding me what life is really about.

To my husband, Rob, thank you for loving me for who I am. I will always love you for the lessons you have taught me about myself.

To my Dad—I know that some of what I have shared in this book may not be easy for you to read. I want you to know that I truly love you and have no regrets about my life. You have helped me be who I am and that is both a gift and a blessing. I treasure our time together.

To my Mom—thank you for writing this book. Thank you for touching my life in so many profound ways. In life and in death, you have shaped me, brought out the best in me, and most of all, loved me. I can still hear you laugh, and that is a beautiful thing.

# Introduction

Life is like a giant Slip N' Slide®. When it's dry, sliding on it will hurt like hell. Add a little water, and soon everyone is slipping, sliding, and having a great time. As a coach, I know that my job is to assist my clients in living the best lives possible for them. I notice how often they're trying to move through life as if they've forgotten to add water to their personal Slip N' Slide®. They screech and grind before coming to a painful stop. Everything seems to be a struggle. Then, as if guided by some unseen force, they open the spigot; the water flows, and so do they. Miraculously, it all seems so easy.

This book is, ultimately, about turning on the tap. Most people sleep-walk through life, hoping they'll somehow make it to the finish line. Life is hard, with one letdown after another. Then, there are those who have figured out some secret formula that allows them to glide from one success to another. I've coached some of these people and seen many in my everyday experiences. So have you. As a coach, manager, consultant, office worker, construction boss, or whatever, you have most definitely witnessed people who fit both ends of the spectrum.

I refer to these two sides of the spectrum as living in scarcity and living in abundance. I admit that people get a little edgy when I start talking about scarcity and abundance. So much has been written in the past 10 to 15 years about abundance, abundance thinking, or having an abundance mentality that it's almost become cliché to talk about it.

Cliché or not, it's a conversation that must be had. I see far too many people living in scarcity to remain on the sidelines about the subject. In fact, it's been the major focal point of my life for the past several years. This book is not the culmination of my investigations and work with scarcity and abundance. Rather, it is an evolution of my work.

Throughout, you'll read much about my personal history. I wasn't always a published author, and I certainly didn't grow up with a silver spoon in my mouth. And, I didn't start out as a coach. I share with you my story, and the stories of successful people you know and don't know, simply as an illustration of what can happen when you add a little water to your Slip N' Slide®. As you'll see, all manner of assistance comes to the forefront, often faster and in greater quantities than you ever thought possible.

My decision to become a coach didn't come from a lifetime of hoping for the right job to come along. It was a whim — a lark, and an intuitive leap of faith into a completely unknown universe for which I felt wholly inadequate. The evolution that led to the writing of this book was much the same process, albeit much more conscious as time went on.

I used to believe that good things would never come my way. I was never "enough" — good enough, smart enough, talented enough, knowledgeable enough. This belief grew out of a series of events in my teenage years. After I lost my mother to cancer when I was 15 and my dad subsequently married a practicing alcoholic, I spent my senior year attending three different high schools. I became very practiced in comparing myself to others (usually negatively), and to the "fact" that struggle was a natural part of life. I also felt very alone.

Being human, I naturally adapted to the events of my life by creating habits and beliefs that made sense of my world. As an adult these same habits and beliefs were holding me back from doing what I wanted to do or having the life I wanted to have. I had developed an innate ability for surviving. But thriving? That was out of the question. Self-limiting habits create a limited life, and I wanted much, much more.

As you know, this quiet life of just getting by is a common theme played out by many. I changed my life dramatically by closely following through with every step outlined in this book. My work resulted in the well-defined process I've used to help hundreds leap from their safe, but stagnant lives, and without struggling, do the thing they most want to do.

I don't care what it is that you, your clients, your colleagues, or your employees want to do. The size, scope, or relative importance of that thing anyone wants to do is irrelevant. What is important is that they do it, and not "someday," but now. I didn't have a minute to spare.

You don't, either.

## PROFILES IN GREATNESS

Throughout this book, you will read the stories of people whom I consider to be Living into their Greatness. "Living into Greatness" is an expression I coined to describe the process of growing into our capacity. Each of us, I believe, is born great. We have within us the blueprint for our unique greatness. Most people run fast and hard away from their greatness. I propose that it is entirely reasonable for each of us to turn back, face our greatness full on, and live into that greatness daily and consistently.

These stories of Living into Greatness are both inspirational and instructive. These aren't rock stars or presidents of nations. These are ordinary people like you and me who simply and purely do what they *can* do, as best they can do it in the moment. Keith Ferrazzi, for example, author of the best-selling book, *Never Eat Alone*, and who has been called one of the most connected people on the planet, grew up very poor as the son of an often out-of-work steelworker.

How does one man who grew up in poverty now see life from such an abundant perspective? For one, he has an abundant belief system. He defines abundance as the belief that "creativity begets more creativity, money begets more money, knowledge begets more knowledge, more friends beget more friends, success begets even more success. And most important, giving begets giving."

Giving is at the heart of this book. Ferrazzi has built his life and his business around his relationships and the idea that "Relationships are like muscles—the more you work them, the bigger and stronger they become." He has what he and I call an abundant attitude about relationships. In *Never Eat Alone*, he shares the story of when he wanted to get into the entertainment industry. He'd already build a successful career by freely helping others, not because he expected anything in return, but because he understood clearly that giving always returns to the giver in greater numbers.

He asked around and was introduced to a man named David who was a smart entrepreneur doing creative deals in Hollywood. Keith asked David if he could be referred to anyone who might help him break into the business. David responded that he did know a senior executive at Paramount, but that he wouldn't give Keith her contact information.

Keith was shocked. David's reply was, "I can't. Keith, here's the situation. It's likely that at some point I'm going to need something from this person or want to ask a personal favor. And, I'm just not interested in using the equity that I have with this individual on you, or anyone else, for that matter. I need to save that for myself. I'm sorry. I hope you understand."

Keith didn't, and neither do I. This is what I call living a scarce life, or living with a scarcity mentality. In my experience, this kind of thinking never works well in the long term. People who live this kind of life live it safely but always yearn for more. They live in what I call a "satin-lined coffin." It's nice, comfortable, and often pretty, but it's still a coffin. They invariably end up with less than they wanted, yet they almost never take personal responsibility for the life they built.

## COACHING INTO GREATNESS

When I talk about scarcity and abundance, I refer to them as states of mind, rather than as wealth or lack of wealth. The person who thinks in terms of scarcity, for example, will say good things never last and there's never enough to go around. People with a scarcity mentality see the glass as half-empty. They are typically motivated by fear, by a lack of something, by a void.

Abundance, on the other hand, is the knowing that you already have everything you need. People with an abundant mentality see the glass as overflowing. They are not motivated by fear but are inspired and pulled forward by an internal conviction that they are on the path meant for them. Abundant people are more than just positive thinkers; they are attraction in action. They accept that life is not always easy and doesn't always follow the straight and convenient path. They let life unfold through them, instead of putting their life into a box of expectations with a pretty red bow on the top. Abundant people simply fall in love with whom and where they are and keep falling in love every single day.

The primary purpose of this book is to provide you with a clear, understandable, and concise process you can apply to your life and the lives of your coaching clients or employees. The intention is to move from scarcity to abundant thinking. It will help you identify scarcity thinking and understand that these are merely illusions or figments of one's imagination caused by past events, circumstances, or experiences. With this awareness, you will learn that you already have everything you need to do the thing you want to do. Put in another way that you'll read repeatedly throughout the book, you will do whatever it is you *can* do.

Greatness is not dependent on anything; greatness simply is. You don't need a single thing more. Most people spend their lives sleepwalking—endlessly searching for the pill, person, information, motivation, or circumstances that will enable them to become great.

I'm here to tell you one thing—*you, and everyone with whom you work are already great.*

What would it mean for you as a leader, coach, or teacher if you could embrace the belief that everyone is already great, that they could put an end to tireless striving and searching, and finally be okay with who they are—right now? What would you create? What possibilities would the people with whom you work say yes to?

As you read the following summary of the seven illusions, practice identifying the attributes of the illusions in yourself and those with whom you work. Is one person hoping for something better, but unable to take action toward it? Is life a constant struggle for another person? As you'll learn, awareness is the first step, and as you improve your ability to detect these illusions in yourself and others, you'll be in a better position to help them improve their awareness, and subsequently take progressively productive action. This is perhaps the greatest gift you can ever give anyone.

Action is the key to Living into Greatness. Without it, all you have are the seven illusions and the satin-lined coffin. Not a pretty picture, is it? If we visualize being buried alive, we're filled with fear and panic, and yet, many people die a little each day, slowly suffocating from unfulfilled dreams and unexpressed desires. However, there is a way to wake up the sleepwalker, and it starts with a simple question. The most powerful question you can ask yourself or anyone else is, "Are you doing what you *can* do today?" Learn to actively apply the four-step process outlined in each chapter. As you do so, you will reach new awareness of scarcity thinking.

As you work the process, remember my favorite phrase: "Struggle is strictly overrated!"

## THE FOUR-STEP *LIVING INTO GREATNESS* PROCESS

Just as actions are critical to Living into Greatness, actions outside of a clear, easily replicated process keep you busy but won't get you anywhere. The four-step process I devised is a never-ending process. It is cyclical, flowing naturally like the four seasons of nature. The process begins with awareness but doesn't simply end when one has established a new behavior. Through authentic action a new and deeper awareness is gained. It's quite a lot of fun once you get into the rhythm and practice of the process! Teach those with whom you work (coaching or consulting clients, employees, etc.) these four steps, and encourage them to practice the steps daily. Better yet, *you* practice the four steps daily, demonstrate success in your own life, and your clients will gladly follow.

The four steps are:

1. *Awareness.* Gain an awareness of where and how a particular illusion is showing up in your life.
2. *Acceptance.* Calmly accept and appreciate what's here now. I love what Thomas Leonard frequently said: "The present is perfect!"
3. *Consistent action.* Once you are aware of the illusion and can accept that the present is indeed perfect, decide what action(s) to take to live into true greatness. Then, incorporate these new actions into your life consistently. It takes time to break old habits.
4. *Authenticity.* Living into Greatness means showing up as one's authentic self. This often takes practice (consistent action) and will certainly give rise to new levels of awareness, starting the cycle all over again!

Within each chapter on the seven illusions, you will be provided one key consistent action step that I have found to be the most helpful in shifting from living in the illusion to Living into Greatness. You may, of course, add as many other actions as you feel are necessary for your clients. The goal should be consistency and authenticity as new levels of awareness are gained and acceptance of the present moment is more solidified.

## A SUMMARY OF THE SEVEN ILLUSIONS

These seven illusions lock people into a scarcity mentality, keeping them from doing the very thing they can do. As an individual dissolves each illusion, his or her entire world opens with new opportunities and fresh ideas. *She simply realizes she's been who she was meant to be all along.* She's lighter, freer, and less encumbered by old beliefs or attitudes. Each of the following seven chapters will provide a more detailed explanation and will include:

- How the illusion typically shows up.
- Patterns of conditioning associated with the illusion.
- Common core beliefs associated with the illusion.
- Common fears associated with the illusion.
- Personal examples from my life and client case studies.
- How to apply the four-step process that will move anyone past the illusion.
- Profiles of living in greatness—stories of individuals who embody mastery of this illusion, including everyday heroes like you and me who are ordinary people Living into their Greatness in extraordinary ways.

THE ILLUSIONS

### 1. The Illusion of Not Enough

Does your coaching client or employee tell you he needs one more piece of information before he can make a decision? Perhaps he didn't know enough, or lacked experience to take the next, potentially risky step. The Illusion of Not Enough is the feeling that one needs more, or has to have his or her act together before taking action. It is at the root of procrastination and is the greatest inhibitor to taking that first big step. The action step for this chapter is to "Stop searching, and start doing."

### 2. The Illusion of Comparisons

When we're comparing ourselves to another, we are not in action. A client who avoids taking action because she doesn't "measure up" is falling prey to this illusion. A chicken may look huge from the perspective of a small bug. That same chicken is tiny from the viewpoint of a giraffe. We're taught to think comparatively, always measuring ourselves against another's standards or views. We project our beliefs onto others, and take on others' limiting beliefs without objection. Dissolving this illusion is critical to Living into Greatness. The action step for this chapter is to "Act intuitively."

### 3. The Illusion of Struggle

Struggle is an illusion that permeates our society to the extent that it has become a virtue. Personally, I feel that struggle is strictly overrated. Struggle isn't hard work, it's working hard ineffectively. My colleagues know I work 10 to 12 hours a day, and that I work hard. But, none of my work is a struggle, although this illusion more than any other was my greatest nemesis. Once your clients let go of struggle all life begins to flow more easily. It's then they find themselves doing that thing they most want to do. The theme for this chapter is, "Struggle is strictly overrated." The action step is to "Replicate simplicity."

### 4. The Illusion of Control

We're always looking outside ourselves for something better. We'll take action, or not, based on our perceived control of the outcome. Things don't always work out the way we want, and the greatest risk is not taking any risk at all. The Illusion of Control keeps us in jobs we don't want, relationships that don't work, and stuck wondering what life would have been like "if only . . . ." Control is different from responsibility and decision. We decide, we act, and then, we take responsibility for our actions. Control is the illusion that certain decisions or actions will always produce certain results; or more importantly that by doing the same thing, we'll somehow get different results. The action step for this chapter is to "Embrace synchronicity."

### 5. The Illusion of Time

Most people waste valuable energy regretting past mistakes or looking toward the future to feel better about today. We have to ask ourselves if our worries or anxieties have any factual basis in the present moment. The Illusion of Time keeps us disconnected from our intuition and stuck thinking about regrets, misgivings, or wistful longings. It is an illusion where true happiness and fulfillment always seems to be in the future or the past. The action step for this chapter is to act, "Not how, but *when*."

### 6. The Illusion of Hope

The client says, "I hope things will improve some day," or "I hope I get a raise." Hope is the dark side of positive thinking—it doesn't require any action and rarely results in the desired outcome. People who hope expect something without working for it and get upset when someone else receives something they deserved. When this expectation becomes an entitlement—something your client feels she deserves; or it dissolves into frustration, loneliness, or even anger, she risks becoming stuck in the Illusion of Hope. Hope creates feelings of disconnection and frustration. To move past this illusion and do that thing one wants to do, one must learn to make failure one's friend. The action step for this chapter is to "Think positively and *act* accordingly."

## 7. The Illusion of Certainty

Do you fail to take progressive or positive action because you feel safe in your current job? Is a coaching client avoiding marketing his business because he's afraid of being rejected? Creating certainty isn't about changing one's circumstances, but about changing oneself. Circumstances will change when you change. The Illusion of Certainty is that certain level of comfort we feel when our current situation is "good enough." We feel safe within the satin-lined coffin. What's outside is the unknown that represents both great opportunity and tremendous risk. The Illusion of Certainty keeps us from the opportunities because we'd rather be safe than take risks. However, circumstances can change in a heartbeat and this supposed safety may disappear. Through the Illusion of Certainty the only light one sees is red—the red stop light. The action step for this chapter is to "Risk life, and live into greatness."

## PUTTING GREATNESS INTO MOTION

You can't and won't Live into your Greatness just by understanding the seven illusions. Imagine trying to ski without ever strapping on the skis! I've organized this book so that you can create a productive, positive daily practice of Living and Coaching into Greatness, just as you would practice skiing, singing, or playing a guitar.

The action steps are absolutely essential to obtaining any positive results from this book. Each illusion has an associated action step; and you can create your own action steps based on your intimate knowledge of your clients and from your personal experience with the four-step process in your life. The four-step process is the same for every illusion: awareness; acceptance; consistent action; and authenticity. Your clients will resonate or connect with some illusions more than others.

Have them start with those to which they feel most drawn, exercising their intuitive powers.

This four-step process is without a doubt the best way I've found to dismantle the illusions and live into greatness.

Begin exactly from where you are today. After all, that's the only place a person can begin, right?

## CHANGING MY CIRCUMSTANCES BY CHANGING MYSELF

As I explored and decided to dissolve each of the seven illusions in my life, new opportunities "miraculously" appeared. I've discovered the true power of synchronicity and I'll never go back to my old hiding places!

In the fall of 2002, I was accepted into a program to create a brand image for my business led by one of the top coaches in the industry. It was here that the hidden gifts offered through past experiences were revealed. I realized how these experiences had given me a high degree of empathy, compassion, strength, and leadership ability. Once I lifted some of the illusions, I began to see myself as a leader.

It was through consistent action that my new thoughts and beliefs about myself began to manifest in physical form. I was challenged to show up in the world, not as the timid person I thought I was, but as the independent and bold person I really am. Struggle isn't necessarily easy to release, but I made every effort to set boundaries and communicate differently.

Again, through synchronistic events, I moved up through the ranks of coaching quickly, establishing respected leadership roles and forming many lasting friendships and relationships. I've learned to see every event as a new opportunity. Everyone I've met along the way has become a friend in some way. I have lost my fear of asking for what I want. I am not afraid to seek and get interviews with amazing, well-known people. I feel that no person is outside my reach, and many of these amazing people were interviewed for this book. I have also created strategic alliances with people and organizations I've long admired. Most importantly, *I have stopped waiting for someone to figure out my greatness.* Instead, I have found ways to live into that every day by continually stretching myself, asking questions, examining my fears, and building a supportive environment.

Finally, this book uses a coaching approach in which service plays a major role. Regardless of your connection to those you're trying to help, you are in their service as a guide, mentor, coach, and leader. I refer to you as the coach and those with whom you work as your clients or coachees as a matter of convenience, but also because you are indeed a coach. You might add water to the Slip N' Slide® or help them get the hose or find the faucet. You are an active participant in their process, and as such, you have as much responsibility to learn and grow as they. You are the coach, just as you are a student. As you read this book and begin applying the principles and practices to your work, remember this key phrase: Struggle is strictly overrated!

## Now It's Your Turn

Everyone has the capability to succeed. As you'll discover by reading the profiles of those who are truly Living into their Greatness, one's current circumstances are irrelevant. Each of these individuals has overcome significant odds simply by refusing to live in illusion and by taking persistent and consistent action. They decided they would, and could, do that thing they wanted to do, and they let nothing stop them. One of my friends and colleagues, Dr. Ivan Misner, who is interviewed in this book, defines success as "the uncommon application of common knowledge." The purpose of this book is to help you uncommonly apply the knowledge that you and your clients are already great.

Decide now that you will no longer just get by in life. Choose to be fully alive and fully engaged in Living into Greatness!

## CHAPTER ONE

# A New Way of Being

*You were born with potential.*

*You were born with goodness and trust.*

*You were born with ideals and dreams.*

*You were born with greatness.*

*You were born with wings.*

*You are not meant for crawling, so don't.*

*You have wings.*

*Learn to use them and fly.*

RUMI

We're built for great things. We naturally want to be a part of and contribute to greatness. It's who we are.

I've had my share of challenges, heartbreaks, and other assorted "human moments." You'll get a glimpse of these throughout the book. It's not that my life is better, worse, or different from yours or the people you coach and work with. That's exactly the point. We all have ups and downs, ins and outs. That's life. It's how we face what happens in our lives that is compelling. In the last few years, I feel like I've come out of a deep sleep, like I've finally understood the point of a movie I've watched over and over for many years.

Here's the interesting part: Even though I'm doing things I've never done, *I feel more like myself than I have ever felt before.*

Truly being alive is the purest intention of this book. As I mentioned in the Introduction, you'll hear me repeat two phrases: *Doing What You Can Do,* and *Living into your Greatness.* When I talk about Living or Coaching into Greatness, I'm referring to the aliveness that happens when we're actively participating in life as our true selves. We've stepped out of the satin-lined coffin, broken the shackles of the illusion that we're anything other than great, and we're embracing every little bit that life has to offer. It's an exhilarating feeling! It's when we do exactly what we *can* do, in spite of any overwhelming odds or evidence to the contrary.

How about you? Are you alive? I mean really alive? Vibrantly, boldly alive? Or are you going through the motions, reacting to life as it happens—simply existing? I'm alive, you say, I'm breathing, aren't I? I have a good job and a family with 2.5 kids and a house. I manage to golf once a week.

But are you *alive?* Are you doing what you *can* or want to do? Are you experiencing the fullness of life? Are you Living into your Greatness? Do you even have an idea what it might mean to Live into your Greatness?

If you can proudly and boldly answer, "Yes! I am living an amazing life and living into my greatness more every day," then hooray for you! This book should give you the perfect tools to get out there and help others live into their greatness.

The truth is that we're all learning all the time. I'm learning and living a little more into my greatness as I write and revise this book. As you read these words you can rest assured that I'm living my life more as me than I was when I started the book. I've chosen to do what I *can* do in spite of all the little voices from the past that wanted me to quit.

## HOW YOU SHOW UP IN LIFE IS WHAT IS MOST IMPORTANT

> *You must first be who you really are, then, do what you need to do, in order to have what you want.*
>
> MARGARET YOUNG

We live in a universe of opposites: up—down; in—out; good—bad. We don't pay a lot of attention to the opposites, but we should. Everything is a choice. We can go up, or we can go down; in or out. We see things as good or bad. Every choice we make is based on some—often long-held— belief. These choices define how we show up in life, and whether we're living a life of scarcity or a life of abundance. Like a teeter-totter, we're always moving from one side to the other, more often than not getting thoroughly stuck on our least favorite side!

We show up in life according to our beliefs. If we think that getting laid off from a job is bad news, then we show up depressed or angry. If we think the layoff is good news, we'll show up excited and relieved. It's the same job, and the same loss. The only thing that makes the difference is our perception of what is happening, and this perception is based on the lens through which we view the world. The amazing thing that many people don't get is that *how you show up in business is directly proportional to how you show up in life.* Your beliefs, perceptions, assumptions, and attitude about life directly impact your career and the way you do business.

Many label this the "soft side" of business and discount the value of such a discussion. And yet, despite all our speeches and charades and hard work, at the end of the day, we can't get away from ourselves. Hard as we try, we can't get out of our own skins. We bring our personal problems to work and we bring our work problems home.

Similarly, whether you see life as abundant and rich or scarce and threatening impacts how you show up in business and in life. The people you coach or work with choose abundance or choose scarcity, and these choices create the results they see every day. In business, many like to keep the personal out of the boardroom, but try as we might, we are not machines. At some point, who we are (or who we are trying to be) surfaces—either causing problems or causing celebration.

This book is about helping you, your coaching clients, or your employees remember who they are so that they can live lives of celebration and can have businesses of celebration. This book is an experience—it's more about unlearning and remembering than learning and discovering. And at the center of this unlearning and rediscovery is the *choice* of abundance or scarcity.

## THE OLD WAY OF THINKING—THE TRUTH ABOUT SCARCITY

> *To live is the rarest thing in the world. Most people exist, that is all.*
>
> OSCAR WILDE

Scarcity is the currency of our times. We hear about everything that isn't working, the devastation, the deception, and the destruction. It seems the entire world population is bent on getting what they can from a limited supply. We're so focused on what we don't have that we think other people have, that we're driven to do more and become more. And yet, we're told that anything we want is just a swipe of a charge card away. Three hundred different kinds of toothpaste — there's something for everyone. Take out that loan, buy that lottery ticket. Which is it? Is the world richly abundant, or limited and scarce?

The topic of scarcity usually revolves around discussions about limited resources — air, water, minerals, oil, money, and the like. It's all about physical limitations and physical scarcity. We all know that the best way to jack prices up for a new and popular product is to create a limited supply. "Act now or you'll miss out!" Society, and especially modern culture, has always focused on *external* scarcity — the scarcity of things, or even of ideas.

In his landmark book, *The 7 Habits of Highly Effective People*, Stephen Covey introduced the idea of scarcity mentality, which took the concept of scarcity from our outside environment to an inner environment. In this context, Covey defines a scarcity mentality to be a belief that the pie of life is only so big and there isn't enough of it to go around.

I'm taking this concept of scarcity a step further. I'm going to push the edge and challenge your beliefs about scarcity. Saying you'll simply drop your scarcity mentality and take on new habits is like saying you'll avoid mosquito bites by pretending mosquitoes don't exist. Scarcity mentality exists in some form in all of us. What's important is understanding how this way of thinking keeps people stuck in business and life, and then changing the thinking by changing what goes on *inside the person*, not *outside*.

At its core, scarcity is a deeply internal matter. When we shift the focus from our environment to ourselves, we can see that the most pervasive form of scarcity in our world today exists inside each of us.

## SCARCITY IS A MINDSET

Scarcity isn't something out there. It isn't the natural law or state of the environment or anything else external. It's a state of mind. *Scarcity is human-made*. It is not thrust upon us; it is created and perpetuated by our unwillingness to be who we are. Is this a harsh statement? It's harsh only if someone is under the illusion that he or she is not enough, which is the vast majority of the educated and advanced civilized culture. We're not as thin as the latest model, as smart as that chess champion, or as visionary as Bill Gates. As long as who we are is defined by external conditions, we can never be fulfilled. It's like jumping on a Slip 'N Slide® without the water. Ouch.

Scarcity happens inside. *Scarcity is trying to rearrange the world so that it aligns with the way you think it should be.* Scarcity isn't a reality; it's a perception. One person's sparse existence is another's abundant existence. Someone who's filled with a scarcity mentality tries to be like someone else. He actually resists being himself. In a greater sense, he resists life itself that wants to unfold gracefully through him. In short, he resists his own greatness because he can't see it. He thinks all that is available to him is what he can see. He *thinks* in terms of lack or scarcity.

*The ultimate form of scarcity is resisting who you are.*

A scarcity mindset is the greatest source of unhappiness in our world today. It happens when you *focus on what you perceive you don't have,* instead of embracing what you do have. Scarcity boxes us in and defines us according to external factors.

## THE SCARCITY MINDSET KEEPS PEOPLE RESISTING WHO THEY ARE

Scarcity is based on the dangerous assumption that we can find the answers to who we are outside of ourselves. We must create new definitions. As long as we use external definitions, we will never be fulfilled; we will remain feeling empty.

When we are in scarcity we are conformists. Scarcity makes us sleepwalk through life, comparing ourselves to the world around us and trying to achieve goals and levels of performance based on outside norms, standards, and ideals. Many people live on the surface of life. I call these people surface dwellers. It's easier to go along with or try to be like everyone else, fitting in, being safe, and never rocking the boat. Earl Nightingale used to say that most people sleepwalk through life, playing it safe and hoping that they get to the other end alive. That's not living, and this isn't a dress rehearsal!

We pay the price of just getting by. It puts us into a satin-lined coffin that feels safe and comfortable, while inside we're dying a little every day. Ultimately, a scarcity mentality leaves us living someone else's life and resisting being ourselves.

As bleak as this seems, we can investigate, understand, and change a scarcity mentality. We're taught scarcity from the time we're infants, so it's no wonder scarcity thinking is so common. After all, "money doesn't grow on trees," does it?

We now have a process for moving people out of a scarcity mindset. Based on my work with hundreds of business owners and my own personal experiences, I've identified seven illusions that are evidence of a scarcity mindset. Most people fall in and out of these sources of scarcity throughout their lives. The illusions are like a fog that very slowly settles over us. Before long, the darkened view ahead seems normal. We forget that only a few feet above us is clear sky. Some people walk their entire lives in this fog, never questioning the source or nature of the fog, and rarely risking the safety of the fog to poke their heads out, if even for a moment. The beauty of this process is that it's simple, and it works.

Is a scarcity mentality really that big a deal? You bet! I think it's the greatest disease of our times. These seven illusions keep us thinking in terms of scarcity, and scarcity thinking destroys us from the inside out. We die a thousands deaths every day in our minds, hearts, and spirits, and we can't help but be affected physically. I wouldn't be surprised if someday scientists discover that scarcity thinking is a root cause of major physical diseases.

Each of the illusions is an example of resisting what is. This will make more sense as you read about each illusion. Illusions are by their nature a filter that keeps us from seeing the truth that's right before us. If we can't see who we are, how can we be and act on the basis of who we are?

When we don't act according to our true natures, we'll naturally become disillusioned with ourselves. The illusions create a kind of self-hatred. It's like the part-time golfer who breaks his clubs whenever he misses a shot. We become afraid that the real person isn't enough (good enough, smart enough, talented enough); we hope. we struggle, and we try on each of the illusions like a new hat with the vague idea that they'll make us feel better. But they won't.

The illusions and scarcity are in fact a form of indentured servitude. The thoughts, beliefs, ideas, and limitations of others are the masters, while we are their slaves. The illusions make us think that the truth is out there, while they hide us from ourselves. It is all a grand scheme of resistance to what simply and irrevocably *is*, right here and now. The illusions each of us chooses to live by are simply the methods of resistance with which we are most comfortable.

Thus, all illusions are make-believe images of ourselves that we hang on the wall as if they really are who we are. They're not us. They're the ultimate illusion of scarcity.


## A NEW WAY OF BEING — THE TRUTH ABOUT ABUNDANCE

> *There isn't any second half of myself waiting to plug in and make me whole. It's there. I'm already whole.*
>
> SALLY FIELD

Abundance is an inside job, just like scarcity. We live in a time of striking contrasts: tremendous prosperity for some, and outrageous poverty for others. Industrialized nations seem to live in an age of abundance. We have *so* much available to us! Yet, we continue to strive for more, more, more.

On the surface, abundance appears as the acquisition of possessions or status. If you've got it, flaunt it. There's something missing, though, and we all feel it. Daniel Pink, in his book, *A Whole New Mind*, identifies abundance as one of the three major trends shifting us from the information age to the conceptual age. He says, "The paradox of prosperity is that while living standards have risen steadily decade after decade, personal, family, and life satisfaction haven't budged. That's why more people — liberated by prosperity but not fulfilled by it — are resolving the paradox by searching for meaning." With all this material splendor, we're still not happy, and we're still stuck.

So what's going on? The secret is to also see abundance as a mindset. We must move from external abundance (materialism) to internal abundance. This kind of abundance is something that can't be achieved or found in other people, things, or events. As much as we're taught to focus on the external abundance, it's the internal kind that gives us the greatest rewards. In business we measure abundance by what we can see, taste, and feel. Unfortunately, this kind of thinking often stifles innovation by cramping creativity and keeping imagination on a tight leash.

We are predisposed to believe in only what we can see and measure. These are the external measures and definitions that lead directly to scarcity thinking! "Seeing is believing." "What gets measured gets done."

I'm not saying that benchmarks and measures are bad—it's when they keep us from seeing possibilities and being open to change that they are no longer helpful. We're so quick to quantify our lives that we've forgotten what makes us alive. Individually and as a society we must move from the external definitions of who we are to remembering the internal definitions of our greatness. Then and only then will be we happy.

Just as I challenged you with a new way of looking at scarcity, we must do the same with abundance. Abundance is not simply the opposite of scarcity.

> Abundance is a state of mind in which individuals exercise the freedom to be who they are.

Abundance is waking up to the reality that you are already the person you yearn to become, and that you already have everything you need. It is the denial, or more likely resistance of one's true nature that keeps you in scarcity. Abundance is about falling in love with who *and* where you are. It is focusing on all that you have, and not losing yourself in all that you don't have. In the end, though, it is an abundance mentality that allows each of us to do what we *can* do in each moment, and that's exactly how we Live into our Greatness.

## Abundance as Freedom

*The sun shines not on us, but in us.*

JOHN MUIR

Freedom is essential to abundance. Freedom is defined in as many ways as there are people to define it. I see freedom as your ability to *actualize* who you are. That is, freedom is your ability to do whatever you *can* do, undeterred by external factors or forces. Freedom is a decision or choice to act in full alignment with your true nature. It is a choice to think, decide, and act according to your capacity.

Choices that are out of alignment with your true self bind you to one or more of the seven illusions, like choosing a direction in a dense fog without any navigational aids. Freedom is like having an internal global positioning system (or GPS) that keeps you on track.

We often think of freedom as freedom from or for something, such as freedom from a bad job or freedom to purchase a new home. When freedom becomes a need, not a desire, and when we equate our worth with what we obtain, we are no longer free. We are controlled by the thing we seek. It defines us. On the one hand, we're running away from something negative (what we don't want); and on the other, we're seeking happiness through something new. In both cases, we're out of alignment with who we are because the focus is on the external, not the internal.

When you're out of alignment with who you are everything seems hard; there is constriction instead of free movement. It's hard to get new clients in business, and even smart business strategies fail. This misalignment shows up in your business on a par with how it shows up in the rest of your life.

Freedom is active, not passive. *True freedom is not hoping to be yourself someday; it is being yourself right now.* Freedom is broken down by scarcity thinking. Scarcity thinking creates resistance, and this keeps us from being free and from Living into Greatness—like the body rejecting an organ transplant.

## ABUNDANCE IS REAL AND SCARCITY IS AN ILLUSION

> *Some of my best friends are illusions. They've been sustaining me for years.*

> SHEILA BALLANTYNE

Most people see themselves in terms dictated or defined by their parents and/or society. Only by falling in love with where you are can you move on to being who you are. We have to see ourselves as we are, and not how we're viewed by society or our parents. That's obvious, you say. Then why are so many of us struggling? Because we don't even realize we've forgotten who we are. This is the power of conditioning that I discuss in Chapter 3.

Abundance is real and scarcity is an illusion. What makes something real? As a child, I loved the story of *The Velveteen Rabbit* (Williams and Nicholson), which chronicles the adventures of a stuffed bunny and his boy companion. As an adult, I've come to love this story for totally different reasons. Now I see it as a powerful metaphor for abundant transformation—the story of a stuffed bunny transformed into a real flesh-and-blood rabbit by loving himself and allowing himself to be loved.

> "What is real?" asked the Rabbit one day when they were lying side by side near the nursery fender before Nana came in to tidy the room. "Does it mean having things that buzz inside you and a stick-out handle?"

"Real isn't how you are made," said the Skin Horse. "It's something that happens to you. . . ."

"Does it hurt?" asked the Rabbit.

"Sometimes," said the Skin Horse, for he was always truthful. "When you are real, you don't mind being hurt."

What I didn't know at the age of five was that the Skin Horse was a terrific coach. Terrific coaches (and consultants, trainers, and managers) inspire greatness in others by reconnecting their coachees to who they are—to those unique qualities that make them real. The Skin Horse, for example, helped the rabbit identify the misconceptions about being real and learn to love being exactly who he was. It's the same for a business coach: You help your coachee identify and correct these misconceptions (illusions) and learn to live into greatness by first loving who and where he is.

The Skin Horse reminded the rabbit of his greatness—the fact that by being loved and loving ourselves we are real. The rabbit became real because he *believed* he was real.

## THE PARADOX OF BELIEVING

> *If you think you can do a thing or think you can't do a thing, you're right.*
>
> HENRY FORD

If your coachee believes herself to be less than, not enough, weak, or flawed, then she is going to be all of these things in her actions and results. Does this mean she is really weak or flawed? No. She was born great. But her inability to see her greatness, to be who she is will cause her to be someone or something else. This is a life of scarcity, but it is the life she lives because it is aligned with what she believes. If, though, she believes she is already great and accepts that she is free, she will indeed Live into that Greatness.

This is the paradox of believing. Who we are is great, and who we *think* we are is how we will show up; but if we are living in scarcity we will never be who we really are. Let that sink in for a moment.

When I was a kid, my dad used to say to me, "Who do you think you are?" This wasn't a contemplative, thought-provoking attempt to help me define myself. This was a condescending kind of question. The question always got the same result: cutting me off at the knees and shutting me up.

I questioned who I was, alright, but not in an abundant way. I questioned who I *thought* I was. I stopped listening to myself and listened more to others. What they believed shaped what I believed. I learned early that what other people think of you is more important than what you think of yourself. At least, that's what I thought.

Now I know that abundance *is* greatness. It's so easy for us to get confused by the combination of the words *abundance* and *greatness*. Does this mean that everyone who lives into his or her greatness will be famous and wealthy? Of course not! These are just external measures. True abundance may never be completely seen by another, yet it will always be felt by the person who is abundant. Abundance is, as I said, the ability to live into your capacity and in alignment with who you are. Freedom is being free of the illusions that keep us living in scarcity.

This reminds me of the time I spent as a VISTA volunteer (Volunteers in Service to America). Fresh out of college, my assignment was to create a grant-writing process for an agency for the homeless in Massachusetts. Although I'd never written a grant, I was an idealistic college grad who believed she would change the world. Interestingly enough, I didn't change the world so much as the world changed me through an unexpected chain of events.

Living on a meager $40 a week with room and board above the agency's family shelter, I discovered that to change the world I had to learn about myself while really engaging with my day-to-day relationships. My best teacher wasn't a counselor or mentor, but one of the residents of the family shelter where I provided direct services.

She had been violently assaulted while in nursing school, and was eventually slipping into mental illness; she had been abandoned by her family and was homeless. In her 50s she found her way to the shelter, where we became fast friends. Quickly, I came to realize how my friend saw the world differently. She noticed and admired the "little" gifts in life — the joy of a long awaited spring day, petting a visiting dog, hearing a long-forgotten favorite song on the radio. Without either of us knowing it, she schooled me on what's important, helping me to adjust the lens through which I saw the world. She was like a visit to the eye doctor, looking through that machine that determines your prescription (a Phoroptor® Refracting Instrument). "Which one is better, A or B?" I soon discovered that every gift I ever gave her quietly and unceremoniously found its way to someone who needed it more than she. She loved the joy of giving to others more than having for herself.

Years later, I helped her move into an assisted living facility. Her greatest joys are caring for the cats and birds living there. We talk regularly, and I often visit, bringing one of my pets along. Every month like clockwork, she sends me exactly $2 for treats for my dogs. She has nothing, but she has everything. Her abundance isn't in material possessions or money (she lives on a meager monthly disability check). But she is a constant example of living a simple and abundant life. She knows exactly who she is and what brings her happiness. So frequently, I'll visit her and be struggling with something in my life and she reminds me of what's most important.

That brings me back to where we started. Abundance is about focusing on what you have and what you *can* do, not on what you don't have and what you think you can't do. I walk my dogs in the park everyday. Earl, a 10-year-old basset hound, usually chooses to graze in the weeds, picking out the most succulent blades of grass like a true gourmet. On the other hand, Newton, a terrier-mix, bolts out into the field as soon as I take her off the leash. I love to watch her lope around like a miniature gazelle, completely free, loving life. Have you ever noticed how happy animals are? A lot of people would say that's because they don't know better. Maybe that's the point. Their heads aren't gummed up with thoughts of what they could be. And so they just are.


THE OPPORTUNITY COST OF SCARCITY

The purpose of the Coaching into Greatness process is to help you and the people you coach realize that *who you are* is everything. It's the *only* thing that really matters because everything hinges on your ability to be yourself, and to do that, you must become intimately aware of the barriers you create along the way.

You'll notice that I sometimes refer to the process as the Coaching into Greatness process, and sometimes as the Living into Greatness process. Which is it? Both, actually. My goal is for everyone who reads this book to *live* into his or her greatness. Then, everyone will be a much better position to *coach* others to live into their greatness. Whether you're a professional coach, a manager, or an executive, this process applies equally to you and to those with whom you work.

To fully comprehend the impact of scarcity mentality on our lives, it is important to be familiar with the concept of Opportunity Cost. In business, the opportunity cost is the cost of passing up another choice when making a decision. For example, if an asset such as capital is used for one purpose, the opportunity cost is the value of another purpose the asset could have been used for. The problem with scarcity thinking is that we don't even *see* the other possible choices, thereby missing the opportunity to make these choices.

In the context of this book, I define *Opportunity Cost* as the tangible and intangible costs to the individual or business when operating through a scarcity mentality. They simply miss or avoid many opportunities.

For example, Steve dreamed of moving his business out of his basement and into a rented office space. To do this, he needed to generate more revenue, which meant taking on more clients. But as a solo-preneur he was already at his breaking point with the volume of work. Steve wanted to bring on an assistant to share the workload and manage his time more effectively, but he wouldn't even consider this option as long as his office was in his basement.

He assumed that he couldn't keep his home life private from the new assistant while working at home. The Opportunity Cost of this assumption kept him struggling to keep up with his workload, like a hamster on a wheel. Exhausted and frustrated, he soon lost clients. Too deep into the situation, he couldn't see the power his black-and-white thinking had over the future of his business and the quality of his life.

When we show up in scarcity, there is always an Opportunity Cost. There is a direct correlation between the amount of scarcity in a person's life and the degree of Opportunity Cost he or she experiences, known or unknown. In fact, it is the unknown Opportunity Cost that is the most insidious quality of scarcity. It keeps us playing small even when we think we're doing just fine.

How does a person know when she's in scarcity or abundance? How do you translate the feeling of unhappiness, of being stuck, or of thinking you're not good enough into an Opportunity Cost? Picture a teeter-totter. On one end of the teeter-totter we have scarcity; on the other end we have abundance (see Figure 1.1).

The Opportunity Cost can be measured by identifying the Tipping Point of any given situation. *The Tipping Point is the moment when thinking a certain way keeps us from doing what we can do.* The Tipping Point is a foundational concept for this book and the Coaching into Greatness process. None of the patterns I'll share with you that make up a scarcity mentality are good or bad in and of themselves. *It is when they keep us stuck that*

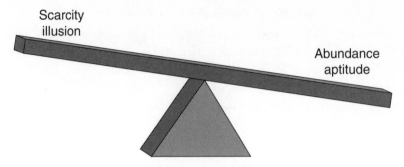

Figure 1.1   The Tipping Point from Scarcity to Abundance.

*they result in an Opportunity Cost.* This point at which the patterns are no longer useful is *the Tipping Point.*

For instance, in Chapter 10 I discuss the Illusion of Hope. In and of itself, hope is not a bad thing. It is a powerful motivator and source of strength for many. However, hope becomes a source of scarcity thinking when we circumvent our personal responsibility and look for someone or something to magically make things better. We put off today what we hope will happen tomorrow. And this decision has an associated cost—the Opportunity Cost.

## INTRODUCING THE ABUNDANCE QUOTIENT (AQ) SYSTEM

This book will teach you a system for identifying where you're under an illusion that creates scarcity thinking, and a process for moving into abundant thinking. Ultimately, we will use this system to measure what I call an Abundance Quotient (AQ). Just as there are systems for measuring your intelligence quotient (IQ) and your emotional intelligence (EQ), this process identifies how your view of life impacts everything else that you do. Another way to look at AQ is that it's a system for measuring the amount of resistance or freedom you have in your life. To the extent we are living abundantly, we are Living into our Greatness.

Remember our earlier discussion about opposites? Associated with each of the seven illusions that are the sources of scarcity thinking, there are seven aptitudes that are the source of abundant thinking. The abundance aptitudes are the competencies that show us how to open up to

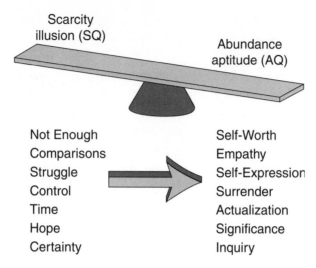

Figure 1.2    Scarcity Illusions and Abundance Aptitudes.

*YES (your extraordinary self)*. They are the essential abilities inherent in *being* who we are. They are illustrated in Figure 1.2.

The Tipping Point is the point at which the source of scarcity thinking prevents you from approaching life abundantly and Living into your Greatness. In upcoming chapters, I explore each illusion, how to identify when you are in that illusion, and how to make the shift to abundance using the four-step Coaching into Greatness process.

In the last chapter, you will find additional information about Abundance Intelligence™. There you will learn more about how to work this process in greater detail. Visit www.coachingintogreatness.com for an actual assessment that gives you a snapshot of your AQ and SQ (Scarcity Quotient) levels and help you to build awareness where scarcity mentality exists, and where to focus your time and energy for the best results. Essentially, the AQ system guides individuals and teams to act more on the basis of who they are, making the concepts in this book directly relevant to your strengths and weaknesses and that of your coachees. This system is a powerful tool for you and the people you coach.

## CHAPTER SUMMARY

Note: Each chapter will include a short summary of key points. These are your vital "take-aways"—thoughts and ideas that, if you take them to heart and implement them daily, will move you several steps closer to Living into Greatness and Doing What You *Can* Do.

How you show up in business equals how you show up in life.
How you show up in life equals how you show up in business.
Scarcity is simply a result of resisting who you are.
Abundance is the practice of exercising the freedom to be who you are.
A scarcity mentality creates Opportunity Cost.
Abundance Intelligence™ is doing what you *can* do in any given moment.

CHAPTER TWO

# Why Greatness?

*Make the most of yourself, for that is all there is of you.*

Emerson

Why greatness? Why not coaching into productivity, or coaching into success? The answer is simple: Productivity and success are fleeting and temporary; greatness is innate and permanent.

Greatness is not dependent on things, circumstances, or people outside of us. When we accept this, we find we no longer have to pursue or strive for greatness. It simplifies life, while simultaneously enhancing life. The army uses the catch phrase, "Be all you can be." What if you knew that you were already all you could be, and that life is a matter of unfolding into this existing greatness? It's like chiseling away at everything that isn't you until what's left is the masterpiece that was underneath all the time.

Another way to look at it is to examine the seed of an oak tree. Everything that defines the oak is already in the acorn. It slowly becomes the magnificent tree by connecting to its environment and using the natural resources of this environment to grow. It never has an illusion that it needs to be something else or needs to strive toward an accomplishment that is not in its nature. It's only we humans who create the illusions that hide our inherent capacities. Greatness is the process of unfolding into who you are, shedding the illusions, and living into your inherent capacities.

We are all born great, like the acorn that grows into the oak tree. We already possess the necessary instructions for being and doing all that's within our innate capacity. As I discuss in more detail in the next chapter, we're simply conditioned to forget who we are. When we begin questioning the answers about life that we've taken for granted, we shed the illusions about who we are and the natural greatness emerges.

## THE CONNECTION BETWEEN GREATNESS AND ABUNDANCE

*When you were born, God said yes!*

UNKNOWN

In the previous chapter on abundance and scarcity, I described the abundance aptitudes as competencies that show us how to open up to YES—your extraordinary self. If the aptitudes show us how to open up to YES, greatness is living into that YES. It is simply doing what you can do in each moment.

Your extraordinary self is your essence, stripped of all the conditioning, excuses, and contingencies that have created a limited life. Coaching into Greatness is the process of helping people open to this YES.

Coaching into Greatness helps you say yes to:

- Life.
- Possibilities.
- Expression.
- Freedom.
- Joy.
- Brilliance.
- Happiness.
- Fun.
- Success.
- Results.
- Awareness.
- Beauty.
- Abundance.

Greatness is transparent. Imagine a clear piece of glass through which others see you and you can see yourself. There's no distortion and no fuzziness. The illusions hide or blur our greatness. It's like looking through a glass block or a piece of etched glass. What feels like the real you is nothing more than a heavily distorted image of the real you. The illusions are opaque layers in between our current life experience and our innate greatness. Greatness is always there, just obscured. We need to see the illusions for what they are and shift from what if to what is.

## IF WE'RE ALL GREAT, HOW CAN WE FAIL?

If everyone is born great, then why are so many people frustrated and stuck? Why do so many businesses fail? Why do we even need coaches?

The answer is actually quite simple. *We are as great as we allow ourselves to be, and most of us don't allow ourselves to be much of anything at all.* We are quick to place huge limits on what we can do, before we've even begun to do it. H. G. Wells said, "What on earth would man do with himself if something didn't stand in the way?"

---

DISTINCTION: POTENTIAL VS. CAPACITY

Potential is based in the future. When we say that someone has the potential to be something, it is about becoming something other than who they presently are.

Capacity is based on the present. It already exists. We are born with greatness. We have the capacity to live into it. The acorn has the capacity to become an oak.

---

We all have the extraordinary coded within us, waiting to be released.

JEAN HOUSTON

Everyone has a secret encoded inside. James Hillman referred to this as his "acorn theory" in his book *The Soul's Code.* Each encoding is specific and unique to the individual, much like an individual's DNA. This book will show you how to excavate the DNA of individual greatness. You'll peel back the layers of illusion that hide who you really are. You're going to become an archaeologist of greatness for yourself and your coachees. There is a Tibetan saying: *"Tashi deley,"* which means *I honor the greatness in you.* Coaching into Greatness is the processes of helping your coachees remember how to honor the greatness inside.

*People living in scarcity see the cup as half empty.*
*People who are positive thinkers see the cup as half full.*
*People living in abundance see the cup as overflowing.*
*But people Living into their Greatness are the Cup.*

This book teaches people how to be the Cup.

## ARGUMENTS AGAINST GREATNESS

*The tragedy of life is not death, but what we let die inside us while we live.*

NORMAN COUSINS

I may as well hit these arguments head-on, because sooner or later you'll hear them in your business. Every great idea and every great movement has been called into question based on the status quo. Few people like change, even if those changes can make their lives better. They'll argue against greatness, against abundance, and even against happiness if these notions conflict with their view of life. Here are a few of the key arguments against inherent greatness that you'll likely hear (or may have said yourself).

### ARGUMENT 1: I'M NOT GREAT. HOW COULD I BE? I'M FAR FROM ACCOMPLISHING WHAT I WANT OR CAN ACCOMPLISH

People are like icebergs. They equate their greatness to what can be seen, measured, or proven. These are the surface dwellers I mentioned earlier. They say, "If I see it, I can believe it; the proof is in the pudding; or, only tangible things have value."

Yet, just like an iceberg, the majority of our greatness lies hidden deep under the surface. The illusions are like the water that keeps our greatness hidden from us and keeps us frozen from living our true nature. The process of Coaching into Greatness is that of evaporating the illusions so that your coachee can clearly see his or her inner core and remember and reconnect with the greatness within.

Help your coachee realize that he has been great all along. The illusions have been operating like smoke and mirrors, so that reality is obscured. When someone operates strictly by the idea that reality is what she can see, and what she sees is obscured by many illusions, she's operating on a false reality! This same person would say that a nearby island doesn't exist because she can't see it through the dense fog. Coaching into Greatness is the process of clearing away the fog so that the island can be seen clearly for what it is. The greatest coaches reveal their clients to themselves.

## ARGUMENT 2: NOT EVERYBODY CAN BE GREAT

Someone has to clean the toilets, right? There's not enough to go around. Some people win, some people lose. These are all common expressions of scarcity mentality.

Inherent in this argument is the assumption that there is not enough to go around and that it's not possible for everyone to live his or her ideal life. This is a model based on scarcity and competition. I can succeed only if someone else fails. My failure equals someone else's success. I can't be an astronaut, so I'm not that great. This argument defines greatness in hierarchical terms. That is, if you're great, I'm not, and if I'm great, you're not.

Greatness is unique to each individual. No one can define it for another. How you define greatness will differ from everyone you meet. More precisely, *your greatness* is uniquely yours. Everyone is great in his or her very own unique way. It's what makes life so richly diverse and ensures that everyone can live into his or her inherent capabilities. Your job is to help your coachee rediscover his or her own definition, shaking off the illusions that were put in place by parents, teachers, friends, family, and society.

Sure, not everyone will become president of a country. Not everyone will become a famous actor who becomes president of a country. Your coachee may not walk on the moon or save the world from itself. But your coachee can, and dare I say it—*should*—fully express his unique greatness as a gift back to the world into which he was born a uniquely gifted and talented individual. For any of us to deprive the world of who we are is a selfish, cynical act. To do what we *can* do and be the person that we *are* is the purest act of love. The world can't live without it.

It is this very questioning of worth that keeps so many people from doing what they *can* do. They can't imagine being president, or some other lofty goal, and suddenly any goal they do have pales in comparison. The underlying assumption here is that anything of value has to be larger than life. Go big or go home. And yet, on further inspection, we find that it is really the little things done consistently that bring greatness. As Mother Teresa said, "We can do no great things; only small things with great love."

After spending two years as a VISTA volunteer working with the poor and homeless, I learned an amazing lesson. I quickly realized I wasn't going to eradicate poverty. But what I *could* do was make a difference one person at a time, one relationship at a time. Cliché, you say? Abundance is all about relationships — first, your relationship with yourself, then your relationship with the world and everything in it. Cliché or not, we cannot have effective relationships with others if we don't know who we are and how we see ourselves in the world.

During those two years, I served meals in the soup kitchen, gave out food baskets in the food pantry, and assisted in the two shelters for the homeless run by the organization. I saw desperation and hopelessness and dead ends. I saw people get shot on the sidewalk and two-year-old kids running around barefoot at 1:00 A.M. But I also saw abundance in action — children getting fed, the homeless receiving access to healthcare, and people making a difference in service to others. The best example of abundance in action is the story of Jerry, second youngest in a family of four who had traveled from shelter to shelter before staying at the family shelter where I volunteered. From the beginning, this family was special to me. Despite the streets, despite the depression of their mom, these kids were happy. When they left the shelter to move into their permanent apartment, it was a bittersweet day filled with the excitement of moving on, but also the fear of letting go.

Last year I ran into Jerry at the local mall during Christmas. The mall was crammed with frenzied, last-minute shoppers searching for the perfect gift. Somehow I heard this voice calling my name. I stopped and looked back through the crowd. There he was. We hugged each other and, looking at him, it was hard to believe this was the same kid who had lived at the shelter 10 years ago, fighting so hard to live an honest life. He told me he was finishing up pharmacy school and how much I and the shelter staff had done for him. He beamed with excitement and pride.

I've thought a lot about Jerry since that day. I've thought about how easy it would have been for him to fall into the scarcity trap of his environment. And I've thought how amazing it was that a few caring people made the difference for him. That experience was an expression of the power of people doing what they *can* do.

*Holding out to do that truly audacious thing keeps us from doing the great things we can do today.*

I once read a story about a developmentally challenged young man who bagged groceries at the local store. Not a very glamorous job, but to him, that job meant everything. He used it as a platform to live into his particular area of greatness. He started printing out inspirational quotes and cutting them up into individual strips to insert into the groceries he bagged. Before long, people formed long lines in his lane, just to get the quote of the day. Who are we to say that he wasn't great? Whatever your vision or whatever your particular expression of greatness, it's time for that greatness to emerge.

### ARGUMENT 3: IF I'M ALREADY GREAT, THEN I SHOULDN'T HAVE TO DO ANYTHING

What a cop-out! Greatness is not an excuse to sit back and watch life go by. What would happen to that poor acorn if it sat on the ground and thought, "I don't have to plant myself, break through this hard shell, reach my roots deep into the ground and push my way high into the sky." That acorn would wither and die, much the same as anyone who thinks he doesn't have to act because he knows he's already great.

There is absolutely nothing more exciting than discovering one's true nature and expressing that nature in authentic ways. Thomas Carlyle said, "Nothing is more terrible than activity without insight." Actually, I can think of something equally terrible and that is insight without activity. If all you do is read this book and think "hmmm, that's interesting" without taking any action, you've missed the whole point. What's the point of having awareness if we don't do something with it? In truth, nothing really changes with awareness alone. That would be like playing a game of baseball knowing you can hit a home run but never swinging the bat. We set ourselves up for failure in all kinds of ways, creating excuses that serve our need to remain safe. Ignoring or arguing away our greatness is remaining safe; it is the greatest tragedy of our times.

> Men are like trees; each one must put forth the leaf that is created in him.
>
> HENRY WARD BEECHER

## THE PROFOUND IMPACT OF EACH INDIVIDUAL

> *I am not bound to win, but I am bound to be true. I am not bound to succeed, but I am bound to live up to the light I have.*
>
> ABRAHAM LINCOLN

*The Man Who Planted Trees* is an inspiring story written by Jean Giono that illustrates the impact one person's actions can have. In this tiny book, Giono tells the tale of an isolated shepherd living just outside the French Alps who takes it upon himself to plant 100 acorns a day throughout his life in an effort to reforest his desolate region. Through extraordinary vision, perseverance, and commitment, the shepherd is responsible for reforesting an entire countryside—transforming the land and attracting people, animals, and communities. What once had been filled with scarcity and hopelessness was now teeming with life and abundance. Giono writes, "When I reflect that one man, armed only with his own physical and moral resources, was able to cause this land of Canaan to spring from the wasteland, I am convinced that in spite of everything, humanity is admirable. But when I compute the unfailing greatness of spirit and the tenacity of benevolence that it must have taken to achieve this result, I am taken with an immense respect for that old and unlearned peasant who was able to complete a work worthy of God."

That's a nice story, you say, but it could never happen in real life. Well, it has! Wangari Maathai, 2004 Nobel Peace Prize winner, founded the Green Belt Movement in Kenya over 25 years ago. Horrified at the environmental devastation of her country, Wangari recruited women to plant trees in their villages, providing them with a source of food and fuel, as well as tremendous environmental benefits. The movement met with great opposition from the government—she was even jailed for her efforts. But Wangari, like the shepherd, had an abundant vision. She persevered to live into her greatness, becoming the first African woman to earn a Ph.D. in Eastern and Central Africa, and the first woman to attain associate professorship at the University of Nairobi. To date, her movement's efforts have resulted in the planting of *30 million trees*. One person's vision is that person's greatness.

If the shepherd and Wangari had both started out with the goal of planting millions of trees, neither of them would have succeeded. Instead, they were aware of their greatness, they accepted their role in the situation, and they consistently did what they could do, thereby Living into their Greatness; and, they just happened to plant millions of trees.

Success is a byproduct of Living into our Greatness. In its simplest form, scarcity keeps us from taking action. It robs us of doing what we *can* do, of being powerful. Our biggest argument against greatness is really our biggest fear. We fear being great. Of all the business owners

# Why Greatness?

I have coached, the vast majority are paralyzed by the fear of being great. Is that surprising? Typically we assume that people are terrified of failure. And yet, in my experience, I have found that what lies under the fear of failure is something much different.

> Our deepest fear is not that we are inadequate.
> Our deepest fear is that we are powerful beyond measure.
> It is our light, not our darkness that frightens us.
> We ask ourselves, who am I to be brilliant, gorgeous, talented and fabulous?
> Actually, who are we not to be?
> You are a child of God.
> Your playing small doesn't serve the world.
> There's nothing enlightened about shrinking so that other people won't feel insecure around you.
> We were born to make manifest the glory of God that is within us.
> It's not just in some of us, it's in everyone.
> And as we let our own light shine, we unconsciously give other people permission to do the same.
> As we are liberated from our own fears,
> Our presence automatically liberates others.

FROM *A RETURN TO LOVE* BY MARIANNE WILLIAMSON

I once coached a consultant who wanted to become a motivational speaker. Her big dream was to travel around the world speaking to corporations and conventions on her area of expertise. Yet, every step of the way, she met with resistance. After working through the Coaching into Greatness process, she realized *she* was creating the resistance. Her fear? It wasn't a fear of failure—it was a legitimate fear of reaching her goal. She could see it. But what she also saw was time away from her young family, disruption of their routine, and disconnection with her way of life. That conflict caused her to sabotage her actions and fueled the fire of her resistance.

We fear that if we actually become the person we know we are, our lives will change and we will leave people behind. We will leave the familiar behind; and so we play just small enough of a game to keep ourselves safe, to fly below the radar. Each of the illusions is a different expression of this fear. That's where Coaching into Greatness comes in. When we can uncover and shed light on the conditioned beliefs, fears, and assumptions that drive us, we can truly be ourselves.

## CHAPTER SUMMARY

GREATNESS IS INNATE.

SUCCESS IS A BYPRODUCT OF LIVING INTO YOUR GREATNESS.

DOING WHAT YOU *can* do today is more powerful than waiting to do a great thing tomorrow.

Greatness is not dependent on things, circumstances, or people outside of us.

We are as great as we allow ourselves to be, and most of us don't allow ourselves to be much of anything at all.

## CHAPTER THREE

# Forgetting Who You Are

*I've often said, the only thing standing between me and greatness is me.*

WOODY ALLEN

When I was 10 years old, I had a conversation with my mom that sticks in my mind like it was just yesterday. It was one of those lazy afternoons in the middle of a humid Wisconsin summer. She and I were talking when her voice suddenly got very quiet and serious. It felt like time stood still. "Kimi, what would you do if I died?"

My answer was automatic. "Well, I'd die, too." What else could I say? I couldn't imagine a life without my best friend and greatest champion. Little did I know, five years later my mom would be gone and I would begin fulfilling my promise to her.

Obviously, I didn't die—I'm here, sharing this book with you. I didn't literally fulfill my promise. I never tried to end my life or do really out-rageous, risky things. But deep down inside, when my mom left me, a big part of me died with her. I didn't realize this on a conscious level. I became the overachiever, super-responsible, independent daughter. My dad never had to worry about me. "She's a rock," my uncle used to say. I could take care of myself, and most of the time, I took care of my dad. My mom's death crushed him, and in many ways, he lost a part of himself, too. He became emotionally absent, unable to deal with the loss and our grief. Eight months after she was gone, my dad met a new woman who soon moved in with us.

The rest of the story might sound like a soap opera, if it wasn't true. He quickly remarried but missed the signs. I choose to remember her as a beautiful, giving, loving person, but in truth she was an alcoholic who would go on weekend drinking binges involving violence, shoplifting, and screaming bouts.

Sometimes I can't believe I survived that period of my life. Still grieving my mother, I was forced to accept this new woman, who boxed up all my mom's possessions, pined over the two daughters she was forbidden to see, and alternately cared for and yelled at me. I never knew what to expect. Within four months, I was sent away to live with my uncle in Nevada—thousands of miles away from my friends and the only lifeline I had.

I didn't realize it then, but I was already fully protected by a full set of emotional riot gear. I'd learned plenty of survival techniques—elaborate strategies for coping with whatever devastation life might offer. I told myself I was strong, and that I had it all together. I was surviving, and to many, it appeared that I was thriving because I had the success to prove it—the good grades, achievements, and recognition. It seemed to work for a while.

I was unconsciously fulfilling my early promise to my mother. I was preparing to die—not physically, but emotionally. I buffered myself against what I saw would be a never-ending onslaught of very bad things happening. This was the start of one of my strongest scarcity beliefs—that good things don't come my way. I lived my life constantly waiting for the other shoe to drop, and I immediately discounted any good that came my way. Like many kids who lose a parent at an early age, I didn't feel that it was right for me to be happy, not when she had to suffer and die.

Unfortunately, this kind of emotional riot gear blocks out everything, good and bad. Just as you don't allow yourself to experience the challenging lows of life, you miss the exhilarating highs. These blocks make you live life like a robot, mechanically going through the motions—superficially efficient, but missing the best parts of being alive.

How do we get like this? How do we end up acting in ways that might destroy our businesses, careers, and lives? It's a matter of conditioning.

# THE DYNAMICS OF CONDITIONING

*The mind, conditioned as it is by the past, always seeks to re-create what it knows and is familiar with.*

ECKHART TOLLE

Quite a bit has already been written on the subject of conditioning, much of it to be found in psychology text books. I am not a psychologist, but, like you, I have a lot of experience with conditioning—mine and that of my coaching clients.

I define conditioning as "living someone else's answers about life." That someone else is a combination of our parents, family, culture, society, school, and religion. It's a form of brainwashing that is so subtle that most of us live our lives thinking we're thinking our own thoughts, when they're not our thoughts at all.

How's that for a mind bender? What you're thinking isn't what you're really thinking at all. I loved the film, *The Matrix*. In this futuristic adventure, we enter a world where humans are all cogs in a machine, seemingly living a life of reality, but what everybody thinks is real is merely an elaborate computer program.

Futuristic fantasy? Maybe. But not too far off base. We learned our beliefs and attitudes from our environment. We've been conditioned to believe that they are our reality. That is the danger of conditioning. Some may believe that ignorance is bliss, but the cost of ignorance in this case is nothing short of death—often a slow and extremely painful one. Many people have lived a long life, but a life of imitation. Let's explore how conditioning occurs so that you can recognize it in your own life.

## THE CYCLE OF CONDITIONING

*Most people are other people. Their thoughts are someone else's opinions, their lives a mimicry, their passions a quotation.*

OSCAR WILDE

Conditioning is an endless cycle of illusion and deception. When you are a baby, you are born great. You already have everything you need. As I discussed in the previous chapter, you are born with your personal DNA of greatness already encoded. I don't mean that you were capable of self-care or self-sufficiency. Greatness is not about being completely self-sufficient; it is about interdependence.

As a baby, you depended on the love and care of your parents to grow and thrive. But who you are was already perfectly defined inside of you. Through the efforts of often well-meaning people who provide us with a steady stream of misinformation about us and the world, we soon become disconnected from who we are.

See Figure 3.1 for the four stages of the Conditioning Cycle.

## Forgetting

Forgetting begins as soon as we start understanding the language of our parents. They teach us about the world and how to live in the world. They show us what is right or wrong and the rules of life. They tell us to color inside the lines and wash our hands before eating. We're often to be seen and not heard. Each of us learns what kinds of actions reward us with love and attention (or a treat), and which actions result in punishment.

Your parents imprint their view of the world onto your little mind, so that you begin seeing it the same way they see it. Your siblings, grandparents, aunts, uncles, and others with whom you have contact also gift you with their worldly knowledge and preconceptions. You start becoming like them, complete with their prejudices and ideas of what and who you should be.

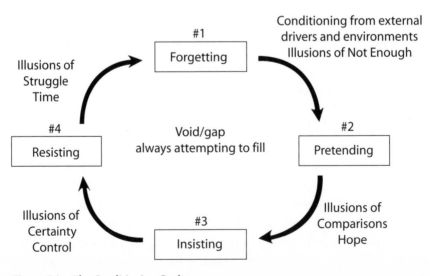

Figure 3.1   The Conditioning Cycle.

As we're normalized by society, we begin to forget our greatness and uniqueness. It's easier, and often safer, to fit in, go with the crowd, or ride the wave of conformity. If as a child you're different, people will call you names, laugh and point, or even take your lunch money. You'll get picked last at recess, or not at all. Being unique or different isn't easy, and it can be downright painful.

## Pretending

As we forget who we are, we naturally begin pretending to be someone else. We emulate the behaviors and appearance of others, taking on whatever image is popular or rewarded by society. If it's cool to wear your pants down to your ankles, you can bet that you'll see all the cool people doing it.

Pretending is a natural way to feel safe, secure, loved, or wanted. There's nothing wrong with emulating others. Often the best way to learn something new is to emulate an expert in that area. Pretending is different. It's not about emulating someone to become more skilled or to enhance your natural skills and abilities. Pretending is simply a way of staying safe in an otherwise scary world where being different or unique is dangerous.

If you can remember who you are, you'll realize there's no reason to pretend to be like, think like, or act like anyone else. But stepping out of your well-defined role can get you slapped around pretty hard, even by your best friends.

## Insisting

After enough time pretending, we insist this is who we are. Listen to your coachee carefully. Does she say that she's stupid or not creative? Does he insist that he's just unlucky by nature? Whatever it is we've been told repeatedly is what we come to believe as the truth, even if it is something that is ultimately harmful. We become the mask we've been wearing. In fact, we insist that the mask is real, and what's under the mask is the illusion.

We can be very unhappy, feeling a deep void within, and still, we insist that this false image is what's real. It's really quite astounding that we play this game with ourselves, since it leaves most of us feeling like something is missing. Something *is* missing from the equation: the real you.

## *Resisting*

With insisting comes resisting—the heart of scarcity and struggle. As we continue to insist we're cookie cutter paper dolls with the matching set of cookie cutter beliefs, we struggle through life. We have a sneaky suspicion that something is out of place, but we ignore the feeling. It's like having a small oil leak in your car. It's nothing to worry about until the little red light goes on.

For us, that red light might be the loss of a loved one, loss of a job, or major life transition. If we're fortunate, we'll have some very powerful feelings of discontent—so powerful that we can't hide from them any longer. This is a critical point in the cycle and the crossroads of decision. Either we look more deeply at the nagging discontent, or we push it aside once more, succumbing to the appearances of life instead of having a real life.

Coaching into Greatness is the process of excavating greatness and remembering who you are. First comes awareness of the resistance. When we have awareness, we have choice. When we have choice, we have freedom. When we have freedom we have greatness.

There's a popular series of television commercials featuring a credit card company portraying identity theft. The 30-second spots feature one person speaking, but with another person's voice. For example, the 85-year-old grandmother speaks in a man's voice about a new surfboard that he rides on several gnarly waves. It's a funny commercial, but there's a deeper message that even the credit card company doesn't understand. It's the theft of identity that occurs through the cycle of conditioning.

I was flipping through a business magazine recently when an ad by Philips Electronics caught my eye. The full-page ad shows the picture of a very happy baby with a big smile on his face, lying on his back. But it wasn't the happy baby that caught my attention, it was the headline underneath:

Things start uncomplicated. Why change them?

Think about that. When you were born, you were uncomplicated—a clean slate waiting to be imprinted by your experiences and by all those willing to define who you are. At the same time, your unique greatness was already encoded and ready to unfold and mature.

44

## A Pattern Language of Scarcity and Abundance

*The sculptor produces the beautiful statue by chipping away such parts of the marble block as are not needed — it is a process of elimination.*

Elbert Hubbard

*There is something in every one of you that waits and listens for the sound of the genuine in yourself.*

Howard Thurman

Coined by Christopher Alexander, world-famous architect and author, in his classic book, *A Timeless Way of Building*, a *pattern language* is a way to describe a series of patterns that identify a recurring problem. It gives language to, and allows people to relate to, a problem in accessible, understandable terms.

Understanding Abundance Intelligence™ is a way to identify and measure the pattern languages for scarcity and abundance. The Scarcity Quotient (SQ) identifies and measures the pattern language of scarcity, while the Abundance Quotient (AQ) measures the pattern language of abundance.

Each of the two pattern languages consists of three parts. The scarcity side consists of conditioned beliefs, conditioned patterns, and the seven illusions of scarcity thinking. The abundance side consists of conscious beliefs, conscious patterns, and abundance aptitudes, the counterparts of the illusions.

We can readily see in people's behaviors the conditioned patterns or conscious patterns. These are the most visible clues to whether someone is living in scarcity or abundance. Conditioned or conscious patterns are the results of conditioned or conscious beliefs. A belief is either created and reinforced by unconscious conditioning (parents, teachers, etc.), or through a conscious effort to instill and reinforce beliefs that are based on our true nature.

Figure 3.2 shows the pattern language of scarcity. An unconscious belief is created, which results in a conditioned pattern. This pattern becomes the reinforcing behavior of one or more illusions that creates a life of scarcity.

Figure 3.3 shows the pattern language of abundance. By using the four-step process, we become aware of the conditioned beliefs and patterns and consciously choose a belief that is in alignment with our inherent greatness. We reinforce the belief through consistent and

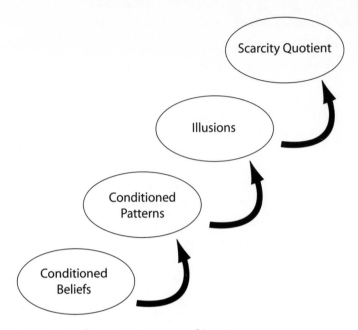

Figure 3.2   The Pattern Language of Scarcity.

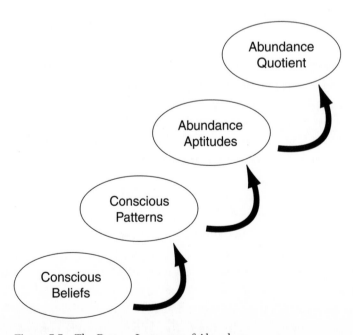

Figure 3.3   The Pattern Language of Abundance.

authentic action; that is, through conscious patterns. Eventually we create abundance aptitudes, which lead to a life in which we live into our greatness.

## CONDITIONED PATTERNS VERSUS CONSCIOUS PATTERNS

*Most new discoveries are suddenly-seen things that were always there.*

SUSANNE K. LANGER

*A conditioned pattern is the culmination of a repeated series of actions and reactions that are based on and reinforce conditioned beliefs.* We learn about conditioned patterns by looking at the results we get in life. For example, someone who has trouble keeping jobs is living in scarcity. When we examine his consistent behavior (conditioned patterns), we find that he takes far longer than his colleagues to complete a project. He can't move to step two until every nook, cranny, and crack in step one has been completely filled. He lives his life under the illusions of not enough and struggle. We find he has the underlying beliefs that he can't afford to make mistakes, or even that he's not worthy of success.

*A conscious pattern comes from repeated and consistent authentic action that is in alignment with our true nature.* Again, we see the conscious patterns through everyday actions. The person in the above example might become aware of the conditioned patterns and beliefs and will want to develop abundance aptitudes to replace the illusions. He'll do this by consciously choosing new beliefs ("I'm capable of correcting any mistakes"), developing an action plan, then taking action in alignment with who he is. Through the four-step process, he'll develop new, conscious patterns that will replace the old conditioned patterns.

*Conditioned patterns are the reasons we keep taking the same unsuccessful actions.* They result in us asking, "Why did I do that again, even though I know it doesn't work?" They're like holding patterns that keep us circling around the landing site without ever touching down. Examining these patterns gives us the information we need to identify why we keep getting the same undesirable results in business and life. They're extremely frustrating because they keep us from doing what we *can* do.

Deepak Chopra says that there are really only two emotions: pleasure and fear. We do something, either because it's pleasurable or out of fear. Conditioned patterns are our strategic responses to fear. While conditioned patterns are a fear-based reaction, conscious patterns are based on a desire for pleasure. When we get to do that thing we want to do, we feel pleasure, but we don't react to fear.

Do you want to know why your coachee's business isn't doing as well as he'd like? Look to the conditioned patterns of each individual in the business, especially the executives or leaders. The collective mindset and culture of an organization is comprised of its individual conditioned patterns. Remember that how you show up in business is directly proportional to how you show up in life. If your business or corporation functions primarily through people, not machines, the way those people show up, or don't, has a huge impact on how the business performs.

## CHAPTER SUMMARY

*You were born an original. Don't die a copy.*

JOHN MASON

A pattern language is a way of describing reoccurring events.

The pattern language of scarcity is made up of conditioned patterns and conditioned beliefs.

The pattern language of abundance is made up of conscious patterns and conscious beliefs.

A conditioned pattern is the culmination of a repeated series of actions and reactions that are based on and reinforce conditioned beliefs.

A conscious pattern comes from repeated and consistent authentic action that is in alignment with our true nature.

## CHAPTER FOUR

# Remembering Who You Are

*Change is inevitable. Growth is optional.*

ANONYMOUS

You can have a great map, but if you don't have a way to get from your start to your end point, that map won't do you much good. When I suggested earlier that simply reading this book from cover to cover (or skimming for the high points) won't help, it's because the content of the book is only a map.

The four-step process is the vehicle through which the map becomes meaningful. The process gets you from point A to point B, which in this case is from scarcity thinking and living to abundant thinking and living.

You can't think your way out of scarcity. Some new age gurus suggest that all you have to do is visualize success. I wish it were that easy, but I don't know of anyone who's been successful. Unfortunately, our conditioned beliefs and patterns are so finely ingrained that they become automatic responses to life's events.

How many times have you had a great Aha! moment, only to discover that several weeks (or even days) later, you're back to the same old habitual patterns? Have you noticed that your clients or employees often have a great deal of difficulty turning an insight into a lasting change in behavior?

We intellectualize new concepts, popping them into our minds like so many tiny placebos. We *think* that by learning new ideas and new theories we're accomplishing something important.

When we intellectualize, nothing changes. The information settles into the recesses of our minds, to be recalled when the need arises to impress a colleague or the good-looking tenant in Apartment 3. But *we* don't change. We're still *acting* and *living* according to the old conditioned patterns and beliefs, while we *pretend* that things are different. New ideas that are intellectualized are filtered by and through the old conditioned patterns. What comes out the other end is very similar to the old patterns and rarely resembles the new idea.

Say, for example, the only way you know how to cook is to boil your food for an hour. You get a new recipe for a chocolate cake about which you're really excited. Unfortunately, all you do is apply these wonderful ingredients to your conditioned and (for you) natural way of cooking. You pour the sugar, chocolate, flour, eggs, and baking soda into a pot, add some water, and boil it for an hour.

That's what happens when we intellectualize something new without taking the steps to *internalize* the new idea. The four-step process is specifically designed to help people internalize new beliefs, ideas, and thoughts until their normal behavior is based on these new beliefs.

When we fully act on the understanding that there is no separation between what we believe and how we act (and consequently, the results we get), we are ready to internalize new beliefs. Then, and only then, will we take responsibility for our actions and the results those actions produce.

We can form new beliefs, and through a consistent process (the four steps) internalize those new beliefs, choosing a new way to act that produces the kind of results we want. As you'll see, a key difference between intellectualizing and internalizing is choice—making decisions, and acting on those decisions. Thus, I can take responsibility for quitting a smoking habit when I have the knowledge of its harmfulness to my body. Awareness alone, without decision and action, won't get me past any addictive or destructive patterns. The four steps are the process for internalizing abundance.

*Welcome to your new vehicle. Drive safely and confidently.*

Make a commitment, for yourself and your coachees, that you'll work the four-step process. Remember the Slip-N-Slide®? By itself, it isn't much fun and can cause some serious road rash. But add water, and you'll slide from one end to the other with the greatest of ease. The four-step process is the water; the principles outlined in this book are the Slip-N-Slide®.

Please add water, and have fun.

## THE FOUR-STEP PROCESS

Before we dive into the four steps, it's important to understand the results that occur with each step. Figure 4.1 illustrates the two ends of the spectrum for each of the four steps.

Step 1 moves us from forgetting to awareness.
Step 2 moves us from pretending to acceptance.
Step 3 moves us from insisting to consistent action.
Step 4 moves us from resisting to authenticity.

Finally, the entire process moves us from conditioned patterns to conscious patterns and from conditioned beliefs to conscious beliefs.

### YOUR DECLARATION OF TRUTH

First, we have step zero. I don't call it the first step, because this step stands alone and isn't a part of the cycle of learning and internalization

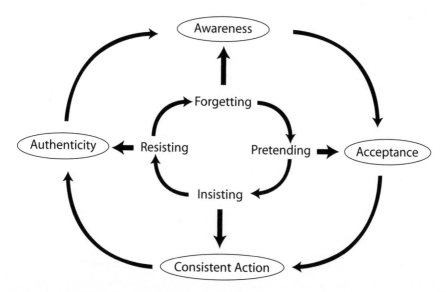

Figure 4.1   Outcomes of Four Steps.

that occurs with the four steps. Step zero is a Declaration. It is the statement about *who we are* that we are living into through the four steps. The Declaration is also the statement of intention and purpose that drives the four steps; and it is the compass by which we can navigate the ins and outs of life and ups and downs of the four-step process.

We continually align our awareness and choices to the Declaration by asking these questions:

- What does it take for me to live into my Declaration?
- What illusions are most prevalent in my life?
- How do those illusions prevent me from living into my Declaration?

A Declaration is a public promise of who, and how, you intend to be in the world. It is a commitment to act on your personal definition of abundance. The Declaration must also be realistic. I'm not going to declare that I am the heavyweight boxing champion of the world, but I might declare that I have a successful and thriving coaching practice, even if I only have one client.

The Declaration is like the dry Slip-N'-Slide®. You must add the water of the four-step process to make it useful; otherwise, it's nothing more than an elaborate fantasy.

A word of caution: When you're working with your coachee, be careful about pushing him or her into a Declaration too soon. Especially when we're living life under several powerful illusions, we can't see the truth of who we are. Declarations made in this state can be a setup for failure. Begin working through the four-step process. Slowly, as your coachee gains awareness, she will begin to accept the truth of who she is. Once this truth becomes more apparent, your coachee will be in a much better place to make a realistic Declaration she is ready to embrace and act upon.

The water does not flow until the faucet is turned on.

LOUIS L'AMOUR

## THE FOUR STEPS

I have two ways of visualizing the four steps. As above, they are (1) Awareness; (2) Acceptance; (3) Consistent Action; and (4) Authenticity. They are also as shown in Figure 4.2.

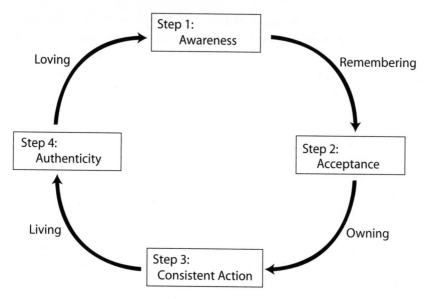

Figure 4.2   The Four-Step Living into Greatness Process.

First you *See It*.
Then, you *Own It*.
Next, you *Live It*.
Finally, you *Be It*.

The four steps, illustrated in Figure 4.3 aren't a one-shot deal. They're a continuous cycle in which new awareness brings acceptance, which leads to action, and then to living authentically. Through the process of living, some things work, and some do not. Sometimes we succeed, and sometimes we don't. Both success and failure provide new opportunities for awareness, acceptance, action, and greater authenticity.

There is no end point, which to me is a good thing. It means there is always a new awareness to be had, and another level of Living into Greatness.

STEP 1—AWARENESS

> *The real voyage of discovery consists not in seeking new landscapes, but in having new eyes.*
>
> MARCEL PROUST

Awareness = remembering who you are

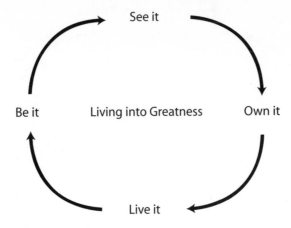

Figure 4.3   See, Own, Live, Be It.

The *process* by which we gain awareness is crucial. We can gain awareness of ourselves and our environment through trial and error, or by
waiting for random events to provide an awakening. Or, we can consciously *create* greater awareness through a concrete process of inquiry.

The process is simple, yet challenging:

1. Identify a situation in which you're stuck or in which you'd like
   greater movement.
2. Isolate the fears (those things that make you feel uncomfortable or
   anxious) that surround the situation.
3. For each fear, identify the illusion or illusions that feed and give
   strength to the fear.
4. Examine each fear for underlying beliefs and assumptions. An easy
   way to identify these beliefs is to examine your behavior patterns.
   Notice what you're doing, then ask, "why do I do this?" Inquire
   into the reasons that you repeatedly act in certain ways.
5. Take the "Truth or Dare" test with each belief:
   a. What proof or evidence do I have that this is true?
   b. How does thinking this way serve me?
   c. What new thought would serve me better?

STEP 2 — ACCEPTANCE

> *Each life is an original work of art. When are you going to start sign-
> ing autographs?*
>
> RUSTY BERKUS

Acceptance = owning who you are

We have free will to accept or reject any thought. You can continue to accept old beliefs and assumptions that no longer serve you; or, you can reject those thoughts and replace them with new thoughts.

All of our conditioned beliefs are beliefs we accepted by choice. They may have been unconscious choices, but they were choices nonetheless. When I talk about acceptance in the context of Living into Greatness, I am referring to acceptance of consciously created beliefs that are based on internalizing and experiencing truth.

There are two parts to acceptance:

1. First, *Own* that a new thought or belief has personal relevance. This involves recognizing the Opportunity Cost, and realizing the Tipping Point of the beliefs and behavior patterns. You can see why and where the old belief is holding you back, and why and where a new belief will move you forward.
2. Based on the recognition of personal relevance, you now *decide* to commit to internalizing the new belief.

You can't realistically move toward acceptance, decision, commitment, and internalization without awareness. Notice that the question in the Truth or Dare test is about *how* the belief serves you, and not *whether* the belief serves you. All beliefs have a purpose and serve a function. Most unconscious beliefs protect our fragile egos, keep us "safe," and maintain our membership or status within a community. They don't help us Live into our Greatness. They do serve a purpose—just not a positive, productive purpose.

Hence, acceptance is a choice. What do you choose to own? To what thought, belief, or purpose do you choose to commit? Your coachee, for example, can choose to own and commit to the belief that she isn't good enough to create her own music CD. She can also choose and commit to the belief that she is a successful musician who easily creates wonderful music and routinely puts that music on CDs.

It may take time for her to integrate aspects of the new belief. Her *Declaration* that she's a successful musician may not come until several rounds through the four-step process. But, it will come; and once it does, she's *accepted* the new belief as the truth of who she is.

Acceptance of the truth is arrived at not *because of* appearances, but is arrived at *in spite* of appearances. We must learn to accept that the truth is in our capacity and not in the appearance of things as they are today.

I didn't know *how* I would become a successful coach or publish my book when the ideas came to me. I *knew and accepted* the truth of my Declarations and took consistent action on the truth and knowledge I had at each step. Each step led beautifully to the next, creating synchronicity after synchronicity until the Declaration had been realized. (And, now, I'm on to my next Declaration).

Work with your coachee to surrender to the process. You've added water to the Slip-N-Slide®. Now, help her glide through the four-step process, letting go of how it's all going to happen.

STEP 3 — CONSISTENT ACTION

*The measure of success is not whether you have a tough problem to deal with, but whether it's the same problem you had last year.*

JOHN FOSTER DULLES

Consistent action = living who you are

Albert Einstein said, "All present results are an expression of a certain way of thinking. As a scientist, I have learned that to change my results requires new ways of thought and new action until we find the new result."

The new result comes not from one action, but from *consistent action.* Consistent action is the process of applying conscious choices to everyday living. You cannot act where you are not. You can't act in the future or the past; you can only act in the present.

Every day we are faced with new situations that require a choice. Do I, or do I not return a phone call? What will I say to my boss? If I believe that nothing I do is good enough, and I decide and act on that belief, I will struggle in my actions, attempting to produce or do "enough." If, though, I *accept* the belief that I produce quality work, I will accomplish my actions with greater ease. I choose to consistently act on the basis of the *conscious* belief.

Consistent and conscious action enables us to replace the conditioned patterns with conscious patterns. Actions aren't random but are consciously chosen and applied daily.

Each day, do all that can be done in that day. Take actions that align with your Declaration (your greatness). If your coachee is uncertain about taking a particular action, ask her how well that decision/action aligns with or moves her in the direction of her Declaration.

Consistent action is the action plan of the Coaching into Greatness process. It is what helps us internalize and actualize the new beliefs and create the new conscious patterns.


## STEP 4 — AUTHENTICITY

> *Our greatest pretenses are built up not to hide the evil and the ugly in us, but our emptiness. The hardest thing to hide is something that is not there.*
>
> ERIC HOFFER

Authenticity = loving who you are

You are authentic when you are living your life according to the truth of who you are, even when the appearance of things in your life would dictate otherwise. How you show up might be scary (for you and others), is almost always difficult, and is generally unpopular. Earl Nightingale said that if you want to follow anyone, don't follow the 98 percent of the population that are headed in one direction. Follow the 2 percent that are going in the opposite direction!

I am often asked why authenticity is the fourth step and not the first. Shouldn't we, people ask, be authentic first? How can anyone be authentic without first understanding what that means on an individual basis? Only you can determine what is true for you, and the only way you'll know the truth is by removing the layers of conditioning and illusions, and replacing them with the truth.

People who start with authenticity are only authentic to their conditioning. We first become aware of truth by observing our present results, realizing we can do better, then deciding and acting on a new set of beliefs. As these beliefs are integrated, we naturally show up in the world more authentically.

When you align with your vision and values, become aware of the illusions under which you've been operating, and begin making conscious choices and actions according to truth, you then have the difficult task of showing up daily in an authentic way. It's not easy, and there will be breakdowns. We all revert back to old conditioned patterns, especially during a crisis or an especially challenging situation.

Rather than see these breakdowns as evidence of the truth of the illusions, choose to see them as evidence that this process is working. Breakdowns are a part of the process. They are evidence that you are alive and changing and exploring what opportunities are out there. They are an opportunity for reflection and recommitment. Remember that the four steps, the cycle of conditioning, and the Living into Greatness process are all continuous cycles.

Developing new patterns and habits takes time. It takes effort and conscious attention. When you experience a breakdown in the process, return to awareness. What is working for me here? What is not working? How has this altered my perception? Keep working all four steps of the process. Remember, *shift happens!*

The following chapters discuss each of the seven illusions in detail. In each chapter, I will provide a case study, which will walk you through applying the four-step process from a coaching perspective.

Remember to keep thinking and acting on truth in spite of appearances.

## CHAPTER SUMMARY

All of our conditioned beliefs are beliefs we accepted by choice.

You can't think your way out of scarcity.

A Declaration is your public promise of how you will show up in the world.

You are authentic when you are living your life according to the truth of who you are.

## CHAPTER FIVE

# The Illusion of Not Enough

*I have enough for this life. If there is no other life, then this one has been enough to make it worth being born, myself a human being.*

PEARL S. BUCK

After my mom died, I was sent to live with my uncle in Lake Tahoe, California. It was an achingly lonely, confusing time. That summer, my uncle got me a job working at a deli on the top of Squaw Valley, the resort that held the 1960 Olympic Games.

In spite of a tremendous fear of heights, each day I took the tram ride up 6,000 feet to the deli. But, it was a job, right? I felt out of place and completely invisible. It seemed as though everyone but me had a busy, normal life. I pretended to be okay.

Soon after, my dad got a new job in Reno, a 45-minute drive from Tahoe. He and my stepmother moved their increasingly codependent relationship to their new home—the place I would also call home at the end of that summer.

Talk about out of place! I felt like an alien in a dust bowl. I yearned for the comfort of my friends in Wisconsin. I longed for the trees and the grass, and, crazily enough, I even missed the humidity. (I must have been out of my mind!)

The first day of school is one I'll never forget. First, I actually *walked to the bus*. As a senior, it was like wearing a huge neon sign that blinked

"LOSER." That I had the ugliest shoes ever made wasn't much help, either. I think I held my breath on the entire descent down the hill to the bus stop. It didn't take a degree in psychology to know what they thought of me, and at the time I would have agreed with their assessment: major loser.

Later that fall, I wrote poetry about my mom in the relative comfort of my uncle's house. Left alone by my dad, who wanted "quality time" with his wife, and my uncle's family, who'd gone out on the town, I wandered outside into a rain just cold enough to feel like thousands of miniature razors. I wore no coat and left the umbrella in the house. I didn't care if I got sick. Maybe if I did, I'd actually get *someone* to pay attention!

It didn't work. I've been blessed, or cursed in that case, with a strong immune system. I yearned for someone to see me, to notice my pain, but I was invisible. Always invisible.

Fifteen years later, a therapist commented that I was "pathetic" on that cold, dreary night. You might agree. It does sound rather pathetic looking from the outside in. Pathetic or not, it was no more or less than the desperate attempt of a young girl to reclaim her place in the world— to *be enough*, to be seen.

Through what was the most difficult time in my life, I didn't trust in my own ability to get me through the tremendous pain I was experiencing. My experiences all pointed to the fact that I wasn't enough, and because I waited (hoped) for others to provide the validation that never came, I built my young life around the belief that I wasn't enough.

## THE DYNAMICS OF NOT ENOUGH

People every day are walking through life, desperate to be seen, desperate to matter. *Because they don't trust that they are enough.*

> The Illusion of Not Enough occurs when an individual believes that they can't trust who they are, resulting in feelings of being incomplete.

The Illusion of Not Enough occurs when you believe that you are incomplete—not good enough, smart enough, resourceful enough; and, the list goes on. It is a *perception of lack.*

The Illusion of Not Enough keeps people striving for something better—some way to fill the void experienced by the perception of lack. It creates a persistent struggle between the unreachable standards we see "outside" and the often huge internal sense of lack.

You'll recognize the Illusion of Not Enough by these fears:

- Fear of missing out on "the good stuff" (it all goes to someone else).
- Fear of being invisible and not mattering to others.
- Fear of being seen for "who you are"—when they finally do see you, they'll see your flaws and confirm you're not enough.

People under the Illusion of Not Enough are just getting by; they can't thrive because every step of the way the perceptions and beliefs of Not Enough are validated by their life experiences. Instead of seeing themselves as the Cup (a sign of Living into Greatness), they see themselves as a crack in the Cup. Sure, we're all flawed, but this idea that any of us can ever be Not Enough is, when you really think about it, quite silly. Who holds the measuring tape?

## A Story of Not Enough

Jim, a management consultant, had big plans for his business. He wanted to double his sales in the next year and hire an operations manager to take over the day-to-day running of the business. In our first session, I discovered that this wasn't the first time Jim had big plans for a business. He'd previously started, and subsequently folded, a similar business, but in a different industry.

Everything he said made some sense. He'd previously focused on high-tech businesses, and when the "dot-com" boom went bust, so did his business. So he reinvented himself and was beginning anew in a different industry that he felt was ripe for the picking. He had a solid plan and a clear vision for his business.

As we worked together, it soon became apparent that Jim was going to have some problems. While his plan called for direct marketing to the Chief Information Officers (CIOs) of his target market, Jim felt that he would be better off networking at various project manager functions. He also hesitated in completing his marketing materials, feeling that he needed more time to get to know the project managers. His inaction and his obvious lack of positive results were powerful clues to the Illusion of Not Enough. We'll get back to Jim later in this chapter. In the meantime, see if you can spot the patterns that might be keeping Jim from following through with his plans and accomplishing his goals.

## THE CONDITIONED PATTERNS OF NOT ENOUGH

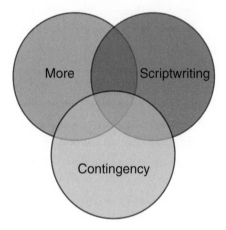

Figure 5.1   The Conditional Patterns of Not Enough.

### THE CONDITIONED PATTERN OF MORE

> *You never know what is enough, until you know what is more than enough.*

WILLIAM BLAKE

The first conditioned pattern for Not Enough is what I call "More." It is the drive to fill the void caused by a deep sense of lack. When I think of the conditioned pattern of More, I imagine Audrey, the blood-drinking plant from *The Little Shop of Horrors*, who constantly pushes Seymour to feed her. Her appetite for blood can never be sated, much as one who is conditioned from lack to want more:

- Evidence before making a decision.
- Talent to take on a new task or role.
- Time to do whatever must be done.

- Energy with which to get through the day.
- Confidence before going public with something new.
- Information before deciding to act.
- Patience to stick with a decision.
- Money for investing in the future.
- Proof before taking a stand.
- Details before proceeding.
- Explanations before expressing an opinion.
- Skills before completing a project.

---

More is characterized by the belief that something or someone outside of ourselves will complete us.

---

Someone who wants More will rarely proceed without things first being "perfect," which of course, they never are. Steven Wright understood this when he said that "You can't have everything. Where would you put it?"

A few of the conditioned beliefs underlying the conditioned pattern of More are:

- I can't be myself and be happy or have what I want.
- Only those at the top get what they want (there's not enough to go around).
- I can be happy if only I can . . . (fill in the blank).
- I'm always the one left out (or left behind).

All you need do is reread my story to get a good understanding of where these beliefs might originate. I wasn't a happy camper, and I certainly believed that the only way I'd ever be happy is if I somehow

---

DISTINCTION: WANTING MORE VS. BEING MORE

We want more because we feel what we have isn't enough. It's a perception of lack.

Being more is at the heart of Living into Greatness!

Who you are *is* enough; and who you are is constantly expanding into greater fulfillment and personal satisfaction. —*See Julia Butterfly Hill's story later in this chapter*

---

became someone entirely else—someone *more* confident, smart, accomplished, talented, and so on.

The conditioned pattern of More is all about filling the void caused by a sense of lack—there isn't enough, and therefore I have to be the best to win any prizes at all. That is, I have to *become great,* rather than realize my greatness. It is a negation of my capacity.

### THE CONDITIONED PATTERN OF SCRIPTWRITING

Everyone is an incredible playwright. Most of us are highly skilled at concocting elaborate scripts to define how we appear to others. Just ask a large group to define who they are, and you'll get a room full of carefully constructed scripts. We are all actors in a play of our own construction.

What do we say about ourselves? "I'm really very analytical." "I'm assertive and bold." "I'm shy." The conditioned pattern of Scriptwriting is that skill we all develop to latch onto a particular image of ourselves and write scene-by-scene justifications of that image.

It's all a great big story—a bunch of hooey that's defined by a big pile of "shoulds" that sit on top an even bigger pile of "can'ts". As Lorretta Larouche, author and comedienne, says, people are "shoulding all over themselves."

> Scriptwriting is characterized by projecting an image of ourselves that is not real.

We project our insecurities out into the world. We fear we're not enough so we overcompensate or manipulate or prove. What we get is reinforcement of our script, which is exactly what a script is designed to do! These scripts are designed as an attempt to make sense of a nonsensical situation—we *feel* lack and *see* lack, while those around us seem to get exactly what we want. So, we create stories to *be more like them,* in the hope that we'll also win. It doesn't work.

Here are a few conditioned beliefs associated with Scriptwriting:

- If I could be more like (fill in the blank), I'll be happy (liked, successful. . . .)

- I'll never amount to anything unless I can be like (fill in the blank).
- If I could only prove that . . . (I'm smart enough, good enough, etc.).

## THE CONDITIONED PATTERN OF CONTINGENCY

*While one person hesitates because he feels inferior, the other is busy making mistakes and becoming superior.*

HENRY LINK

You'll recognize this conditioned pattern in an "If—then" or "If only" statement. It is the type of conditioning that leaves the individual always waiting for an external event to occur before making a decision. His or her decision is contingent upon something or someone else.

These should sound familiar:

- When I get a new job, I'll finally feel good about myself.
- If only I was married. Then, I'd be happy.
- I won't be satisfied until I get that new car.
- If I create a killer product, I'll make a lot of money; and *then* I can relax.

> Contingency is characterized by the need for a condition outside of ourselves to happen for us to do or be something.

Contingency makes us dependent on outside or external sources. We make success contingent on someone or something else. That something else is usually time or money.

Fill in the blank:

Money doesn't grow on _____. <Trees>
I didn't do it. I didn't have the _____. <Time or Money>

Lack of time and lack of money aren't real. They are conditioned beliefs that create the conditioned pattern of Contingency. For example, I was working with a coaching client to create a strategic alliance strategy for growing her business. We'd identified her ideal alliance partners and an implementation plan during several coaching sessions. At our next session, she admitted she hadn't done a thing. Her reason? She didn't have the time!

Of course she had the time. Like many of us, she found plenty of distractions to fill her days so that she could avoid making the phone calls. She was terrified that these alliance partners would find her lacking; that is, not enough. She was actually afraid they would agree to the alliance.

Time and money are typical reactive responses to the call to Live into Greatness. In their groundbreaking book, *The Power of Full Engagement,* Jim Loehr and Tony Schwartz demonstrate how managing time is rarely the issue. "Every one of our thoughts, emotions, and behaviors has an energy consequence, for better or for worse. The ultimate measure of our lives is not how much time we spend on the planet, but rather how much energy we invest in the time that we have." The Illusion of Not Enough sees us as flawed, thus stealing our energy. Living into our Greatness is how we *invest* our energy.

I've had my own struggles with contingencies. Toward the end of my eight-year career in health care, I was involved in a great culture change movement, called The Eden Alternative™. The Eden Alternative™ works to deinstitutionalize nursing homes and make them more like human habitats. As a trainer for The Eden Alternative™, I became friends with the founder, Dr. Bill Thomas.

Near the end of my health-care career, I was terribly burned out. I visited Dr. Thomas in his home in New York and asked for his help in making my decision to leave the industry or stay. His eyes welled with tears at my statement, and he said, "That makes me so sad because we need people like you. Can't you think of a way to make it work?"

I said that one way was to start my own business, but I simply wasn't ready. It wasn't the right time, and I didn't have enough money. I felt in need of that steady paycheck. Looking me straight in my eyes, he asked, "When is there a right time?" We sat in silence for several moments before he continued, "Kim, there never is a *right* time."

His words have stayed with me. Six months after I met with Dr. Thomas I discovered coaching and started my own business.

Circumstances are never perfect. He or she who waits lives a life of forgotten dreams and promises. Do the thing, and you will have energy to do the thing.

## THE TIPPING POINT OF NOT ENOUGH

We all want More. The nature of the universe is to seek expansion and growth. We tip toward the downside of Not Enough when the search for more comes from a strong sense of lack instead of a desire for something greater. We continuously attempt to fill the void.

When the teeter-totter has shifted to Not Enough, people see themselves as "the problem." Self-ridicule becomes the rule instead of self-exploration or self-evaluation. It's hard to become self-aware when beating yourself over the head with your own mistakes and insecurities.

There is a marked difference between someone who wants more out of life because he's enjoying the fullness of an already abundant life, and someone who wants more because he feels a deep sense of lack.

---

### DISTINCTION: MOTIVATION VS. INSPIRATION

When you feel Not Enough, you are *motivated* to do something or get More. You're trying to get away from an emotional discomfort that's the result of a perceived lack. Motivation is initiated *externally*.

When you feel enough, you're *inspired* to attain or achieve more—to grow and prosper through expansion. Inspiration is initiated *internally*.

---

The teeter-totter tilts too far toward scarcity when More means "I don't have enough to be content, happy, or comfortable." This is when we create scripts to pretend we're happy, content, or good enough. It moves toward abundance when More means "I enjoy who I am and what I have so much that I desire even greater things."

It's useful to gather facts, investigate opportunities, and conduct all the appropriate due diligence before making a decision. There are always contingencies. The question is whether those contingencies are keeping us from getting or doing what we want. If they are, then we've tipped toward scarcity. Your coachee may not be the "fire, ready, aim" type, but he or she can still move forward without having every little detail in place.

## PROFILES IN GREATNESS: JULIA "BUTTERFLY" HILL

On Dec. 10, 1997, a 23-year-old woman named Julia "Butterfly" Hill climbed onto a 180-foot-tall California redwood tree. She put her life on the line for just over two years, living high up in the tree year-round to save the life of the tree ("Luna") and the forest where it had lived for a millennium. Hill became an international symbol of nonviolent environmentalism and has been an inspiration for thousands around the world. She continues to this day campaigning to heal the divide between humans and nature.

Julia wasn't born rich or privileged. She grew up wondering where she'd get her next meal, often feeling afraid of looking stupid or worthless. She wasn't particularly braver than anyone else and suffered from the same fear-based scarcity thoughts as the rest of us. What differentiates her, though, is her openness to abundance. She associates abundance with a kind of magic — a miracle of life.

"I was literally freezing to death in the tree," says Hill. "My hands and feet were frozen and I had every ounce of clothing and my sleeping bag on. I was completely drenched, sleep deprived, food deprived, and freezing. I thought that if I can make it through this breath, I might make it through another." It was a profound moment in which she could easily choose to fall into the abyss of the Illusion of Not Enough, thinking that "I don't have enough food. I don't have enough sleep. I'm going to die." She could give in to the fear, or take each moment as it comes — one breath at a time.

But the transformation really started before Hill ever set foot onto Luna. This is what is so beautiful about her story. Had you or I approached her before she climbed the tree and suggested that she'd be up there two years, she says, "I would have laughed and then screamed and run in the other direction." In this way, she's no different from most of us.

Much of her success has to do with facing the fear of not being enough, both before she climbed Luna and while she was facing the many physical, emotional, and mental hardships during her two years in the tree. When she faced the base of the tree, all her fears were magnified. She was no environmentalist, and certainly not an activist. She'd never done anything like this before. She thought, "Oh, I should do something." But, what came up then was, "Well, I don't know anything about this issue. I don't know what an activist is. I don't know anyone who's involved. I'm not smart enough. I am not connected enough. Then, at the base of the tree, it was just hyper intensified. All those concerns I had had before are even stronger."

Then, she thought, "Julia if you walk away from this injustice, your inactions are as much a part of the injustice as the actions of others."

She equates people's inaction in the face of feeling not enough to clear-cutting a forest. "We clear-cut ourselves over and over in our lives, especially living in that space of fear and lack and scarcity. We take chain saws to who we are on a very deep level. We're wounding not only our external world, but our internal world."

So, Julia climbed to the top of Luna. While there, she came front and center into the public eye. Everyone had opinions about her, who she was, and what she was doing. They told her what she should or shouldn't say, and how she could, should, or would act.

Hill says that she felt like she was developing a personality disorder, "trying to be everything to everyone and it was ripping me to shreds." At one point, she says, she had to put herself under her own microscope. Like most of us, she'd spent most of her life trying to please her parents, teachers, and everyone else. Of course, she says, none of this worked. "I had spent years, afraid to put myself under the microscope because there's some not so pretty stuff in there. So, we tend to hide from that and in the process we're not being who we authentically are, and we're stuck in the same pattern over and over again."

There were times when she dangled in the fetal position, begging and crying for help. She wondered what kind of karma she was working off. Then it struck her: "You asked for strength." She got just what she was asking for! Julia continues, "You don't get muscles by sitting on the recliner with potato chips in your lap and a remote control. You get muscles by exercising them and the heart is a muscle. Our brain is a muscle. Our spirit is a muscle."

The gift of Hill's self-inquiry is getting to the core essence of who she is. The investigation was, to Hill, much like using a magnifying glass to start a fire. "When we choose to really delve into ourselves," she says, "is when we turn the magnifying glass toward the sun. That's when it gets fierce." We're so afraid of this intensity, we keep the magnifying glass turned the other way. "The results," she continues, "can only happen in the space of that intensity, so that in the process of being pulled in a million different directions and being unhappy most of my life, I can finally say 'Okay, I'm going to take it on now.'"

She did burn, but as she puts it, what burned were the illusions she had about who she was, and the illusions about not being enough. She switched from "being in the world of fear to being in the world of joy." She's learned to laugh more easily, and she can see more clearly the way our existing systems feed off our scarcity and fear. "Can you imagine," she asks, "what it would be like to walk down the store aisles and see magazines covers, '101 ways to be perfectly happy and satisfied with who you are, where you are, with what you have?'"

Living in the tree wasn't two years and eight days as one event, she says. "It was two years and eight days of moment by moment access of who am I choosing to be in this moment, and recognizing that all we need to be is who we are." When asked "What can I do?" she responds: "What do you love to do? Find a way to offer some part of that. Who we are is exactly who we were meant to be."

Hill concludes: "Everything I needed to be is already within me, but I had to be willing to embrace the real burning of the illusions; the letting go of the illusions. In the butterfly analogy, the melting of myself so that I could become who I already am—a newer, more vibrant expression of who I am."

Are you feeling jealous or envious of Julia Butterfly Hill? She'd say that if you're jealous, it's because you haven't claimed your own power and your own responsibility. It's like you want to have the fierceness of the magnifying glass without wanting to do the work of getting there. Are we not enough? Hill says that it is more likely that "we are afraid of our own divinity. We are afraid of our own power, our own light, but it's because making this manifest in the world today takes responsibility."

## SHIFTING THE BALANCE FROM NOT ENOUGH TO SELF-WORTH

*How much easier is self-sacrifice than self-realization.*

ERIC HOFFER

On the opposite side of the teeter-totter from Not Enough is Self-Worth (see Figure 5.2). It is a simple formula. If I'm not enough, then I'm not worthy of all the good things that life has to offer. If, on the other hand, I know my worth, then the idea that I'm not smart enough, talented enough, clever enough, or prosperous enough to do what I want to do in life is preposterous!

Unfortunately, much of the self-help industry thrives on the Illusion of Not Enough. Personally, I'm not very fond of self-help programs. The whole idea that we can generate a sense of Self-Worth by doing a bunch of exercises is baffling. How can it be that by meeting certain conditions

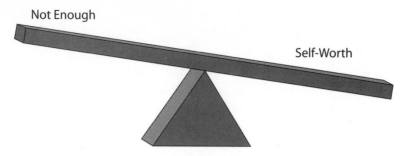

Figure 5.2   Tipping the Balance to Self-Worth.

of the self-help program I'll suddenly have Self-Worth? Isn't that something of a contradiction?

George Carlin captured this best when he said, "If you're reading it in a book, folks, it ain't self-help, it's help." This is why the role of a great coach can make the difference between acquiring knowledge and getting lasting results.

You can see through my own story and that of our case study how Self-Worth is intricately tied to the Illusion of Not Enough. So many are addicted to self-help programs in a futile attempt to satisfy the insatiable appetite for *More*. Through self-help, we strive to be someone or something other than who we are. The Illusion of Not Enough does this to people.

Self-Worth is a state of being, while self-help comes from a striving to be someone or something else. The idea of Self-Worth is not to *become* who you are, but to live, today, according to *who you already are.*

You are not improving yourself or becoming yourself. You are *being* yourself. Self-help works from the perspective that we need to be fixed. Dogs get fixed. People don't get fixed. Our worthiness is completely independent of any external events or circumstances.

Said another way, if where you are today isn't good enough, then nothing you do or find or achieve will ever be good enough. You can't be fixed because nothing is broken. As soon as you or any of your coachees are able to view yourselves as complete, you're on your way to Living into your Greatness.

Let's go back to the acorn and the oak for a moment. The acorn is complete; still it is not yet an oak. It contains the blueprint for an oak, and by realizing its capacity to be an oak on a day-to-day basis, it grows into the fullness of that blueprint. We are all like that acorn, and each of us has the ability to embrace the perfect blueprint of our greatness.

---

DISTINCTION: SELF-HELP VS. SELF-WORTH

At its very core, self-help says that we are broken, needing to be fixed. Who we want to be is outside of ourselves, something to be attained, something to strive for, our potential to reach.

Self-Worth is believing that you already have everything you need, that you are the person you've been waiting for, that you have the Capacity of greatness. You don't have to strive, achieve or reach your potential. There is nothing to reach. There is only living who you are.

---

Don Ward said that, "If you're going to doubt something, doubt your limits." To doubt is to lose touch with who you are. If your coachee doubts his or her ability to accomplish a goal, no matter how far-fetched (space travel was once considered far-fetched), what he or she is really doing is resisting the natural inclination toward expansion and growth.

Doubts cannot be corrected externally. You can't wish a doubt away; nor can you ever really eliminate a doubt just by reading books, taking classes, or following a guru. *The only way we can really continue to be abundant is to look inward and fill this gap with our internal resources.*

## THE WEEDS OF YOUR GREATNESS

*A weed is just an unloved flower.*

EDITH WHEELER

Have you ever seen a butterfly bush? In bloom, they're beautiful, attracting an abundance of butterflies and bees. Many people plant them intentionally. In some states, though, they're considered a noxious weed.

We are all many things. The Illusion of Not Enough says that some parts of us are good, and others are weeds. We're taught to reject ourselves because someone else thought what they saw in us was nothing more than a field of weeds. Fortunately, those "weeds" never die. A friend of mine once had a butterfly bush that became too big for his yard. He laboriously dug out the entire bush, roots and all. That bush is now thriving in another person's yard. What's even better is that my friend used one of the "dead" branches to mark a planting in his vegetable garden. By the following spring, that dead branch had rooted and was rapidly growing into a new butterfly bush.

What are the weeds of your greatness?

Your greatness is unchanging, unconditional, and unlike the script you've written, it is real.

## SELF-WORTH AFFIRMS GREATNESS

*I never saw a wild thing sorry for itself.*

D. H. LAWRENCE

The three conditioned patterns of Not Enough—More, Scriptwriting, and Contingency, are fear-based—they are based on external definitions and assumptions. Just look at anyone who's created an elaborate script in which he or she looks cool, collected, and totally in control (like I used to look to others). Or, you may know people who've created a script in which they come across as whiners. Both of these scripts are Illusions of Not Enough, and both scripts protect and affirm the conditioned beliefs of Not Enough. In other words, the scripts absolutely serve the purpose for which they were created!

> Self-Worth is characterized by the belief that you are complete, that you are more than enough exactly as you are.

When you fear life because you are Not Enough, you lose yourself to that fear. Nobody can show up abundantly who isn't also thinking and being abundant. You can't fake your way to abundance, or talk your way to abundance. Abundant people show up abundantly because they *know* their worth. They don't assume or even announce their worth. They don't need to. They live it—from the inside out.

When I show up authentically, I receive so much more, which reinforces who I am. There's no waiting involved. Don't wait! Start applying

> ## DISTINCTION: WORTHINESS VS. MORE
>
> Note that the opposite of Not Enough isn't enough. Worthiness recognizes completeness, in which growth occurs as a natural unfolding of something already complete in itself.
>
> More is a facet of lack. It is the perception of incompleteness in which growth is forced in order to compensate for the incompleteness.

the conscious patterns of Self-Worth today (see Figure 5.3). Affirm your greatness, right now. *You* get to define who you are. Instead of thinking of yourself as just enough, see yourself as just right.

*The key action step of Self-Worth is: Stop searching and start doing.*

## THE CONSCIOUS PATTERNS OF SELF-WORTH

*When you realize there is nothing lacking, the whole world belongs to you.*

LAO TZU

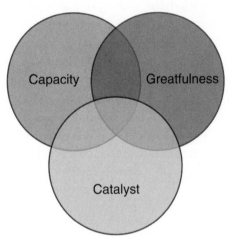

Figure 5.3    The Conscious Patterns of Self-Worth.

### THE CONSCIOUS PATTERN OF CAPACITY

*Only what we are not giving can be lacking in any situation.*

A COURSE IN MIRACLES®

What's the capacity of your computer? Is it the amount of disk space you have available? The amount of RAM? Or is it the CPU speed? If you're a Mac lover, you might say capacity has a lot to do with the type of machine you're running.

Capacity is all of these things combined. Any one of the three parts of your computer (disk, RAM, CPU) can cause the system to slow, or even crash (the "blue screen of death" for Windows users). I consider a person's Capacity to be a combination of their Personal RAM (mental, physical and emotional capacity), their creative energy, and the amount of flow they have in their lives.

> Capacity is defined as the belief that you already have within you all that you want, need, and choose.

When people get stuck, it is because of the focus on *becoming* something. Capacity says you already are that person. You may not be actualized yet, but that Capacity for who you think you should become is already there. People spend their entire lives in a pursuit to become someone, when what they really are is more than enough if they would recognize and live into it.

Capacity is not just the recognition that you are standing on top of a treasure chest of gold. It is owning that *you are* the treasure chest. The gold is inside you, waiting to be invested.

Relate the conscious pattern of Capacity to our brain. It's said that, at most, we only utilize 10% of our brain's Capacity. Does that mean that the other 90% doesn't exist because we fail to use it? *This is exactly the same concept with our greatness.*

Notice that there are no external qualifiers in this formula. Nobody — not your boss, job, house, car, husband, wife, or dog — can add to your Capacity. They can provide support as you expand your Capacity, but they can never complete you or give you more Capacity.

When you are conditioned to want More in order to feel fulfilled, you're likely asking the following questions:

What else do I need that will make me happy?
What can I get from others that will enable me to do what I want or feel better about myself?

Once you gain awareness of your conditioned response to need more, you can start asking these questions in a different way:

What do I want?
What will that give me that I believe I don't already have?
How can I get this from within instead of without?

The conditioned pattern of More assumes that you don't have the Capacity within to do or get what you want. Shifting from this conditioned pattern to a conscious pattern of Capacity assumes that you do have what it takes. It *doesn't* mean that you already know everything you can know, or have all the skills of which you're capable. What the conscious pattern of Capacity does mean, though, is that you already have within you all that is needed to pursue and gain that knowledge and those skills.

For example, if I'm conditioned to need more (I'm not enough), I will avoid making calls to the executives of the companies with whom I'm trying to do business. I'll always feel like I need to prepare more or create better marketing materials. The calls never happen because I need more.

Once I'm aware of this conditioned pattern, I can decide that I'll take action as if I have all the Capacity that I need to succeed. I'll make the first few calls, see what works and what doesn't, and build my skill level and confidence until subsequent calls become easy (or, at least not as scary). I'll assume that I have the Capacity to handle whatever comes up. The conditioned pattern of Not Enough assumes I don't have this Capacity.

## CULTIVATING THE CONSCIOUS PATTERN OF CAPACITY

We are the Cup. It's a Cup that naturally expands to make room for Living into Greatness. Instead of trying to enlarge the Cup, practicing the conscious pattern of Capacity will have you filling the Cup now, knowing and trusting that the Cup will expand on its own as necessary.

Understand that the Cup is plenty big enough for where you are now. Evolution and growth occurs *when we consciously fill our current place or position.* Joe, who desperately wants a better job, but fails to move forward because he feels he needs more experience, will get that new job when he realizes that he doesn't need more—he simply needs to live into his present position fully. If he truly owned and believed that he has the Capacity to be the person who gets the job he wants, he doesn't need more, but he will take the actions that naturally lead him to the new position.

By realizing his Capacity, Joe does what is necessary to move him into a position for the new job. There is no perceived lack; there is only a desire for something greater that is fulfilled by *living into his Capacity.*

## THE CONSCIOUS PATTERN OF GREATFULNESS

On one side, we have what I call Scriptwriting—the conditioned pattern of projecting an image of ourselves that isn't real. At the heart of this conditioned pattern is the belief that we aren't enough or don't have enough, or don't have what it takes to be successful.

If I could create a pill that would cure people of this belief, I'd call that pill *gratitude*. Gratitude can be defined in many ways. I think of it as an appreciation of the truth that you are already great—you are *the Cup*. Gratitude, like greatness, knows no bounds.

---

> Greatfulness is characterized by a combination of elements including gratitude, appreciation, and Capacity. It is the internal knowing that you are "the Cup."

---

As I write this, we are experiencing the aftermath of Hurricane Katrina. I've been struck by the amazing acts of kindness from strangers. In one story, a woman in Texas took in 50 evacuees. 50! When asked why she did it, she responded gratefully, "This is a blessing. It makes me think, where would I be?" This woman recognized her Capacity and was grateful for the contribution her Capacity allowed her to make to the world.

I use a simple equation to understand the power of Greatfulness:

$$\text{Gratitude} + \text{Appreciation} + \text{Capacity} = \text{Greatfulness}$$

There is nothing, and I do mean nothing, that we cannot accomplish by appreciating who we are, being grateful for our infinite Capacity, and then Living into our Greatness. *You* determine how you'll fill your Cup of greatness. You are the Cup, and you choose what goes in and you define the results. That woman in Texas understood this principle clearly. She *is* the Cup, and her Capacity expanded to take in 50 people simply because she was grateful for the opportunity.

See how powerful this concept is? Every single experience you've had—every encounter, success, failure—has helped you to Live into your Greatness. How can you *not* be grateful for all that you are? Whatever you put your attention to expands. By cultivating the conscious pattern of Greatfulness, you quite naturally find and create more things for which you can be grateful.

## CULTIVATING THE CONSCIOUS PATTERN OF GREATFULNESS

While there are many ways to cultivate Greatfulness (practicing it daily as a matter of course is an obvious approach), I really like using a gratitude journal. Every day I record the events, situations, circumstances, or people I've met, and I express gratitude for each and every one. Gratitude can also be expressed for events that have yet to happen. I can easily express gratitude for the new house I see in my mind, or the success of a new business. This kind of gratitude strengthens my awareness of how I might be limiting myself and gives me the confidence to go beyond those limitations.

## THE CONSCIOUS PATTERN OF CATALYST

Imagine working a jigsaw puzzle. You can pick up a piece and search existing holes in the puzzle, or you can take the same piece, set it down, and find the pieces that fit around it. The latter is the way of the person who acts as a Catalyst. Instead of conforming to the existing external environment, the Catalyst chooses to be a center of creation, building what's needed around him as he Lives into his Greatness.

> A Catalyst is a person who has the ability to take what is available in his environment, use it to create what he wants, and leverage it to Live into his Greatness.

The conscious pattern of a Catalyst involves a combination of intention and action. First, initiate or create an idea (or concept) that is in alignment with your greatness. You're not waiting for others to bring you the circumstances you want. You *create* the circumstances you want through conscious Intention. Then, take action. The Catalyst understands that Intention is no more than a fantasy without action. It's the action that pulls in the pieces of the puzzle and aligns them around the creative center.

## HOW TO CULTIVATE A CONSCIOUS PATTERN OF BEING A CATALYST

Since the conditioned patterns imply waiting until things are just right, or until some external event says you're ready, to be a Catalyst requires a greater degree of acceptance without judgment. That is, replacing "if" or "if only" with "what is." Nothing is right, wrong, good, or bad in and of itself. We are not flawed, and what makes us different is a unique gift. It's a part of our greatness.

A coachee who's cultivating a conscious pattern of being a Catalyst analyzes, but doesn't judge the past. He accepts what is with gratitude, and then sets a clear Intention to learn, integrate, and grow, deciding to Live into his Greatness. He becomes a Catalyst for creating his own circumstances instead of waiting for others or looking for that perfect amount of More that will make things right.

We are the only catalyst for living the greatness that exists in us. No one else can do it for us. Life either consumes us or catapults us. It's our choice.

## THE FOUR-STEP PROCESS APPLIED TO THE ILLUSION OF NOT ENOUGH

*He who knows he has enough is rich.*

TAO TE CHING

Remember our management consultant coachee, Jim? Let's quickly apply the Coaching into Greatness four-step process to his situation, particularly his inability to market directly to the CIOs—the people who are the ultimate decision-makers for his services.

The following sections will apply the Coaching into Greatness four-step process to Jim's situation.

### AWARENESS

First, Jim needs to become aware of how the Illusion of Not Enough is expressed through his actions and produces the results that keep him from being successful. We do this by asking the coachee very pointed questions about his results and the actions he is or isn't taking. For example:

- What are your current results?
- Are they satisfactory? (Obviously, no; but if Jim thinks they are, we've got bigger fish to fry.)
- What are you doing or not doing that might be producing these results? (If he has no clear answer, be specific: Your plan calls for direct marketing to the CIOs; yet, you're not doing this. What are you afraid might happen if you do?)

Don't be afraid to get to the point. To shift from the Illusion to the Aptitude of Self-Worth, Jim needs to become aware of the impact of his inaction, and understand its origination in his belief that (among other things) he's not qualified or good enough to go to the top. (Jim's biggest fear was being seen as a fraud.)

## ACCEPTANCE

With awareness of the impact of the Illusion of Not Enough on his life, Jim can accept that it is a lie, and simultaneously accept the truth. While he might not be the most knowledgeable consultant on the planet, he has the Capacity to do good work for his clients. He can accept, with gratitude, the beauty of his current circumstances. Had the "dot-com" bubble not burst, Jim may not have had the opportunity to face the illusions that controlled his life. Now, he is aware of his Capacity and his ability to be a Catalyst for his own success, instead of trying to rely on the project managers he was meeting.

Questions to ask Jim include:

- What do you want to have happen?
- What do you need to believe in order to have this occur?
- What do you need to decide so that these beliefs are fully integrated?

This would be a good time to either help Jim create, or review, his Declaration. What is it that Jim is creating? What greatness is unfolding in him as he lives that greatness?

## CONSISTENT ACTION

It's planning time. Jim already has a plan, so we take the opportunity to refine that plan. We define clear and specific actions that Jim will take that are in alignment with whatever new beliefs he's decided to integrate. For example, he's decided to believe that these CIOs are his peers. Hence, his plan might include both direct contact (via voice, e-mail, or personal letter—or a combination of the three), and contact through networking. Instead of attending the project manager functions, he'll go straight to events attended by the CIOs.

We expect that Jim's old fears will rear their ugly heads as he takes consistent action, and that's when the fourth step kicks into high gear.

## AUTHENTICITY

By now, Jim has his plan and is starting to act on his plan. His Intention is to connect with the CIOs authentically, that is, *according to the truth that he is their peer.* Jim may still not feel like their peer, but it is purely authentic for him to engage with them *as* their peer.

Jim's job is to maintain a high level of awareness as he shows up authentically. Other aspects of this and other illusions will reveal themselves, both in how he feels (trepidation, fear, uncertainty), and in any procrastination. Your objective as his coach is to keep him in consistent action while you assist him in gaining greater awareness.

New awareness brings new acceptance, which leads to refined or new consistent action, and eventually greater authenticity. And, the cycle continues.

## CHAPTER SUMMARY

When you see yourself as not enough you are not trusting who you are.

Fear is a loss of who you are.

Self-Worth is trusting who you are.

We are the only Catalyst for Living the Greatness that exists in us.

Self-Worth is characterized by the belief that you are complete, that you are move than enough exactly as you are.

For additional information and chapter resources, visit http://www.coachingintogreatness.com/the_illusion_of_not_enough.

## CHAPTER SIX

# The Illusion of Comparisons

*The less satisfaction we derive from being ourselves,*
*the greater is our desire to be like others.*

ERIC HOFFER

As you know, I wasn't always a coach. What few people know, however, is that I almost didn't become a coach. My clients wouldn't recognize the confused and scared seeker who literally stumbled upon the coaching profession. I remember quite clearly hesitating before making the decision to break through my fears.

As the director of volunteer services for one of the largest long-term care companies in the country, I knew I was doing something worthwhile. I'd worked in this field for seven years, and although I loved what I was doing, I became bored. I had reinvented my job until there was nothing left to invent. I was in a position similar to many of my coaching clients—comfortable, but never fulfilled. This, for me, was the satin-lined coffin.

I was just getting by in life, not being fully alive. Even though I couldn't see it then, I was on a path of synchronicity. I made one simple, unconscious decision that changed my life. With one more selection required from my book club, I was drawn to the book *Coach Yourself to Success* by Talane Miedaner, for no better reason than the title. I just liked the sound of it.

I had no concept of coaching or the existence of the coaching profession. Only one quarter into the book I knew I'd found my destiny. Talane's description of her work as a coach and the impact she had on her clients resonated with some long-forgotten knowing deep inside me. I thought, "I can do this." The more I thought about it, the more positive I became. "Yes, I am doing this!"

I quickly went online and Googled "coaching." Right at the top of the list was a man named Thomas Leonard and his CoachVille site. I'd found my home. Thomas was so incredibly accomplished and prolific, and the coaches profiled on the Web site appeared successful and confident. What began with excitement, however, quickly diminished into dread. My heart sank as I read profile after profile about their accomplishments. Looking at the enormity of the site brought me to tears. As much as I knew coaching was my destiny, I couldn't help but question myself.

Bang! I ran right up against a big wall of comparisons. I believed that to become successful, I had to somehow already possess the requisite skills and knowledge. Because I felt unequal to the coaches on the CoachVille Web site, I questioned my ability to make it happen.

I did it, anyway.

I took a huge leap of faith and joined the CoachVille community in spite of the negative internal chatter. My very first step was to realize that I had to start from exactly where I was. As much sense as this statement makes, it's a major reason most people never start toward their dreams. I started by learning everything I could about coaching. I enrolled in the new Graduate School of Coaching at CoachVille and took every class I could fit into my schedule. More importantly, I began coaching other people.

My story epitomizes the Illusion of Comparisons. My coaching career, the people I've met, and this book would never have happened if I'd given in to the Illusion of Comparisons. When I saw myself as inferior and the people listed on the Web site as superior, I could have given up right then and there. Fortunately, I didn't.

## THE DYNAMICS OF COMPARISONS

We can't avoid comparisons. They're everywhere we look. But the Illusion of Comparisons comes into play when we think, even for a moment, that these comparisons somehow define who we are. An extreme example would be to compare myself as a person to Lindsay Davenport, the current top-ranked women's tennis pro. I wouldn't last one game with her, let alone even hope to come within five feet of one of her serves. Does this mean that I'm inadequate as a person? Unfortunately, this is exactly what happens with this illusion!

> The Illusion of Comparisons is the habit of consistently comparing ourselves to people and things in the external world to validate our belief of who we are.

The basis of this illusion is that our capabilities are somehow dictated by comparisons to people, events, or things in the external world. The truth is that who we are is in no way dependent on anyone or anything outside of ourselves. I'm short. You're tall. I'm a woman. You're a man. I don't have a Ph.D. in nuclear physics. You do. So what?

My worth, your worth, and our unique capabilities are completely independent of how we stack up against each other—in size, intelligence, gender, education, experience, hair color, or even in the clothes we wear. That we are inundated with comparisons on a daily basis is, however, a fact of living in today's hyped-up, fast-paced world.

Of all the illusions, comparisons may cause the most unhappiness for people. Rarely will anyone be the best in the world at anything, and even then it happens for only a very short period. Comparison to others is normal but is also a conditioned response to life.

> DISTINCTION: COMPARISON VS. EVALUATION
>
> Comparison involves judgment. He's smarter, which implies I shouldn't even try to be in the same field.
>
> Evaluation is a factual analysis that leads to a conscious choice. He may be smarter, but I can choose to enter the same field with a different strategy that plays to my strengths. There's no judgment of good/bad or right/wrong.

## A STORY OF COMPARISONS

One of my clients, Eileen, was torn—pretty much in the proverbial spot between a rock and a hard place, about whether to take a new position in her company that offered a little room for growth and was significantly more interesting than her current job. On the one side were all the reasons she *should* take the new job—better pay, more responsibility. On the other were all the reasons she shouldn't take it—more responsibility, a new boss.

It was an excruciating process (for both of us) to get to a point of decision. She'd asked everyone she knew and of course got as many opinions as there were people. Her gut said, "Take the job!" Finally, she followed her gut, ignoring the many contradictory messages from her family, who thought she should play it safe.

Within months of taking the new job, Eileen faced yet another difficult decision. In her heart, she knew she wanted to work in the human service industry, but she was making good money in the business sector. Out of the blue, a nonprofit company offered her a position at two-thirds her salary, but essentially doing the same job she had now.

What to do? Eileen's immediate reaction was to ask for advice—from me, her parents, and her friends. Back came the lists of comparisons—plus, minus, positive, negative. Here we go again.

## THE CONDITIONED PATTERNS OF COMPARISONS

*He who trims himself to suit everyone will soon whittle himself away.*

RAYMOND HULL

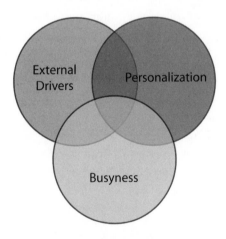

Figure 6.1   The Conditioned Patterns of Comparisons.

### THE CONDITIONED PATTERN OF EXTERNAL DRIVERS

It's simple, and it starts early in our lives. We see really happy kids on TV and think that we'll be just as happy if we get that cool toy. Mom tells

Johnny that she'd really like him to be more like Bill, his older brother. We notice that a certain type of kid seems to get all the attention, or that we get a little more attention if we act in certain ways.

We're conditioned to be motivated by External Drivers pretty much from the day we're born. Studies have shown that as a rule, boy babies aren't held or cuddled as much as girl babies. Clearly, boys are supposed to be one way and girls another (and, no, I don't think males and females are from different planets!).

These and other conditioned patterns soon form in which our interpretation of who we are and the Capacity we have is dependent on outside sources. These are the External Drivers that dictate who we are and of what we are capable.

Eileen, can't seem to make a decision without first evaluating all the External Drivers, which include:

- The anticipated opinions of others.
- Her odds of succeeding, based on a comparison of others making similar decisions.
- Social norms and standards.
- What she currently has or doesn't have (resources, knowledge, experience).

These External Drivers tell Eileen what she should or shouldn't do. She's like a poor little ping-pong ball, smacked from one side of the table to the other on the basis of opinions, thoughts, ideas, circumstances, and customs that are for the most part irrelevant to her decision.

---

External Drivers are characterized by the interpretation that who you are is dependent on sources outside of yourself—people, circumstances, or events.

---

External Drivers are:
- Other people—
  - What they have that we want.
  - What they want that we have.
  - Their intelligence, knowledge, experience, or success.
  - Their upbringing versus ours.
  - Their history or past experiences.
  - Their opinions or views of the world.

- What they do or don't do (do we follow the crowd, or not?).
- Their permission (we often ask for advice as a means of getting permission).
- Events and circumstances —
  - Past failures (ours or others).
  - Past successes (ours or others).
  - World events—for one person, a recession offers tremendous opportunity for growing a business; for another, it's a sign to close shop quickly.
  - Natural disasters (good or bad luck?).
  - Opinions about trends (see the example below).
- Societal norms and standards —
  - What works or doesn't work (according to societal definitions).
  - Religious tenets or beliefs.
  - What we learn from our parents ("Kids today are so lazy.")

Clearly, I could go on. It just goes to show how truly remarkable it is that anything new ever gets invented or accomplished.

Here's a little bit of truth I've learned through experience: *Every time you focus on External Drivers you lose power—the power to be yourself, to be great.*

People will believe all sorts of falsehoods and call them the truth just because they've been repeated for decades. Take these, for example:

- Coming in second is never good enough. I have to be number one, or I'm not even going to try.
- How else will I know if I'm doing okay if I don't compare myself to others?
- There's no way I'll ever be as good as _____ (fill in the blank).
- I won't believe it can be done until I've seen someone else do it.
- I should care what others think.
- Every time I did it my way, I failed; so why bother trying?
- I have to heed the advice of others. I can't see my own blind spots.
- And, of course, "The grass is always greener. . . ."

## THE CONDITIONED PATTERN OF PERSONALIZATION

> *When we take something personally, we make the assumption that they know what is in our world, and we try to impose our world on their world.*
>
> DON MIGUEL RUIZ

"Don't take things so personally," he said. Ha! How can I not take it personally when he said that he didn't think I was qualified for the job?

Sound familiar? We are conditioned to take things personally. I call this the conditioned pattern of Personalization. That is, we're like sponges sucking up the criticism, comments, or experiences of others as if they had anything to do with who we really are.

I have a friend whose sister called him by the nickname "ugly" all through middle school. That's a pretty vulnerable age, so it was natural

> Personalization is characterized by consistently taking on the opinions and beliefs of others as the ultimate truth, even when those beliefs feel contradictory to our inner knowing.

for him to enter high school with the firm belief that he was, indeed, ugly. Personalization is about identification. We hear something said about us, and we decide that it must be true. We identify with the comment, even if we can joke about it at the time. We end up making other people's experiences into *our* experiences! It's the emotional equivalent of carrying some part of everyone else's suitcases. That's a lot of baggage to cart around.

It's not that we're taught to personalize everything. But, we're not taught how to deflect these comments and see the truth. How many kids have been traumatized by a parent who said in anger, "Stop being so stupid?" Said often enough, we *become* stupid.

Developmentally, we understand that children initially see everything as a part of themselves. There's no separation. Slowly, they begin to see that mom is separate, dad is separate, and the rest of the external world is not "me." If they're fortunate enough to be reinforced in the natural development of an individual ego, they learn to separate "me" from "not me."

Unfortunately, this doesn't happen fully for most people. So, we end up personalizing just about everything that goes on around us, especially comments from others. This is unfortunate because we end up being controlled by the opinions of others. We're just not ourselves. In fact, we're trying to *be them.*

Say I'm at my home in Massachusetts, and you're at your home in San Diego, California. I look outside at the six inches of snow on the ground, call you, and say, "It's so *cold* out today!"

You giggle, replying, "You silly girl. It's really quite a warm and lovely day. You're always so negative about everything."

Now, I can personalize your comment, even though I know it really is cold where I am. I'll think, "Yes, I do tend to be negative." And, off to the conditioned pattern races we go.

The conditioned pattern of Personalization is this pervasive—and this subtle. I certainly wouldn't think, "I'm now going to personalize her comment." I end up seeing the world through *your* eyes instead of my own because I'm so concerned about what you think. After all, you're my friend, so I trust and respect your valued opinion.

See if some of these beliefs sound familiar:

- My friends (or family) know me better than I know myself.
- I can't help but take things personally. I'm just sensitive.
- They must know better. They're more experienced (smarter, more knowledgeable).
- Feedback is important. I don't know what I'd do without honest feedback.
- If it's important to him, it's important to me.

## THE CONDITIONED PATTERN OF BUSYNESS

Have you ever had one of those days when you've felt like you've run around like a madwoman, but at the end of the day can't for the life of you remember what you accomplished? Me, too.

Bob Proctor tells the story of having lunch with Earl Nightingale and asking him how he manages to get so much accomplished in a short day. He asked how on earth Nightingale did so well with managing his time. Earl laughed. "Nobody can manage time," he said. "Time can't be managed. What I do is manage my activities."

We have so many activities to manage! All the time-saving devices of the late twentieth century have given us far more things to do, and of course all of them are extremely important, or so it seems.

We're conditioned to be busy from a very young age. Imagine the child who dares to sit idly in class, daydreaming about someday being president or a major league baseball player. He or she will, of course, be told to stop that silly daydreaming and to do something "productive."

> Busyness is behavior driven by the belief that our worth is tied to how much we accomplish that can be seen by others.

The conditioned pattern of Busyness (being busy simply for the sake of being busy) is a mindset many, if not most of us, have today. The pace of the world has been greatly accelerated, and the belief is that in order to keep up, we must do more. We think that our worth as workers, entrepreneurs, business owners, managers, or even coaches, is directly related to how much we can accomplish.

To take it a step further, it's not so much about being busy as it is about *looking* busy. I know I certainly get caught up in the Busyness whirlwind. If I lead more classes, facilitate more groups, and conduct more interviews, then I'll be rewarded by the praise of my peers. I get the instant gratification of praise or positive comments. I've even been known to write something on my to-do list that I've already done, just so I can then cross it off!

Even so, I might look back at the end of the day and realize that I may have accomplished few things of any real substance. It's something of an act, but mostly it's an addiction and fascination with the art of being and looking busy. This kind of thinking and behavior is rewarded everywhere today.

Say you're managing two people in the same department. You give both a very similar assignment. Joe jumps right on it, making phone calls, taking notes, and creating reports. He's busy all day, and maybe all week, running hither and yon on tasks related to the project. At the end of the week, he turns in his final report, which is thorough but doesn't offer anything new.

Mary spends the first two days alone in a conference room, staring at a blank white board and occasionally taking notes. She makes an occasional phone call that is followed by even longer moments of staring at the blank wall. You are one concerned manager, so you have a talk with Mary about her lack of performance. Fortunately for you, she listens politely and then decides to ignore what you've said.

The next day, you are pleased to see that Mary has brought several other people into the conference room with her. Ah, you think. Finally she is working on the project! Early the next day (one full day before Joe has completed his report), Mary hands you the most exquisite

---

DISTINCTION: SHORT-TERM REWARD VS. LONG-TERM GAIN

A short-term reward is the instant payoff for acting immediately. We have proof that what we did mattered. This often comes at great costs — robbing us of the benefit of bigger, long-term gains.

A long-term gain is the ability to postpone short-term rewards for greater gains in the future. It is the ability to persevere, sometimes with no direct evidence that a payoff will occur. It involves faith and trust and staying the course.

---

and insightful analysis you've seen in your 20 years as a manager. You're baffled. How could she have done this without working as hard as Joe?

We look at Self-Worth as what we can produce and what we can measure, just as we are too often caught up in what we do (being busy), and not who we are.

Conditioned beliefs of the conditioned pattern of Busyness:

- I get more done when I stay busy.
- Idle hands are the tool of the devil.
- I just feel better when I'm busy. I feel like I'm accomplishing something.
- It's not real if I can't see it.

---

DISTINCTION: BUSY (EFFICIENT) VS. EFFECTIVE

Busyness is the illusion of productivity. Busyness is when we appear to be accomplishing things, but our activities do not add up to anything of significance. People can be busy rearranging the chairs on the deck of the Titanic. The end result will be the same — ineffectiveness. In business terms, this is what we would refer to as efficiency. One company can be extremely efficient in operational capacity but go broke because *what* they do is not effective; that is, it fails to produce sales!

Effectiveness occurs when your actions are in alignment with your purpose, vision, and values. Your strategy is combined with focus and accountability to move you *effectively* toward a clear and compelling goal.

---

- I'm only as good as what I produce (you are what you do).
- And, my favorite, the one who dies with the most toys wins.

## THE TIPPING POINT OF COMPARISONS

*Let me listen to me and not them.*

GERTRUDE STEIN

Dreams come, but far too often they're stopped in their tracks by the Illusion of Comparisons. The decision to stop pursuing a goal or dream occurs because outside influences have become more important than internal guidance. Maybe someone else has already done what you want to do, and you don't think you can improve on what they did. A business owner might continue forever taking low-paying clients because she doesn't have the same experience as the high-paid consultants or coaches. Instead of positioning herself according to her Capacity, she only sees the illusion that she is inadequate because of the comparison. Bob Proctor says that, "if you're going to compare yourself to anyone, make it in something in which you're better!"

Better yet, just go do what you can do, and don't even bother with comparisons. Like so many other illusions, the Illusion of Comparisons seeks to fill an internal void with external information. It doesn't create much happiness, but it certainly creates huge amounts of revenue for a lot of companies.

Great advertisers understand the Illusion of Comparisons. They use it to their advantage by showing both what *you're not,* and what you *could be.* The implication is that who you are isn't good enough. And they'll prove you're not good enough by putting on display people who clearly *are* good enough. What do you do to take away the feelings of inadequacy? You buy their product!

And, here's the real kicker: You already know it won't work. It's not real. It's just another illusion that sends you down the yellow brick road in search of a wizard that's not really a wizard.

The Tipping Point occurs when we allow External Drivers to dictate our capacity to be great. We begin to think in terms of short-term rewards instead of long-term gain.

Essentially, we fail to do what we can do because of one or more comparisons. That's when you know you've hit the Tipping Point of comparisons.

## PROFILES IN GREATNESS: DR. IVAN MISNER

Dr. Ivan Misner is the Founder and chairman of BNI (Business Network International). BNI was founded in 1985. The organization has over 4,000 chapters throughout every populated continent of the world. Last year alone, BNI generated over 3.3 million referrals resulting in over $1.5 billion dollars worth of business for its members. Dr. Misner has written eight books, including his *New York Times* best-seller, *Masters of Networking,* and his number one best-seller, *Masters of Success.*

Misner knows a lot about abundance, having founded BNI on the principles of abundance. The company motto is "Giver's Gain." Instead of looking at relationships and situations and focusing on the problems, you look for the opportunities, he says. "Giver's Gain" is based on the idea that you build relationships by contributing to other people. He's also run into his share of scarcity thinking, particularly as it relates to the Illusion of Comparisons.

Misner shares a story from the early 1990s when we were in the midst of a deep recession, especially in Connecticut, where he was attending a network meeting. All everyone talked about was the recession, and how it was negatively impacting their businesses. The atmosphere, he says, became rather gloomy. When introduced to one of the many real estate agents attending, he reluctantly asked about business. Miraculously, the man shared that he was having his best year ever.

Misner was curious, asking how this could be. The man pulled a card from his pocket and read it aloud: *I Absolutely Refuse to Participate in the Recession!*

The man continued, saying, "While most of my competitors are crying the blues about how bad business is, I'm out drumming up a ton of business networking with my contacts and generating referrals by talking about the great opportunity that exists right now to purchase real estate."

Misner has seen this scenario played out many times since. He concluded that "very few people were actually networking and working on seeking new business. Instead, they were merely commiserating with each other."

This is how we are so severely impacted by the Illusion of Comparisons. It's what Misner calls a "why me mentality, the victim mentality, or scarcity mentality. If we can focus on the solutions rather than the problems, we're going to have better results."

He's noticed that people who haven't achieved success almost always point the finger and assign blame (Comparisons). "It often ends up defining who they are," he says. Successful people, however, almost never point fingers or assign blame. They see their failures as temporary conditions from which they can learn. Taking responsibility is a critical factor. Misner points out that "Unsuccessful people generally point to others for their failures, and successful people tend to point to others as contributing to their success."

One of the traps of the Illusion of Comparisons is that we look at successful people, especially dynamic and powerful speakers like Misner, and we say, "there's no way I can do that. I'd be terrified to stand on stage and deliver a speech to hundreds of people." When asked if successful people have no fear, Misner laughed. "That is so untrue, I don't even know where to start with that. Yes, success does help breed some level of confidence, but along the way, you certainly have the fears that anybody has. I love speaking and I still get nervous going up and speaking in front of a large group of people. I'll stand there and go 'I'm not nervous. I'm not nervous; I'm too laid back. Wait, if I'm too laid back, I won't do a good presentation. Wait, I'm nervous—that's good.' I've done thousands and thousands of presentations and I generally get nervous. If I don't get nervous, I get nervous that I'm not nervous!"

This from a man who runs a successful worldwide organization and does a large number of public presentations each month. He also scoffs at the notion that anyone cannot do what they want to do because there might be a better alternative elsewhere. Here's his analogy for the idea that the grass is greener on the other side: "The grass is greener where you water it. If successful people lack the fear that you have, it's because they haven't been watering those fears."

What can we do to stop comparing ourselves to others, buying into mass-market thinking, or holding back because of fear? Being the ultimate networker, Misner suggests cultivating relationships that go both ways. You might provide information that helps another person, and he might give you a referral. Giving, or the law of reciprocity, is something that colors everything we see, he suggests. "Successful people see it as where are the opportunities for us *both* to do well, and unsuccessful people see it as where is the opportunity for *me* to do well."

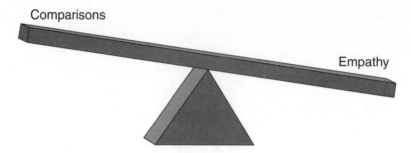

Figure 6.2    Tipping the Balance to Empathy.

## SHIFTING THE BALANCE FROM COMPARISONS TO EMPATHY

Typically, Empathy is used to define our ability to feel what another person is feeling. We feel empathetic for them — not sorry, sad, or angry. That is, we can sense what another person is feeling, identify those feelings, and adjust our behavior accordingly (see Figure 6.2).

We're all empathetic. Your spouse, for example, comes home a little late. You ask if everything is okay, and he says, yes, everything is fine. You know better, though. You can feel the disappointment, anger, or sadness that lurks beneath his attempt to hide his feelings. Likewise, you don't need someone with a bullhorn announcing to all concerned that your daughter is in a bit of a funk.

Walk into any room, and you'll immediately sense what's going on inside the minds the people in the room. To whom do you feel attracted? Who are you scared of? This is Empathy. Most of it happens at an unconscious level, and almost all is directed outward, toward others.

It makes sense on a primordial, primitive level. Our ancestors had to develop empathetic abilities as a matter of self-preservation. There wasn't room to be thinking about your own feelings if you wanted to avoid a tussle with the burly guy wielding the enormous club.

And, yet, life really is about relationships. We're always in relationship to someone, and typically those "someones" are people we care about. We're not living in caves anymore, and even though for many the world isn't a very safe place, most of us won't be clubbed to death by those we meet.

Today, more than ever, we have the opportunity to embrace our relationships with ourselves — not as a means to protect ourselves

96

from others, but as a way to develop even deeper relationships with others. How deep can we go in relationship if we're focused on self-preservation?

*Being abundant is a way of developing relationship equity.*

We change the world by being ourselves, and by embracing the notion of abundance.

The only shortages we face are in our own minds, and in the way we view and treat ourselves. How we view ourselves creates a domino effect for everything else in our lives.

Daniel Pink, in his book *A Whole New Mind,* states that not only does Empathy build self-awareness, but it is also an essential part of living a life of meaning. What if we could turn our deeply ingrained practice of

---

Empathy is the abundance aptitude of compassionate internal awareness.

---

Empathy inward? Self-Empathy does just that.

Self-Empathy does just that. It is the abundance aptitude of compassionate *internal* awareness. It is the degree to which an individual consciously directs his or her awareness inward, with the same amount of compassion that might be directed toward others. We learn to detect our own feelings as a means of making more conscious decisions. Do I feel angry at Jane for saying that my new hairstyle looks "strange"? Am I feeling scared to move forward because I don't think I'll measure up to what others have done before me?

Self-Empathy is that capacity that allows us to reflect inward to what we're really feeling, and to separate what's real from the Illusion of Comparisons.

Thomas Leonard often spoke of viewing people as always doing their best. He didn't imply that people would constantly perform at their optimum best; nor did he intend this would be an excuse to let people off the hook. Rather, the ability to view people as always doing their best is an opening of awareness — an opportunity to invite compassion for the other person and remove judgment.

When we say that someone is doing the best they can in a given situation, it doesn't mean that there isn't room for improvement. It means that we recognize their humanity, and that, given any number of circumstances and mitigating factors, that person is doing their best based on what they know and feel at that time.

Self-Empathy is extending this notion of doing the best you can *inward*. When we're comparing ourselves to others, the tendency is to beat ourselves up. We are our own worst enemies. And so our internal boxing match ends up being projected on the people and situations in our external world. It's not often a pretty sight.

Self-Empathy is the ability to internalize loving kindness, and at the same time relate to others more powerfully and authentically because we're no longer defending ourselves. The key to Self-Empathy is an internal inquiry process in which we learn to see the truth in spite of any existing conditions or circumstances.

Author Joyce Meyer says that you are the one person you can never get away from. Yet, so many lives are spent searching furiously for the things that will help us do just that, as if we can ever leave ourselves behind.

To break this cycle, we must practice Self-Empathy:

- Acceptance of who you are *and* who you'll never be (both are true).
- Separate the intended outcome from the actual outcome.
- Practice the Tibetan philosophy of loving kindness—compassion for ourselves and all living things.
- Celebrate what is, not what was or what could be.

For example, say that your client is experiencing a huge downturn in his business. In fact, his bank account is rapidly approaching zero. He's scared and desperate for some answers. His view of the world at

---

DISTINCTION: EMPATHY VS. SYMPATHY

Empathy is feeling what another person is going through, relating to their situation or experience. It is relating in a compassionate way.

Sympathy is feeling for someone else and taking their burdens as your own.

Sympathy can be damaging if we let someone else's situation overcome our own or keep us from being who we are.

this moment is one of lack—there isn't enough. He begins to compare himself to others, feeling more inadequate as time goes on. He sees himself as a failure, and can't figure out how to get out of the hole.

The Illusion of Comparisons would say that he is inadequate. He's a bad business person, and probably incapable of running an effective business because his peers are successful and he is not.

Self-Empathy has him reflecting on what is true and what is an illusion. He can inquire (Self-Inquiry) into the nature of his beliefs and feelings *with compassion,* and determine what's really true. Perhaps he is in the wrong business (for him). It then becomes a decision to move to a new business, not because he's a failure, but because he now understands himself better. This is Self-Empathy.

*The key action step of Self-Empathy is: Act intuitively.*

## THE CONSCIOUS PATTERNS OF SELF-EMPATHY

*If you love something enough it will reveal its secrets to you.*

GEORGE WASHINGTON CARVER

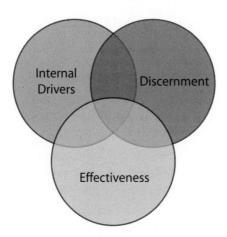

Figure 6.3   The Conscious Patterns of Empathy.

### THE CONSCIOUS PATTERN OF INTERNAL DRIVERS

*Listen to your intuition. It will tell you everything you need to know.*

ANTHONY J. D'ANGELO

Internal Drivers are simply the opposite of External Drivers (see Figure 6.3).

Instead of thinking and acting (or not acting) according to what others say, or reacting to external events as if you're a ping-pong ball, you want to develop a conscious pattern of following your Internal Drivers.

Internal Drivers are:

- That quiet inner voice urging you to make a call, follow an idea, read a book, listen to a tape, or introduce yourself to someone new.

> Internal Drivers are beliefs, thoughts, and attitudes that are of your design and making, not of external sources.

- The sudden inspiration to write a poem, start a new business, or change the direction of your current business.
- Internal conditions and circumstances that are aligned with your core purpose, vision, and values.

When we're inspired by Internal Drivers, we tap into a wellspring of knowledge that increases our focus and our conviction in what we're doing. Doubt may still be present, but it is tempered by a deeper knowing of truth. You get to practice self-definition and self-reflection, as Julia Butterfly Hill did (described in the previous chapter). Then, the information you follow emanates directly from your own internal wisdom.

Internal Drivers aren't whims or flights of fancy. They are based on the often long accumulation and awareness of truth. Over time, you learn for yourself what is true and what isn't. You learn these things through experience and reflection. The Coaching into Greatness four-step process clearly identifies the cycle of fine-tuning your awareness of these truths. Then, when the inspiration comes—and it will—you're ready to trust the inner guidance.

Sure, all this can sound a little "woo-woo." But ask any top executive how big a part intuition plays in their decision-making, and they'll unanimously agree that most of their big decisions are made on a gut feeling. The trick is that this gut feeling comes after a great deal of investigation and research. Then, once they've gathered all the information available, they turn inward—to the Internal Drivers—for the answer to the ultimate question.

This is how you tip the teeter-totter to Self-Empathy and abundance. Gather information; then, trust the internal wisdom instead of External Drivers. Greatness is orienting yourself around your Internal Drivers.

Tim Sanders, author of *The Likeability Factor* and *Love is the Killer App*, relates one of the most powerful lessons his grandmother taught him about life. She always encouraged him to "love people for who you are, not for who they are." This is the opposite of External Drivers, isn't it? What would it mean for you and the people you inspire if you could "love people for who you are?" How would that paradigm shift change the relationships you have with clients, family, coworkers, or even strangers?

Taking this a step further, if we can love people for who we are, why can we not love ourselves for who we are? Now things really get interesting! If you want to shift the balance to abundance, then trusting your Internal Drivers is the ultimate form of love, and the most profound source of abundance.

## CULTIVATING THE CONSCIOUS PATTERN OF INTERNAL DRIVERS

Do you want to start trusting your internal wisdom more? Begin practicing the following beliefs:

- The grass is greener where I water it. (Thank you, Dr. Misner!)
- Ultimately, it's up to me.
- Wherever I place my attention is where I'll end up.
- There are no wrong decisions—only decisions.
- I trust that I am capable of handling any challenges that arise.
- I am unaffected by the good and the bad opinions of others.

The only way to cultivate a conscious pattern of using your Internal Drivers is to understand that your decisions are *your* decisions. You are always the best judge of what is best for you. Take action on the basis of the truth as you understand and know it today. If adjustments need to be made, you can be assured that you'll get plenty of clues.

## THE CONSCIOUS PATTERN OF DISCERNMENT

*The fundamental qualities for good execution of a plan are first; intelligence; then discernment and judgment, which enable one to recognize the best method as to attain it; the singleness of purpose; and, lastly, what is most essential of all, will—stubborn will.*

FERDINAND FOCH

Discernment is the process of chipping away everything that isn't the truth for you to reveal what *is* true for you.

Most of us have been in situations where we had to choose one of many options. With the conditioned pattern of Personalization, we learn to take on the opinions and beliefs of others as the ultimate truth, even if those beliefs feel contradictory to our inner knowing. My friend whose sister called him ugly in his formative years came to believe she was right. He relied on external validation, and when his attractiveness wasn't validated, he felt he had to believe his sister.

Years later, he had to learn how to discern the truth. Rather than limiting his options, the conditioned pattern of Discernment gave him a sense of freedom. Personalization says, "Take what others say about you to be true." Discernment says, "Judge what is said on its truth *in your life.*"

In fact, there is little freedom in Personalization. Your self-esteem and happiness is completely dependent on the opinions of others. What kind of life is that? For some, it might be following one fad diet to another. For others, it results in a kind of indecisiveness that leaves them wallowing in a mud-puddle of hopes and dreams.

Discernment takes practice. How do you know what's true and what's not? How do you judge one opinion as useful and another opinion as irrelevant? There aren't easy answers—no magical litmus test of truth. If I could create such a test, my guess is that few would buy it. It's much easier to make excuses and blame other people (Personalization) than to take responsibility for *discerning* the truth.

Discernment takes thought. George Bernard Shaw said, "Two percent of the people think; three percent of the people think they think; and ninety-five percent of the people would rather die than think." You've got to develop the conscious pattern of Discernment, because it doesn't align with our training. We're not taught to think in school, but to pass tests and get good grades.

Practicing Discernment is very much like learning to sculpt. In a sense, you chip away everything that isn't the truth, until the truth is finally revealed clearly. Each little chip is a choice made. Those who constantly seek external approval and validation often don't see that they have a choice. You'll hear this all the time: "I felt I didn't have any other choice." That's a major cop-out.

To discern feels like limiting choices. People believe that it infringes upon their freedom, but quite the opposite is true. We are only truly free when we can discern the truth and act on that truth, thereby Living into our Greatness and having a more significant impact in the world. This is a modern-day version of holding ourselves hostage, and the ransom is no more or less than the decision to seek the truth.

True freedom is breaking away from the conformity of conditioning. Stop being held captive by the Illusion of Comparisons, and in particular the conditioned pattern of Personalization. Practice: "If it has to be, it's up to me."

## CULTIVATING THE CONSCIOUS PATTERN OF DISCERNMENT

Here are a few beliefs you can practice that will enhance your ability to discern the truth:

- The truth shall set me free.
- Anything that's said about me is no more or less than an opinion, and I have every right to reject it outright.
- The most compassionate thing I can do for anyone is to discern the truth for myself.
- Everyone is better off when I think for myself.

## THE CONSCIOUS PATTERN OF EFFECTIVENESS

The conditioned pattern of Busyness is a sad illusion that has been foisted on an unsuspecting public. When someone says that he "works harder and longer than anyone in his business," what ultimately matters is his degree of success, and not the number of hours he puts in. While one person may set a goal of earning $100,000 a year in his business, he may work 8 to 10 hours a day to achieve it. Another person can set a goal of earning $50,000 and work 12 to 15 hours a day to achieve his goal.

Both people work hard and long, and both are probably quite busy. Yet, by most people's standards, the first person was clearly more effective and successful.

But let's swim a little deeper into the pool, shall we? Even the person who earns $100,000 a year, working 8 to 10 hours a day may be ineffective. He may also be working day-to-day under the illusion that by doing a lot of things every day, he's Living into his Greatness.

Could he consider, even for a moment, the possibility of earning *twice* that amount in half the time? Probably not. Most of us aren't taught to be effective; we're taught to be busy. We far too often sell ourselves short.

Effectiveness can be hard to quantify. How do we measure Effectiveness? The person earning $100,000 may *say* he's effective, but is he truly Living into his Greatness? He most certainly could *decide* he wanted to double his income and work fewer hours. To do so, he would have to change both his thinking and his behaviors. He'd have to alter what he believed could be done, and change how he went about doing it. That is, he'd have to be considerably more strategic in his thinking (and much more discerning).

> Effectiveness is doing what's most essential without compromising who you are being in the process.

Thinking is important. It's what motivational speakers often refer to as the difference between doing and being. Joe, in the story earlier, who is busy *doing,* often misses opportunities to be more effective. Mary, who spent her energy *being* great was able to accomplish far more, and in less time.

Mary showed up authentically, even though she was chastised for doing so. She worked in alignment with her visions, values, goals, and her inherent greatness. Effectiveness, then, is about both *what* you do or don't do, and *how* you do or don't do it. Busyness, on the other hand, is only concerned with doing—it cares not one iota for either what you do or how you do it.

Effectiveness freely incorporates *both* being and doing. It's easy to see which of the two will create the greatest amount of personal satisfaction, fulfillment, and happiness!

### CULTIVATING THE CONSCIOUS PATTERN OF EFFECTIVENESS

If you're still operating under the belief that being busy will get you what you want, then stop. Start being Effective instead. To cultivate the conscious pattern of Effectiveness, you'll also have to practice discipline. Our culture abhors discipline, but Effectiveness demands discipline. It's not just about doing the right things. Living into Greatness is about doing the right things *for the right reasons and in the right way.* Like it or not, this does take discipline—perhaps more discipline than you've ever been accustomed to.

Cultivate the following beliefs:

- If I take the time to *think about* what I'm about to do, then when I do it (or not), the results will be that much better.
- Once I understand where I'm going, and why I'm going there, the journey will be much more pleasant and easy.
- I really can stop, turn around, or change directions if it means reaching my goals sooner.

## THE FOUR-STEP PROCESS APPLIED TO THE ILLUSION OF COMPARISONS

*Fundamentally, the marksman aims at himself.*

EUGEN HERRIGEL

Remember the story of Eileen at the beginning of the chapter? She has quite the dilemma—she just took on a new job and now has an offer for a more pleasing job at two-thirds her present salary. To whom does she listen, and why? Many of us are faced with similar situations, and our impulse is often to seek outside assistance and guidance. While there is nothing wrong with seeking guidance from others, doing so tips toward scarcity when the external guidance takes precedence over the ultimate source of truth—the internal guide.

The following sections will apply the Coaching into Greatness four-step process to Eileen's situation.

## AWARENESS

If you're walking through a dark tunnel, headed toward a low-hanging beam, how do you become aware of the beam without banging your head? Simple: Turn on your flashlight. In Eileen's case, the flashlight is her willingness to see that her reliance on External Drivers is getting in her way.

People under the illusion that their answers about life can be found by comparing themselves to others haven't learned to trust themselves. Eileen then needs to build faith in her ability to make good decisions. She'll do well by focusing her natural Empathy inward. She'd probably been deeply hurt by a past self-made decision and needs to learn how to go easy on herself when a decision doesn't turn out perfectly (which is exactly what happens to all of us).

Everyone has had positive experiences from following their gut instincts or intuition. Don't let your coachee get away easy, because awareness is absolutely critical to developing Self-Empathy.

You can ask Eileen:

- How do you feel after you've made a decision (even if that decision was to not decide) based mostly on the suggestions of others?
- Describe a time when you followed your gut. What happened? What were the results, and how did you feel?
- If you had to decide right here and now, and your life depended on your decision, what would it be?
- What would you do if you weren't allowed to ask anyone for advice?

## ACCEPTANCE

Like all illusions, the Illusion of Comparisons requires a bit of a balancing act. Others often *do* have more experience and more knowledge. Some have less experience and knowledge. While we can always learn from those who've gone before us, we have to remember and accept that our experience is unique. What works for Oprah might not work for you. However, you can still learn from her experiences.

Eileen must accept her own unique skills, talents, and wisdom. She can gather research and learn from observing others, but ultimately she must accept that the decision is hers to make. If she knew there was no way to fail, what decision would she make? I might ask her to flip a coin—heads she stays, tails she takes the new job. After she flips the coin, I'll ask which side she *wished* would come up. Invariably, this will provide the true internal direction.

Acceptance requires understanding the reasons a particular decision is made, as well as the reasons you're hesitant to decide. Usually, hesitance comes from either a real lack of information, or from the Illusion of Comparisons. Awareness of the reasons for the resistance will help facilitate acceptance of both the illusion and the aptitude.

## CONSISTENT ACTION

The consistent action that helps to develop Self-Empathy is the process of Self-Inquiry. Doubt often stems from a lack of trust in oneself. This trust begins with an internal investigation into the fears and doubts that keeps people from trusting their inner knowledge, wisdom, and intuition.

This self-exploration naturally leads to physical and concrete actions. For example, as Eileen accepts her Capacity to decide on her own, she'll come to a decision point about her work. This is the moment of truth when she either accepts or rejects her gut instincts. One way to help her get beyond the external voices is to put a time limit on the decision process. Then, and this is important for someone like Eileen—once a decision is made, she can't reverse the decision.

Her consistent action will be an unwavering allegiance to her decision— no matter what happens. It is also crucial that the *cycle* of the four-step process be followed. Doubts will form, and Eileen may sabotage her own efforts as a way of proving that she can't believe her own intuition.

Each action must be evaluated on the basis of whether it helps her to achieve her goals, and not whether it is a good or bad action. She'll want to put things in terms of good/bad or right/wrong. Actions are neither good nor bad—they either help you to get what you want, or they don't.

## AUTHENTICITY

> *The "what should be" never did exist, but people keep trying to live up to it. There is no "what should be," there is only what is.*
>
> LENNY BRUCE

There's a saying that when one finally moves beyond the struggle over how to choose, there is nothing left but a choicelessness. Ideally, Eileen will understand her own greatness. Then it's not about making a right/wrong or good/bad choice, but rather about simply Living into her Greatness in each moment. She sees what she wants to create for herself, and day by day takes action to get what she wants. She realizes that it may not turn out exactly as she envisions (it most likely won't), but rather than living a life based on Comparisons, she authentically lives *her* life.

## CHAPTER SUMMARY

External Drivers cause you to focus on someone else's greatness.
Greatness is orienting yourself around your Internal Drivers.
Love people for who you are.
Being abundant is a way of developing relationship equity.
True freedom is breaking away from the conformity of conditioning.

For additional information and chapter resources, visit http://www.coachingintogreatness.com/the_illusion_of_comparisons.

## CHAPTER SEVEN

# The Illusion of Struggle

*What are we but our bad habits? They make us feel alive, don't they?*

MARILYN HARRIS

My mother died when I was 15 years old. For the next 20 years, I did everything I could to resist the impulse to grieve. I had to be strong. God knows why I ever thought that, but I did. Well after leaving my dad and my first stepmother to figure out their dysfunctional relationship on their own, I carried the grief with me like a 16-piece designer set of luggage. For 20 years! I thought I had everything in check—the luggage looked good, I looked like I had it together, and I had achieved a lot of success. But that luggage was pretty damn heavy, and by my 30s the wheels were starting to fall off. The Opportunity Cost to me was huge.

I thought this was how things were supposed to go. Life was supposed to be hard. It was designed to be a struggle. Struggle meant I was courageous and strong. I may have been miserable, but at least I looked good in my misery. I was one of the strong women—able to withstand enormous adversity and come out of it looking like I had everything together.

But, damn, life was hard.

## THE DYNAMICS OF STRUGGLE

Struggle is not a business strategy. Struggle is not a life strategy. Struggle is a cop-out strategy. It is like taking a cross-country road trip with the emergency brake on. You may get there, but you are burned out at the end, and you have missed most of the cool sights on the way.

We always face challenges and hardships—that is just part of living. Through these hardships we learn valuable lessons. *It is what you do with struggle on an ongoing basis that matters most.* As it turns out, *struggle is strictly overrated.*

It is persistent and pervasive, making everything seem so serious! Even in writing this chapter I felt the stranglehold of struggle urging me to treat this topic with all the seriousness it deserves. I guess the joke is on me. When I'm struggling, I find myself pulled in two directions at once. Should I be serious or light; light or serious? It is like having an internal tug-of-war where as soon as I head in one direction I feel an immediate pull in the other direction. Back and forth I go, not getting anywhere in particular, being conveniently distracted, and feeling outright exhausted.

Every tug-of-war needs two sides. In camp it was the boys against the girls or one cabin against another. In life I have found the two sides to be "insisting" and "resisting." I am a bit of a perfectionist, and somehow perfection and seriousness have gotten all wrapped up together. While I know that struggle is strictly overrated, I will still get very serious about the subject. So I resist the seriousness and my tendency toward perfection. It can be a vicious cycle.

As a society we like to struggle. We are admired for it. It gives us that little extra something that makes us appear hard-working. Do you remember getting an "A for effort?" No pain, no gain. Bleed to succeed. These are the mantras of our culture. We hear inspirational stories about people who have "struggled against all odds" to become successful. How often do we hear positive things about the people who are successful because they *do not* struggle?

In his book, *Achieving Success Through Social Capital,* Dr. Wayne Baker defines the myth of individualism as "the cultural belief that everyone succeeds or fails on the basis of individual efforts and abilities." The trailblazer is glorified, even made a martyr for his long-time individual suffering. Personally, I am not at all interested in striving toward martyrdom.

The radio show *Prairie Home Companion* with Garrison Keillor had a humorous episode in which a very politically active organization was given one wish. They thought about wishing for total worldwide peace but realized that if there was nothing to protest or struggle against, they would lose all purpose to their lives!

Struggle has become a part of our heritage. It gives us meaning, and for many people it provides enough resistance to prove that they are alive (as if anyone who constantly struggles is truly alive).

The real question to ask yourself is this: Are you fully alive, or are you just getting by? You will know the answer if you experience yourself plodding through life, feeling weighed down by it and simply existing day to day. There goes that serious side again.

*We lie loudest when we lie to ourselves.*

ERIC HOFFER

## STRUGGLE IS LIFE'S TREADMILL

I'll often notice when coaching someone who is "stuck" that he or she is struggling with a particular fear or belief. There is some initial progress (insisting), often followed by a period of doubt (resisting). He may repeat this cycle several times, eventually quitting or feeling so frustrated that he is on the verge of quitting. Basically, if you are stuck, you are struggling.

Bob Parsons, founder of GoDaddy.com and Parsons Technology, has been a very successful businessman, but he has had his share of challenges and struggle. At Parsons Technology he lost thousands of dollars before eventually discovering the success formula and selling the business to Intuit for $64 million. He then started GoDaddy.com, working through similar frustrations and fears before achieving success. Parsons shares his story:

> At both Parsons Technology and GoDaddy.com I went through some very difficult times. There were times during both startups that I didn't see any possible way that what I was doing could succeed. Coupled with these dismal prospects was the fact that both times I was personally taking a financial beating. As if this wasn't bad enough, I also had to deal with all the "non-risk takers" giving me that "that's too bad" look, or worse yet, shoveling patronizing sympathy my way.

111

The easiest thing to do in the world is to quit and give up on your dreams (and quite frankly, that's what all the non-risk takers want you to do).

What kept me going through the hard times was the vision I kept in my mind's eye and seldom let go of. This vision always dealt with the rewards of succeeding. While I thought often and long about what I needed to do to succeed, the vision that kept me going had nothing to do with the mechanics of success.

Struggle creates the impulse to quit. When struggling, our vision is usually out of mind and out of sight. All we see is the challenge. Then we struggle against the fears and beliefs that feed off the challenge. Many aspects of life are challenging, but as Parsons demonstrates, we do not have to give in to the struggle.

Parsons says that once he evaluated "the worst possible scenario" he realized it was not so bad. He stopped struggling against this unknown outcome and his fear of losing everything and moved fully toward his vision. GoDaddy turned around within a year and is now a very successful operation.

---

DISTINCTION: SEEKING VS. BEING

Seeking is becoming (greatness is still outside of you). Being is embracing the greatness of who you already are and always have been. You can then live into it, without having to recreate yourself.

---

## A STORY OF STRUGGLE

As Jane tells it, her mother had plans. She knew exactly who Jane would become and how she would get there. In other words, Jane's mother was a control freak who thought she knew what was best for Jane. Jane was constantly compared to her "good" cousin, and no matter how hard Jane tried, she could never live up to her mother's expectations. She was simply never good enough, which made her mother try all that much harder to mold Jane into a particular image.

Jane did as many do who suffer from over-controlling parents. She moved away, not just a few miles, but to another country. As you can imagine, this did not rid Jane of the Illusion of Struggle that had been so ingrained in her from childhood. Consequently, poor Jane has struggled with everything. From the outside she looks successful. Sometimes she makes it look easy. On the inside, she is filled with doubt and insecurity. It is not hard to figure out why Jane struggles, but let's look a little deeper into the conditioned patterns that keep struggle in place.

## THE CONDITIONED PATTERNS OF STRUGGLE

*The best way to predict the future is to create it.*

PETER DRUCKER

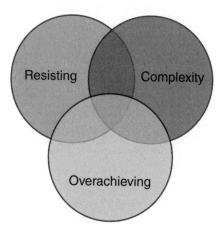

Figure 7.1    The Conditioned Patterns of Struggle.

Struggle is a frustrating mode of travel. When we struggle, we feel exhausted, weary of the constant battles, and ready to give up. Of course most of us do not give up. We keep on struggling, as if that is the only option. Thomas Edison did not invent the light bulb through trying (struggling). He invented it because he *did not* struggle.

Big breakthroughs do not happen when we are stressed. They happen when we finally let go and stop struggling. When dating, is it not true that you always hear that you will not find your mate until you stop looking so hard?

As with all seven illusions, we buy into the illusion that struggle is a good thing because of certain conditioned patterns. The three core conditioned patterns that keep us in the Illusion of Struggle are illustrated in Figure 7.1.

## THE CONDITIONED PATTERN OF RESISTING

> Resistance is the pattern of rejecting people, events, or things for being anything other than what we expect them to be.

Resisting is at the heart of struggle. Although whatever it is we're Resisting feels "out there," the resistance is really inside. That is, if you're Resisting anything, you're really Resisting yourself. That's what makes it the essence of scarcity.

When we resist something, we increase the amount of struggle in our lives, and this in turn increases how much scarcity we experience. A friend recently told me that her partner's worst fear was having all three high-energy kids return home and destroy his quiet life. Guess what happened?

---

### DISTINCTION: STRIVING VS. THRIVING

Striving is pushing yourself toward becoming something other than who you are. You are chasing something outside of yourself, depleting significant amounts of energy and Opportunity Cost.

Thriving occurs when you fully accept the present and live with today's opportunities. You do not live *in* the future, but you create today what will become a future in which you *also* thrive.

---

Perhaps resistance is best understood by example. Although there are many things we resist, there are some we resist more often or harder than others. Four things most people resist to varying degrees are:

- Uncomfortable feelings (or for some people, *any* kind of feeling).
- Circumstances that feel awkward or uncomfortable, or that have the possibility of feeling awkward or uncomfortable.
- Almost any kind of fear.
- Taking action, especially something new.

I've learned by experience that the anticipation of the feeling is worse than the actual feeling. Those 20 years of resisting dealing with the loss of my mom was like walking around with a constant wall of fire in front of me. My biggest fear was that walking through the fire and facing my pain would burn and consume me. When I finally embraced those

114

feelings of loss, I experienced the emotion moving through and out of me. Stepping through the fire (my perception of the grief) did not burn me; it cleansed me.

## THE CONDITIONED BELIEFS OF RESISTING

Why do we resist? Part of our resistance comes from fear—some rational, and some not. Mostly, however, resistance comes from our conditioned beliefs. These conditioned beliefs can include:

- Conditioned for lack: I don't deserve good; or I'm never good enough.
- Conditioned to expect the worst: If I allow that to happen, then . . .
- Conditioned to compete: Someone's got to lose, and it's not going to be me.
- Fear of the unknown: I don't know what I'm doing.
- Conditioned to avoid pain: I've been hurt by that (him/her) in the past.
- Fear there's not enough.

The bottom line: When people resist things being a certain way in life or resist what's happening to them, they're really resisting their own greatness. They are denying the world the best of who they are.

## THE CONDITIONED PATTERN OF COMPLEXITY

Complexity occurs when we make things more difficult than they have to be to avoid doing what we *can* do.

We make things harder than they have to be. By making things difficult, we create struggle and prolong getting to where we want to be. It's ironic when you think about it. In order to appreciate the prize, we feel that we have to struggle to earn the prize. Sure, it can be a lot of hard work, but it doesn't have to be complex. Do you want to run a marathon? Then go out and run a lot of training miles. The solution isn't complex.

*Complexity stalls us from our greatness. It is the quicksand of our intentions.*

---

DISTINCTION: THE OVERACHIEVER VS. THE HIGH ACHIEVER

Overachievers define their Self-Worth or value by what they do, by what they produce, by being busy, or by the sheer quantity of things they're doing at one time. They are defined by External Drivers.

High Achievers are not defined by what they do; they are defined by who they are *being*. Their value doesn't depend on what they achieve or on the feedback and acceptance of others. They define themselves.

---

We make things complicated because we are afraid to decide. It's partly a fear of the unknown (what will happen if . . .?), and partly a fear of making a mistake. Perhaps the excuse I hear the most from my coaching clients is that they're afraid it might be the "wrong" choice. There's a gnawing fear that somehow we will be permanently locked into the consequences of our decision.

But consider this for a moment: what if there were no wrong choices, only choices? Deepak Chopra, in *The Book of Secrets*, says that life is self-correcting. We can make no wrong decisions. Even if we don't choose the optimum choice, we will be guided to what we need to learn. Athletes understand this concept. They know they can only anticipate so much but have to make constant instantaneous decisions *in the moment* as each new situation arises. In the end, we'll probably say that missing, losing, or failing was the best thing that could have happened.

## THE CONDITIONED BELIEFS OF COMPLEXITY

The following are some of the conditioned beliefs that lead to the unnecessary creation of Complexity. Don't be surprised if your coachee absolutely insists that things have to be complex. We do amazing things to ourselves (and others) to prove we are right! Here are but a few of the conditioned beliefs of Complexity:

- I've got to fight for what's worthwhile.
- "On the one hand . . . ; but on the other hand"—I've got to weigh all the options.
- Success means sacrifice: The good things come at a price.
- Life is hard and then you die (humorous, but you might be surprised at how many people live this belief).

We are complex beings, but what we create doesn't have to be complex. Most Complexity is created as a means to avoid making decisions. Illusions appear to be complex. Like a dense fog they obscure reality, creating a vast unknown and unseen world. Many people stumble or stop when they step into the unknown. That next step may be off a cliff! Creating Complexity where there is none is a wonderful way to avoid taking that step.

---

### DISTINCTION: STRUGGLING VS. WORKING HARD

When you are struggling, you are out of alignment with who you naturally are. You are not experiencing Flow (defined as your Capacity to express who you are) because all of your effort is tied up in the struggle, not in being. The Opportunity Cost to you is great.

You can work hard but still be in the flow of experience, embracing who you are. It's not the amount of effort you put into something that brings results as much as it's the alignment of that effort with your true nature, strengths, and desires.

---

### THE CONDITIONED PATTERN OF OVERACHIEVING

We've all known Overachievers. Some of us (me included) have been Overachievers. Overachieving occurs during those times when you're driven to accomplish the impossible, not because of a higher purpose, but because you're desperately trying to fill an empty void.

---

Overachieving occurs when you're driven to meet unrealistic expectations that reinforce a false identity.

---

This is really hard work. The need to overachieve comes up when people go looking for happiness outside of themselves. We can seek comfort from others and comfort from external factors like wealth, but these things can never create lasting happiness because they are based on conditions outside us that we cannot control.

Overachievers have a way of continuously trying to prove themselves. High Achievers, on the other hand, continuously prove themselves without trying. Sometimes there's a fine line between a High Achiever and an Overachiever. As I write this chapter, Lance Armstrong, a High Achiever, just won his seventh consecutive Tour de France. He managed to make the ordinary seem extraordinary and the extraordinary seem ordinary. Armstrong's story is a good demonstration of the line between Overachieving and High Achieving.

He is a man of amazing physical ability who overcame adversity to Live into his Greatness. Armstrong set a new precedent for off-season training, hitting the road several hours a day when his competitors were drinking beer by the fire. While he achieved greatness, he didn't struggle. He worked hard, overcame many challenges (not the least of which was testicular cancer), and accomplished a feat that may never be matched. Without trying to prove his greatness, he Lived into his Greatness.

## THE OVERACHIEVER EXHIBITS GREAT WILLPOWER

Just like struggle, willpower is overrated. I suspect that Lance Armstrong has a very strong will but doesn't resort to exhibiting willpower. If you have to resort to willpower to get something done, it's a good indication that your goal is out of alignment with who you are. You're going to be struggling uphill against odds that aren't in your favor.

---

### DISTINCTION: WILL VS. WILLPOWER

We often confuse having a strong will and willpower. To have a strong will is to have an ability to focus our attention sharply in a given direction for an extended period. It is a relaxed focus that comes from practice. Once one develops a strong will by staying focused, an idea or activity is effortless.

Willpower requires exertion. When we're unable to stay focused, we feel the need to exert willpower. Willpower feels like and is a struggle. While exercising a strongly developed will leaves us energized, exerting willpower leaves us exhausted. The Opportunity Cost is high.

---

Although I accomplished a lot after my mom's death, I did so as an Overachiever. It was *after* my mom's death that I kept a 4.0 grade point average. Who knows whether I would have achieved more or less without struggling, but I'm convinced I would have enjoyed my life much more.

The price I paid was high. I went through three different roommates in my first two years of college. It wasn't because I wasn't a good friend or left my dirty socks in the middle of the floor. They couldn't tolerate my intensity. I'd stay up until 2 A.M. furiously calculating my potential grade in a class based on the results of a particular paper or project.

I thought this was normal. I had something to prove—most of all to myself that I could survive on my own.

I identified with Overachieving. I measured my worth by my grades, my debate championships, or the number of extracurricular groups I led (it wasn't enough to simply participate in the groups).

### THE CONDITIONED BELIEFS OF OVERACHIEVING

There is a strong correlation between Overachieving and hopelessness. When you peel away the layers of the conditioned beliefs you'll find that the Overachiever has a certain amount of hopelessness about life. While she's always striving to be recognized, she rarely believes it will happen. The recognition that does come (and it will) isn't enough. Sure, I got all those As in college and won numerous awards. I received a lot of recognition, but I was never satisfied. I always felt like something was missing. Endlessly trying to fill the big black void inside of you is a sure sign of scarcity.

How can you recognize this pattern in your coachee? Some of the conditioned beliefs of Overachieving you'll recognize include:

- The odds are against you. Others are more talented, smarter, more experienced.
- All good things come to an end.
- Winning is everything.
- I can do anything with enough willpower.
- If I work hard enough, my purpose will eventually become clear.
- If I can prove how good I am people will like/love me.

## HOW STRUGGLE SHOWS UP IN BUSINESS

I've included an extra section in this chapter. I think that of all the illusions, we see the Illusion of Struggle show up more in the business world. I interviewed Richard Reardon, organizational development consultant and executive coach for over 22 years and author of *The Business Development Guide,* to get some of his thoughts on the Illusion of Struggle. Here's what he had to say:

> I define struggle as constantly pushing against whatever current conditions you face. People struggle because they don't know how to change, and it ends up being a fight between them and the issue.

A successful business owner knows that it's the vision that's most crucial to his success. He doesn't struggle with every little problem that arises. People have all kinds of anxiety about what they don't have instead of dealing with what's right in front of them. They forget they have freedom of choice.

As a business owner I can choose two things: what I want and what I'm going to do with the situation I've created. Then, I take it a step further. I can learn from every situation I've created in my business, no matter what it is. It's when I complain about what I've created that I'm struggling.

I call this a company's operating system. It's the way they do things day to day. Some companies, and I've been a part of at least one, think that every day has to be a struggle to just get by. As a coach and consultant I like working with companies who finally realize that there has to be a better way.

The better way is to start working towards what you most want to create. It doesn't come just because you want it; it comes because you're willing to work and change your orientation on how you view the world and how you view yourself. You're ready to change your operating system.

Living without struggle is an opportunity to transcend old limiting beliefs. Most businesses are living in limiting beliefs, limited capacity, and limited potential. That's a very serious operating philosophy. The key is to get them vision driven. Get them to say, for example, "We could become a world-class sales team" or "We could become a management team where we really do communicate." When they see they have an alternative, they don't struggle.

The next step is sticking with the vision long enough so that it feels real. This increases the desire to have that vision, and the degree of commitment to the vision goes up automatically. They naturally create a new business reality that has nothing to do with scarcity or struggle.

## THE TIPPING POINT OF STRUGGLE

Of course we'll struggle from time to time. But when struggle becomes a way of life, it has tipped toward scarcity. Hardships and challenges happen, but that doesn't mean we have to keep struggling. It's when we think we're supposed to struggle, or struggle because we can't see any other options, that we're in danger of missing opportunities. When you're relaxed, you can see the opportunities coming, and you may work hard to bring them to fruition, but it won't be a struggle.

When does Resisting, for example, keep you from doing the thing you *can* or want to do? Resisting that grief for me was a huge energy drain, and it resulted in many missed opportunities—not just for personal growth, but also for better relationships, better health, and who knows what else. That's why I call it an Opportunity Cost. It's like trying to swim against a riptide.

The most successful people I know love what they are doing, and although they may even work harder than most people, there is rarely any struggle. They know that when they feel like they are struggling, then something is off. Push too hard, and you end up going the wrong direction, hiring people who do not work out, and having to reshuffle all your projects.

## Profiles in Greatness: Korrahn Droku

Let's say you or your coachee are contemplating upgrading your business and operations to use more technology, particularly Internet technology. Perhaps you've read something about digital audio or video conferencing or want to provide automated PowerPoint presentations to an e-mail-based audience. But you don't know a thing about the technology.

You then discover a man named Droku—a coach who's committed to helping others embrace and fully utilize technology in their businesses. During your telephone and Internet-based class, you find him to be informative, articulate, and very knowledgeable about his chosen field. What you don't know is that the entire presentation you've just witnessed was accomplished by a man who's unable to move his body from his neck down. Droku is a quadriplegic who has diligently worked through a myriad of obstacles to own and operate his own coaching business.

Approximately 16 years ago, at the age of 34, Droku was like any other young working-class man. He struggled month to month to pay his bills, while casually playing around with several hobbies, including martial arts and music. While not necessarily an accomplished musician, he loved the creative aspect of playing his keyboard.

Then, while visiting his parents, Droku was caught in a drive-by shooting, shot in the neck by a stray bullet that wasn't intended for him. He was instantly paralyzed. His three months in intensive care gave him plenty of time to consider what had happened. He went through the usual cycles of denial and anger before finally realizing that what had happened couldn't be reversed. By the time he was released into six months of rehabilitation, Droku knew that he had to move forward with what he had.

Helped considerably by his mother, an experienced private-care nurse, Droku began his new life. He was provided with a new computer and soon discovered the gift of voice recognition software. "Things happen for a reason," Droku reflects. "Through my computer I started exploring the Internet, eventually stumbling upon CoachVille and Thomas Leonard."

Droku took a gamble. Rather than reading Leonard's Laws of Attraction with the skeptical eye of someone who takes life for granted, he embraced Leonard's philosophies. He says that for him, "There is a way that the present is always perfect. I've been able to embrace the perfection of everything that happens in our lives, and that it's up to us to find the reasons things happen. I end up trusting that everything is happening for the good."

Some might look at Droku and say that he has a life filled with struggle. He'll tell you that he has many challenges to overcome that most people can't dream of, but he rarely struggles. "I define struggle as fighting against what is going on in your life," he says. He adds that "I've been disabled for 16 years, but I've met so many people who are walking but more disabled than I. They complain about things I'd love the opportunity to do—even something as simple as getting up and going to work in the morning!"

Droku learned that, as he says, "what will be, will be." Instead of fearing struggle, he has chosen to learn from life's challenges as an exercise of growth and expansion. Part of the problem people have, he says, is that they keep expecting too much, while taking everything else for granted. "I don't expect anything anymore," Droku claims. "I'm just exploring possibilities."

All this from a man who could have given up, resisted what happened, and then tried hard to be accepted for what he wasn't. "Greatness," Droku says, "is something from deep within. It's just how you choose to show up moment to moment." He fully embraced the idea that the present is perfect and looks for that perfection every day in whatever challenging events or people come his way.

For Droku, struggle is a thing of the past. Every day is a day of reaching forward instead of holding onto the past or trying to recapture what he once had. For him, life is a great fresh canvas just waiting for him to paint himself a brand new life.

•

I think Droku said it best when he said: "I'm just exploring possibilities." He's a shining example to us all of the possibilities we have in front of us.

## SHIFTING THE BALANCE FROM STRUGGLE TO SELF-EXPRESSION

> Self-Expression is the ability to consistently give voice to your authentic self.

On the opposite end of struggle is Self-Expression (see Figure 7.2). Self-expression occurs internally and externally. It occurs internally through self-reflection—inquiring into your values, desires, and beliefs—and through your body as an examination of feelings and sensations. Self-Expression isn't about being seen, but simply about showing up authentically. For one person this might mean being the life of the party, while someone else would engage in intimate and quiet conversation.

While struggle is the result of resistance, Self-Expression is the result of an open flow. It is time to remove the flow inhibitor and reach for full Self-Expression. It's not enough to simply know the answers. To express is to Live into Greatness, while to merely know is still living in the satin-lined coffin. Remember, knowing you're great isn't an excuse for doing nothing.

This distinction becomes particularly important when you're working with people who make bold statements about who they are but struggle to act in a way that reflects this understanding. For example, the small business owner who's struggling to find new clients might say he believes

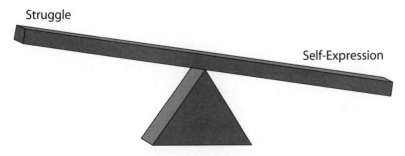

Figure 7.2   Tipping the Balance to Self-Expression.

he's the best in his business, but he resists actively marketing and selling himself. He may have some internal understanding of his greatness, but he is *not* Living into that Greatness.

Struggle is a way of hauling around old baggage. Self-Expression involves examining the baggage by putting it through the X-ray machine of awareness. Your job is to bring conditioned beliefs to light. Once the conditioned beliefs that underlie and create struggle are identified, you are on your way to shifting the balance from struggle to Self-Expression.

And, as with all the illusions, bridging the gap between the illusion and its corresponding aptitude requires a decision.

### Deciding to Move from Struggle to Self-Expression

Who wouldn't want to stop struggling? More people than you can ever imagine! I faced my own challenges in giving up on the Illusion of Struggle. *The power of an illusion is in its ability to keep us thinking that the illusion is reality.* For me to give up struggling would mean admitting to myself that I wasn't a superwoman who could do anything as long as I tried hard enough. I thought I was *supposed* to struggle. It's what defined me as a hard-working and diligent person who should be appreciated for effort. If I gave up struggling, I thought I would be giving up my identity.

We often have to make decisions without any certainty that it will turn out the way we want. We won't always know the exact outcome of a decision, but making decisions is easier with a strong desire. Someone who's "tired of struggling" but doesn't have a strong desire for something new (Self-Expression) will end up struggling to stop struggling. Imagine hearing: "It's so hard to stop struggling!"

*The key action step of Self-Expression is: Replicate simplicity.*

## The Conscious Patterns of Self-Expression

*We shall not cease from exploration*
*And the end of all our exploring*
*Will be to arrive where we started*
*And know the place for the first time.*

T. S. Eliot

124

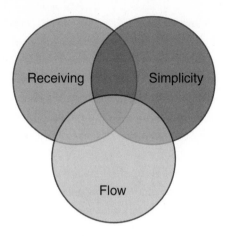

Figure 7.3 The Conscious Pattern of
Self-Expression.

## THE CONSCIOUS PATTERN OF RECEIVING

Now is a good time to refer back to or create the Declaration we
discussed in Chapter 4. Is there a sense of struggle to the Declaration? Does it feel impossible to reach without carefully planning out
every last detail? The Illusion of Struggle will create a need to know
the outcome before stepping forward, while the conscious pattern
of Receiving involves completely letting go of both the past and the
future to actively receive whatever is needed to take the next step.
This point is crucial.

Early sailors were terrified that they'd fall off the edge of the world.
Somebody had to take a chance and move forward without knowing
what would happen. Receiving involves actively moving forward knowing that you can handle whatever comes your way.

> Receiving is the ability to consciously choose to receive the opportunity
> before us, especially when it is not expected, planned, or thought out.

The only limitations on receiving are the barriers we put up. The
conscious pattern of Receiving is like viewing ourselves as giant
conductors—lightning rods of strength and creativity and prosperity.
It is an active state that's also like placing a fan in an open window to
help blow cool air into the room. Some people think in terms of allowing
things to happen. Allowing is a passive state in which all we do is open

the window and hope a cool breeze happens by. To receive is to place the focus of responsibility for creating something new inside oneself.

We get to decide what we want and don't want. We take the steps that put a grand universal machine into action, leading what we want directly to us. Receiving is making a conscious choice to accept, embrace, and internalize. Receiving is a welcoming state of mind that encourages, appreciates, and attracts more of whatever it is that's already being received.

The conditioned beliefs of struggle form a filter or film over our receiving mechanism. Over time, these filters get clogged with debris. What we get is more of the same instead of Receiving more of what we want. Resistance strengthens the filters. It limits and reduces our ability to receive, as if we're pushing away the very things we say we want. We end up going through life like a stubborn child trying to fit a square peg into a round hole.

Receiving in the context of Self-Expression is a conscious choice, like Receiving an award after conscious and consistent action. The true reward is being ourselves. Like the Olympic athlete who monitors her progress closely, we are constantly monitoring where and how we resist or insist. We're always at choice, and constantly making choices. We can consciously choose to receive the opportunity before us, or conditionally resist those same opportunities based on the old conditioned beliefs, stories, and assumptions.

To receive is to fall in love with self and to remember that the present is perfect (maybe it's not ideal, but it's perfect in the opportunity that is always present to learn, grow, and expand into who we are).

### CULTIVATING A CONSCIOUS PATTERN OF RECEIVING

*The problem isn't having it all but receiving it all, giving ourselves permission to have a full and passionate life. . . . [T]he biggest limit to our having is our small reach, our shy embrace.*

MARIANNE WILLIAMSON

Many people walk around with the attitude that they deserve rewards for their hard work. We don't deserve anything, and that kind of thinking usually gets us into big trouble. It's pure scarcity thinking. However, through consistent actions that embody authentic Self-Expression, there is much that we can receive from life.

126

Cultivating a conscious pattern of Receiving goes hand-in-hand with the lessons learned from Ivan Misner of BNI. Through building mutually beneficial relationships, we create more for everyone. Then, by believing that we will receive what we want, we remain open to the opportunities to receive. How often do people walk away from an opportunity because it's not exactly what they want? There are opportunities to receive that happen every single day.

Part of this cultivation is in an increased awareness. *Look* for reasons to be grateful every day. Look for evidence that opportunity exists and that you are Receiving what you want. Instead of focusing on what you don't have, focus on what you do have with an eye toward what you'll receive in the future.

Believe that what you can have is only limited by any old beliefs that you can't have it. See yourself as the Cup, not just that the Cup is half full. Then, take action. Act consistently and in harmony with who you are and what you want. You had the power to create the life you have today, so what's stopping you from creating the life you want tomorrow?

## THE CONSCIOUS PATTERNS OF SIMPLICITY

We often don't trust simple things, or even Simplicity for that matter. Yet, Simplicity is more often than not where we'll find the answers to a particularly vexing puzzle. Simplicity ranks at the top of the acceleration strategies.

> Simplicity is the ability to let things be as they are and let ourselves be as we are.

Complexity has the marathon runner jumping hurdles throughout the race to make it feel like she's accomplishing more. Simplicity removes the hurdles and obstacles that Complexity creates. The clutter of Complexity slowly suffocates us, robbing us of our energy, our creativity, and our vibrant way of being. Complexity clogs our engines, stalls our progress, and flattens our intentions. Complexity eventually dulls the mind to opportunity.

Struggle gives us a feeling of control, while Simplicity asks us to let go of control. As I discuss in depth in a later chapter, control is also a powerful illusion. When we think we're in control, we actually have the least amount of control. Simplicity requires a letting go — of expectation and the need to control the outcome.

We can see the simple beauty of nature and the simple elegance of mere existence. Simplicity serves us in a way that Complexity never can. Simplicity creates clarity and ease of movement. Remember the motto of this chapter: *Struggle is strictly overrated.*

### CULTIVATING A CONSCIOUS PATTERN OF SIMPLICITY

Simplicity is all around us already. To create Simplicity, find out what already works in your life. If you want to expand your customer base, for example, instead of creating a whole new and complex marketing system, identify what already works. Then, replicate those things through a simple and straightforward process.

*Simplicity is created by systems.* Solo-preneurs especially shy away from systems. Usually, this is because they're too caught up in wearing all the hats of a business to work on it at a higher level. To them, struggle is a brand of courage and strength. Simple systems in fact allow for greater creativity by relieving people of unnecessary and energy-draining actions. Systems should be as simple as the steps and processes that make up the system.

Finally, conscious patterns of Simplicity involve making quick, intuitively based decisions. Stop agonizing over making the wrong decision. There are no wrong decisions; only decisions. Any decision can lead to positive results so long as it is acted upon consistently and consciously. Adjustments and new decisions can be made. It happens all the time; you just do not notice it.

People unnecessarily struggle over decisions. Gather the facts, follow your gut, make the decision, and follow through 100 percent according to that decision. You can't go wrong. When you're making decisions in this way, you're allowing life to Flow through you instead of fighting against the current of life.

### THE CONSCIOUS PATTERN OF FLOW

Mihaly Csikszentmihalyi, the author of *Flow: The Psychology of Optimal Experience,* defines Flow as "the state in which people are so involved in an activity that nothing else seems to matter." I'd like to take this a step further, relating the Flow of optimum experience to greatness. Flow is much more than a physical state of being; it is your ability to Self-Express, your ability to temper the outer world's demands of normalization and conformity to honor the truth of your greatness, and it is your core uniqueness. Therefore, Flow is not just an occasional phenomenon to be experienced while getting "lost" to time (painting, rock climbing, writing, etc.). Flow is a state of mind — a conscious choice to be on the path of Self-Expression.

> Flow is allowing life to unfold through you, not because of you or in spite of you.

Flow happens when we accept and embrace what is. Flow happens when we release our death grip on the resistance–insistence tug-of-war and instead step back to take more conscious actions. Flow is a lack of resistance — it's like riding the jet stream or a magic carpet. It is effortless. The magic is in believing in possibilities and then getting out of your own way.

CULTIVATING A CONSCIOUS PATTERN OF FLOW

There are three key steps to creating a conscious pattern of flow:

1. Identify natural talents, inclinations, abilities, and strengths.
2. Focus on those natural talents and strengths.
3. Embrace the fullness of who you are.

The first two steps are fairly obvious and have been discussed in numerous books. The third step, embracing the fullness of self, is a bit more challenging. Who is this full self? Who am I? You can spend months working with your coachee on this self-identification process. But it's time well worth spending.

I may sometimes not like it that I spend so much time on the details, but if I embrace this as a strength and as part of my who I am I'll experience more Flow. It's simply who I am, and no amount of wishing I was different would change this. Some people are naturally more introverted than others. Rather than try to change this personal trait, see it as a strength and build on it. Be who you are. You are great!

Identify what comes naturally. Focus on your strengths. Embrace who you are. Flow is a choice you can make daily to set your life and synchronicity in motion. As Marianne Williamson says in her book *The Gift of Change,* "Synchronicity is the handwriting of God." Flow is the pen.

## THE FOUR-STEP PROCESS APPLIED TO THE ILLUSION OF STRUGGLE

As you recall, our coachee Jane had a very controlling mother who left Jane with the conditioned belief that life would be a continuous struggle in which success, if even possible, would only come after a great deal of very hard work.

In reality, nothing came easy, and much came at great expense to her personal relationships, friendships, and health. She had to work twice as hard and long as others in her field, all the time presenting the outward appearance of calm and ease.

For years, Jane thought that struggle was just a part of life. It's what one does to get ahead. Her first glimpse that life could be different came when she fearfully passed up a golden opportunity for a new job. While the new job would have made her life simpler, she was afraid that people would put her down for taking the "easy road." In retrospect, she realized how her fears and conditioned patterns were controlling her life. For the first time Jane questioned her need to make life overly hard. She wondered if life really needed to be a struggle. What if she embraced and lived according to who she was instead of who her mother wanted her to be?

The following sections will apply the Coaching into Greatness four-step process to Jane's situation.

### AWARENESS

What were Jane's primary conditioned patterns? You can begin to tease her story apart by looking at the fundamental themes that ran through her life. Ideally, you'll help Jane come to her own conclusions. Although the answers may be obvious to you, as her coach you'll want to guide her to a greater awareness of her conditioned patterns. You might, for example, consider the following questions:

1. How did Jane respond to her mother's controlling behavior?
2. What did Jane hope to avoid by moving away?
3. More specifically, what *feelings* did Jane try to leave behind by leaving her mother?

4. What did Jane believe was required of her to succeed?
5. What has been Jane's Opportunity Cost (even beyond the lost job) resulting from her fears?

As you pull back the layers in Jane's story, you'll likely see patterns of Resistance, and some overlapping and interweaving of other illusions. But remember: while the illusions may be complex, the process of moving to the flip side of the illusions is not.

Is Jane an overachiever? How might you determine this? The Illusion of Struggle for someone like Jane might show up through workaholic patterns, a lack of close personal friendships, or even physical symptoms of stress. Generally, she'll always appear to be in control (or try to take control of every situation).

The next step in awareness is uncovering the conditioned beliefs that have created the conditioned behavior patterns. What are Jane's conditioned beliefs? Take a moment and see what immediately pops to the surface. As you practice this four-step process, you'll quickly see patterns and beliefs. Even when you do, be careful to work with your coachee to help her or him uncover the conditioned beliefs.

- What did Jane fear would happen if she jumped on the new opportunity?
- What would happen if she tried something new and failed?
- How would others perceive her if things suddenly got easy?
- What would they think if they knew how hard she really worked?
- Who's in control of her life (trick question—see Chapter 8 on the Illusion of Control)?
- What would happen to her life if she "lost control?"

An Overachiever will identify with her Overachieving. She will believe that nothing good in life comes without struggle, and that *eventually* she'd be rewarded for all her hard work. For her, happiness is always one perfect step away.

Acceptance

As I've suggested, acceptance is the process of owning the conditioned patterns and beliefs with as little regret or remorse as possible. As Jane's coach, you'd help her to recognize and accept these as unconscious conditioned beliefs and patterns—not her fault, but her responsibility to change.

Especially when the conditioned beliefs of struggle are deeply ingrained, bringing a coachee to the point of a clear decision and commitment to change can take time. The Overachiever, for example, may force the issue by wanting to "do it right" this time. What I've found is that when the coachee is truly ready to make a commitment to change, she's already thinking about *how* she'd like to change.

People under the Illusion of Struggle might think in terms of what they *don't* want instead of what they do want. This isn't acceptance. Acceptance involves letting go of the past in favor of a better future. Encourage them to think about what they want, and then challenge them to consciously create new beliefs that align with who they truly are.

When you're helping your coachee develop new beliefs, be careful to help him or her stay grounded in reality. As a recovering Overachiever myself, I know how easy it is to set incredibly high expectations, such as "life is always easy" (it isn't ) or "I'll succeed at everything I do" (I won't). What's interesting about this process is how easily you as the coach or manager can spot the illusion coming to life right in the midst of the process of shifting from illusion to aptitude. Someone who struggles will quite naturally make this process a struggle.

## CONSISTENT ACTION

There is not any one step in the four-step process that is more important than any other. However, without consistent action the old patterns will remain in tight control. Jane, for example, was under the illusion that struggle was proof she was making some progress. Her mother controlled so much of Jane's comings and goings that she developed two conditioned beliefs: first, that she was incapable of doing anything successfully on her own, and second, that to succeed at all would require tremendous struggle.

For people like Jane, who is accustomed to struggling through everything she does, doing anything simply can feel like a perfect setup for failure. It will be enough for her to create some semblance of simplicity in her life. Replicating simplicity may at first feel impossible, but you can't replicate anything until you've first created the thing you're going to replicate.

Jane, for example, might be encouraged to create a very simple action plan. We might even restrict her to three or fewer simple actions that can be replicated (repeated) daily. The last thing you want to do with someone under the Illusion of Struggle is to give him or her more proof that life is a struggle.

The purpose of the action step *replicate Simplicity* is to nurture the new conscious beliefs and prove through experience that struggle is strictly overrated and unnecessary. Jane might learn that she doesn't have anything to prove, can take risks, can fail, and has the ability to bounce right back and succeed without struggling.

Exercising consistent action that is aligned with new beliefs leads into step four of the process: authenticity.


AUTHENTICITY

By exercising her daily plan of action, Jane will begin living and loving authentically; that is, according to her inherent greatness. Jane's authenticity shows up when she stops Resisting and starts allowing simple things to be meaningful. She'll take an action, make a comment, or interact with people honestly, even if it means facing their disapproval.

When Jane pushes too hard, she'll see the results in a higher level of stress or an increased fear of disapproval. Because someone like Jane has such a long history of both feeling inadequate and trying to prove herself, it will be easy for her to fall back into the comfort of struggle. To Jane, struggle actually feels better than seeing the disapproving face of a colleague, boss, client or friend. At least when she's struggling, people can't disapprove of her effort, and if she fails, it won't be for any lack of effort!

Anyone who's under the Illusion of Struggle might feel inauthentic if he or she isn't struggling. That's why I keep emphasizing that this is a *process*, not a cure. Bring them back through the cycle of awareness (as to why it feels inauthentic to not struggle), acceptance (of the conditioned patterns and beliefs), consistently finding new ways to replicate simplicity (action), and back into living into their greatness daily.

As Jane cycles through the four-step process, she'll stop Resisting, stop struggling, and spend more of her time and energy expressing her true self, not the person her mother wanted her to be (or the person she tried to be as a means of proving something to her mother).

## CHAPTER SUMMARY

Struggle is strictly overrated.

The greatest form of resistance is Resisting who you are.

The power of illusion is in its ability to keep us thinking that the illusion is reality.

Self-Expression is the manifestation of living who you are.

For additional information and chapter resources, visit http://www. coachingintogreatness.com/the_illusion_of_struggle.

## CHAPTER EIGHT

# The Illusion of Control

*We must be willing to get rid of the life we've planned, so as to have the life that is waiting for us.*

JOSEPH CAMPBELL

Over the years, my relationship with my father has been challenging. Don't get me wrong, I have always loved my father and known deep down that he loved me, but we never really "got" each other. Or so I thought.

I had many expectations of the way my dad should be, speak to me, or understand me and what I was going through. I usually ended up disappointed. Rarely was he the way I expected him to be. Sound familiar? I didn't realize until years later that these expectations were purely mine.

The problem was that I spent far too many years trying to control something that was completely out of my hands. I learned early in my life that my dad often wasn't who I wanted him to be, but like any child, I did my best to control the situation so that I'd get my needs met. And, like most adults, I carried these control patterns into my adult relationships.

For years, every time I visited him, we would be like oil and water— so awkward and unnatural together. We developed a routine in our attempt to understand our father/daughter relationship. I'd want him to go through a miraculous transformation into super-dad. He'd be himself. I'd get very disappointed, and he'd become frustrated. He didn't know what to say, and I expected him to read my mind. We were like a new pair of shoes that never fit quite right, pinching with each step.

Something wonderful happened two years ago. I made a conscious decision to let go of any and all expectations about my father's behaviors toward me. I realized that when I attempted to control what he did I was focused on something completely out of my hands. I decided to take myself out of the struggle and just accept my father for who he is and where he is.

That one simple action created the miraculous transformation I wanted. By surrendering to what is, I let go of my end of the rope, and the tug-of-war ceased. My father actually began to show up as I always wanted him to. It's as if he sensed that I had dropped the rope. I was no longer a victim; and letting go made the relationship that we have today possible.

I now visit my dad more frequently and look forward to the visits. We laugh, reminisce, and share stories, resulting in the best conversations of our lives. Instead of putting on my riot gear, I started meeting my dad halfway, and that made all the difference. I choose to love him for who I am, and that enables me to love him for who he is. In a particularly synchronistic way, being closer to my dad also allows me to be closer to my mom — he is the one living link that can keep those memories alive within me.

## THE DYNAMICS OF CONTROL

*Take your life in your own hands and what happens? A terrible thing: no one to blame.*

ERICA JONG

I don't know if we're born with a particular image of what the world is supposed to be like, or if this image is developed over time. Starting at a very young age, we somehow figure out whether our parents and siblings are up to par. Normally, they're not. So we do what any intelligent young child will do. We bribe, cajole, scheme, have tantrums, and do whatever we can do to manipulate our environment to meet our needs.

Control seems like such a struggle early on. You can really see it with some parent-child relationships, especially in grocery stores. Who's going to win control of the relationship, with Johnny screaming his lungs out because Mommy won't buy him that cool toy in aisle 12?

We mostly learn about controlling our environment through painful situations. One embarrassing comment in front of your third-grade class about your art project, and you'll never again pick up a crayon. I don't mean to point my finger at third-grade teachers, but it's in these early years when most of us experience the many forms of physical and emotional pain that give us the incentive to avoid pain at all costs.

We don't like it. We hate feeling pain, emotional, physical, or otherwise, so we start developing defense patterns to keep the pain away. I did it with my dad. Because he didn't protect me from feeling pain, I tried really hard to get him to change so that he would protect me. I wanted him to say the right things to make me feel better.

When I talk about the Illusion of Control, what I mean is the deep need to control our external world—people, events, situations. We do this because we've failed at controlling ourselves. We think we should be able to keep the pain away, and when we can't, we try to control our external world. The Illusion of Control is the illusion that we can change the world to fit our idea of how things are supposed to be. Only then will we finally be happy (or so we think).

Have you ever been around someone who's so used to being miserable that she makes everyone else miserable? She's controlling the situation in an attempt to lessen her own misery. We all know that it only works short-term. Soon, everyone is miserable. It's a comfort factor. We try to control others so that they're more like us, or more like how we think everyone is supposed to be.

> The Illusion of Control occurs when a person's happiness depends on rearranging the world to fit their idea of how things should be.

Control is personified by the need to fix and solve everything, to make it happen. It's a need to know *how, when, and where*. No stone is left unturned in the search for making it all okay. In this way, the Illusion of Control is very closely related to the Illusion of Certainty.

Control is perhaps the ultimate form of denial. It goes something like this: We get hurt. We're afraid of getting hurt again. We try to control ourselves. We get hurt anyway. We try to control the external world. We get hurt anyway. Then, we deny that we're trying to control anything. We're just being cautious. That, my friends, is denial.

## FORMS OF CONTROL

Control isn't just a pattern for really aggressive people. Here are a few other forms of control. See if you can spot yourself or your coachees in any of these:

- Overachieving.
- Showing up unprepared at a meeting but expecting a certain outcome.
- Blaming someone else for your life circumstances or events.
- Controlled feelings (unemotional — see distinction below).
- Procrastination (if I ignore it, it might go away).
- Tardiness or being late for an appointment or meeting.
- Incessant talking with little listening.
- Attaching guilt or blame to someone else.
- Refusing to take responsibility.
- Belittling yourself as a means of apologizing for a mistake.

I remember that my dad was always very visible in the community. It was so important to him that we look and act just right when in public. He considered how we looked a direct and personal reflection on him, and he was terrified of looking bad. One day, on the way to church, I was crying because my parents had had an argument. He glared at me in the rearview mirror and said, "What's wrong with you? Stop that! What will people think?" Feelings were to be stuffed and hidden away from public view. *The Rock* was born.

---

DISTINCTION: CONTROLLED FEELINGS VS. CALMNESS

Someone who attempts to control feelings is really trying to deny those feelings. Doing so creates tension, and usually keeps the person from doing what he or she *can* do.

Someone who is calm can still feel and express a full range of emotions but is not controlled by the emotions. Anger occurs, then passes. Sadness occurs, then passes. They tend to think instead of react and can feel things more deeply because they don't fear the emotions.

---

## A STORY OF CONTROL

While there are many forms of control, what I call "the Lone Ranger syndrome" is one of the most prevalent in our highly independent culture. Control often occurs within the context of a relationship, but as in Rita's case, it can cause people to work alone and work much harder than they would with a good team. Rita is a brilliant entrepreneur. After hearing about the value of owning real estate, she hardly blinked before purchasing a few properties for herself, smartly using other people's money to complete the transactions. Then, using the equity in her new homes, she started three new, and very different, businesses.

Many people do what Rita has done, and some would say that she's very successful. She has money to spare and an exciting life. But when we met, she wasn't happy. She worked 60 hours or more a week and had the social life of a zombie. She had constructed for herself the most elegantly satin-lined coffin, and she was tired of living in it.

Rita's problem was that she was leaning heavily toward the scarcity side of control. Everything she did, she did alone. Whenever she took the risk of hiring someone, she couldn't leave them alone. Within weeks, and sometimes sooner, her new hire would fail in some grand fashion, validating Rita's belief that bad things would happen if she didn't maintain control of every detail.

Was she Living into her Greatness? No, not even close. The poor girl was always so nervous about losing her carefully constructed empire that she started developing physical symptoms of stress—she was easily irritated, frequently tired, and unable to focus her attention on any one thing for more than a few minutes. As you'll see, Rita didn't have all the conditioned patterns of control, but the Illusion of Control certainly kept her from doing what she could do in some of the more important parts of her life.

## THE CONDITIONED PATTERNS OF CONTROL

> *Success isn't a result of spontaneous combustion. You must set yourself on fire.*
>
> ARNOLD GLASCOW

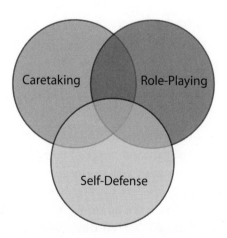

Figure 8.1    The Conditioned Patterns of Control.

## THE CONDITIONED PATTERN OF CARETAKING

*If your house is on fire, warm yourself by it.*

SPANISH PROVERB

I met a woman recently who'd gone through a series of relationships with very needy men. She wanted to complain about the men, but I wouldn't allow her. No, I said. There's a very good reason these needy men are drawn to you.

She was a classic caretaker. She maintained control of her world by taking care of others. As long as there was someone who was more needy than she, she'd be there in full force, ready to take on whatever suffering or pain necessary to help the other person feel better. She's the sort of person who watches her ex-boyfriends move on to vibrant, healthy relationships with other women.

> A caretaker derives her identity from transforming others to fit her view of herself.

It's a good idea to stay away from caretakers because in the midst of their control is a person who feels desperately in need of attention. If I accept their care, there's a price to be paid, and it isn't pretty. They'll eventually make me responsible for their happiness, and I'm not willing to take it on.

The Caretaking pattern often develops because a child will feel responsible for the emotional or physical well-being of a parent. Thus begins an endless pursuit for happiness that (apparently) can only be obtained by taking care of others. Ultimately, it becomes a form of control—controlling one's own emotional state by projecting feelings onto someone else, and controlling relationships through a subtle form of emotional bribery: "I'll take your pain away if you agree to take my pain away."

The problem is that it never works and it always backfires. Nobody likes being bribed or controlled, and sooner or later the Caretaking will be resented. And, just in case you're thinking about people like Mother Teresa, that's not the kind of Caretaking to which I'm referring. She was a shrewd businesswoman who played hardball when necessary to get things done. She helped those in desperate need, but she wasn't a caretaker.

A caretaker uses this pattern to avoid personal responsibility for her or his own emotions and situation, and attempts to get outside help by taking care of others. It is giving with a major agenda. Caretakers focus responsibility outward, while making it appear as if the motives were altruistic.

They attempt to make others better (control) without ever having to face themselves. They stay small and "humble" but never really Live into their Greatness or do the things they really *can* do.

The subtle differences between Empathy and Caretaking are important. In business, you want your employees and peers to generally care about each other. Watch closely, though. The caretaker will often fall behind in his or her own duties (and self-care) because he's more focused on "helping others." The empathetic person also takes personal responsibility for caring for himself and completing his own work. That is, the empathetic person has no need to live through others but is able to help those in need. The caretaker gets his or her sense of well-being through the act of caring for others. If she had nobody to care for, she would not know what to do.

As a coach or manager, there is often a tendency to take on other people's problems. It is easier for us to do something ourselves because it will be done right. It is easier to coach the coachee around a solution to their problem than to go deeper and explore why a solution is needed in the first place. Caretaking is a socially acceptable way to be and remain a surface dweller, and a very convenient excuse for not Living into Greatness.

## SOME CONDITIONED BELIEFS OF CARETAKING

Caretaking is not only socially acceptable; in some circles it is expected. Let's contrast two beliefs:

Whatever I give will be returned to me tenfold.
You cannot give what you have not got. (Originated by Horace)

Both, in my experience, are true. Yet, caretakers focus on the first by disregarding the second. They give, hoping that they will receive abundance in return. Unfortunately, they often give what they have not got themselves, and so the giving is done from the perspective of scarcity. What they get in return is more scarcity. Here are a few conditioned beliefs of caretakers:

- As long as others are suffering, I cannot enjoy life myself.
- I feel better when I take care of others (when used as a way to mask one's own loneliness or self-hatred).
- I am responsible for the happiness of those around me.
- When everyone else feels good, I feel good.

The clue to Caretaking is the direction of one's focus when seeking happiness: internal or external. Caretakers attempt to control the well-being or happiness of others as a way to feel better themselves. Thus, they almost never really do what they *can* do in their own lives.

## THE CONDITIONED PATTERN OF ROLE-PLAYING

*No sooner do we think we have assembled a comfortable life than we find a piece of ourselves that has no place to fit in.*

GAIL SHEEHY

The roles we play are like magic robes. They hide and protect us from all the nasty things that threaten our safe worlds. It's much easier to push aside a snide remark when we're simply playing a role. But if someone jabs at your authentic thinking or actions, it feels like you've been sliced in two.

Have you ever worn a Halloween costume that completely masked your identity? I have, and it gives me a sense of power and control over the situation that I didn't feel when it was just me. I could do things, say things, and act differently. The roles we play are no more than costumes, but they give us the same feeling of control as a physical costume.

Role-Playing, like all patterns, can have a positive or negative side. Clark Gable said that he had played the role of the dashing gentleman so often that he became that dashing gentleman. If we emulate those we admire long enough, we'll eventually think and act more like them while maintaining authenticity. However, most people don't take this conscious route. Instead, they unconsciously wear masks that serve to protect them from outside dangers and keep them from doing what they *can* do.

> Role-Playing is characterized by the persistent obligation to be who you *think* the world should see but often may not be who you are at all.

Role-Playing is characterized by an identification with what we think the rest of the world wants to see. Within the safety of the role, we create well-defined lists of what we can or can't do, and these lists are almost always limiting. For example, do you know any "nice people?" These nice folks are often the ones who blow up if pushed hard enough. The niceness is a role that's played to maintain a sense of control. They'll avoid taking risks because they don't want to hurt anyone (meaning, primarily, themselves).

Some roles are handed to us by our family, but most we create to control the external world. Middle children often end up as mediators, older children as leaders, and the youngest children as rebels. Bossy people are often the most insecure. Habitually shy people control their world by remaining hidden from the dangers that lurk outside.

These roles are *not* who we truly are. The chief executive officer (CEO) might feel obliged to ignore the thoughts of others. The factory worker might in turn feel obliged to feel morally superior to the CEO. *Any time we play a role that becomes an excuse for not doing what we can do, that role is a conditioned pattern of scarcity.*

We often become so attached to our roles that ditching the role feels like running naked through a crowded room. We put ourselves in narrow cages with very little light. It feels safe but offers little opportunity for expansion.

Where does the Role-Playing come from? We're conditioned not to trust that who we are is worthy, important, or good enough. We feel safer in the role than outside the role. The danger of dropping the role is that our greatest fears will be revealed as the truth. Am I really stupid, ugly, insignificant, bad, not good enough, or unimportant? Will anyone love me if I drop all illusions of who I think I am, or who I pretend to be?

Some roles are culturally conditioned. Are women in certain cultures less capable than the men in those cultures? Should a child be seen and not heard? Will a good wife support her husband but expect no support in return? Am I un-American if I question the decisions of our leadership? Again, if any of these roles keep us from doing what we *can* do, they are patterns of scarcity.

A role *feels* like the path of least resistance, but in reality it creates *more* resistance. It's not natural, and it's counterintuitive. We assume that things will run more smoothly when we are in the safety of the role. Instead, we are faced with even greater obstacles. The Caretaker feels safe, but unfulfilled. The problem solver creates more problems to solve. The mediator (nice guy) gets used and abused. The leader feels isolated.

The follower accomplishes little in life. The perfectionist accomplishes even less.

## CONDITIONED BELIEFS OF ROLE-PLAYING

Roles are played out at a very subconscious level. However, the underlying beliefs are very easy to find. You'll discover these beliefs in matter-of-fact statements, such as:

I'm naturally shy.
I'm a go-getter.
I'm not afraid of anything.
I'm just a follower by nature.

## THE CONDITIONED PATTERN OF SELF-DEFENSE

*A desk is a dangerous place from which to watch the world.*

JOHN LE CARRÉ

If someone started to punch you, you'd naturally defend yourself. See a bear on the trail ahead, and the first thing you'll think about is self-preservation. These are very natural forms of Self-Defense. Who wouldn't do all they could to protect themselves from dangerous people or situations?

We are also conditioned to fear situations or people without just cause. While it makes sense to tell your child not to speak to strangers, it's not helpful to instill a deep fear of speaking. Why do you think public speaking is said to be people's greatest fear? People are terrified of feeling stupid or humiliated, so they defend themselves by rarely or never speaking up—in meetings, in groups, or even to loved ones.

---

Self-Defense is characterized by the need to protect oneself from perceived fearful situations and individuals and is inherently tied to the belief that good things do not come your way.

---

Self-Defense is a good thing, except when it causes the person to avoid doing what he or she *can* do. We learn to over-defend ourselves, forming immense and elaborate walls to keep out the boogeyman. The boogeyman comes in many forms: fear of poverty; fear of ridicule; fear of failure; fear of emotional pain (getting dumped by a lover). So, we hide under the covers, hoping that these bad things will just go away.

Guess what? Poverty is still there. Ridicule is still there. You might lose everything and be dumped by a dozen lovers. What's really lost are all the opportunities we don't see when our eyes are covered by thick blankets of fear. The irony of this is that in the process of defending ourselves against life's dangers, we still suffer from them.

The conditioned pattern of Self-Defense can show up in many ways. My coaching client Jan is a good example. She wanted to create her own business but was afraid to venture out on her own. Instead of surrounding herself with a good team, and leading that team, she tried to defend herself against failure by joining up with a business partner for all the wrong reasons. Over the three years they were together, Jan became increasingly resentful of her partner Betty, feeling that Betty was holding her back from growing the business. And yet, Jan was afraid to do what she knew needed to be done. Betty became a convenient excuse for Jan to avoid facing her own fear of failure, and her even deeper fear that she was incapable of creating a successful business. Betty became her defense and her albatross.

Once Jan understood how she was working under an Illusion of Control and scarcity, she was able to clear the situation with Betty. They soon amicably parted ways, and Jan took the risks she was avoiding, eventually experiencing the steady business growth she knew was possible.

## CONDITIONED BELIEFS OF SELF-DEFENSE

*We most often see the conditioned pattern of Self-Defense come up when we inappropriately rely on others for our success.* There is a distinction between building a team and over-relying on others. While I know that I can't possibly do everything, I'm not going to willy-nilly turn my life over to someone else. Consciously choosing to surround yourself with high-quality people who can help you succeed is an abundant action. Defending your pride, ego, or self-esteem by turning your life over to these people is an act of scarcity. Here are a couple conditioned beliefs of Self-Defense:

- Other people will know what's best for me.
- Vulnerability is a sign of weakness.

## THE TIPPING POINT OF CONTROL

It's not wrong to have goals and intentions about the way we want our life to be. This is a good thing. The question is always "what is it that we are attempting to control?" The Tipping Point is reached when we become inflexible and stagnant, when what we are trying to control causes us to struggle and suffer and stay stuck. Most often, this is caused by attempting to control things outside of our realm of influence. We want and expect change on our terms only. We want things to get better, but we don't want to accept that the changes may not be according to our plans or view of life.

When we're under the Illusion of Control, we're constantly trying to shape life according to our current view. We don't see the Opportunity Cost we're incurring because of our rigidity. We negate all the possible options and opportunities because they don't fit neatly in our boxed view of the way things should be.

The challenge of control is that it's exhausting, and in the end it doesn't serve us or our needs. This is also a paradox—we may actually want to stay stuck and have an excuse for not being able to do what we *can* do, because then we don't have to confront our fear of greatness. Control serves us in a very negative way.

The fact is that bad things happen. Hiding in a cave will only get you cold and wet.

## PROFILES IN GREATNESS: SUSAN ANNUNZIO

Let's assume for a moment that you're an executive coach, an executive, or a manager at any size company. Either you (if you're the manager) or your coaching client is in the position of managing a team, whether it's one person or 20. You have two concerns: (1) ensuring that the team performs its purpose effectively; and (2) ensuring that each individual on the team also performs effectively.

Susan Annunzio, author of *Contagious Success* and several other books, teaches the master of business administration (MBA) course on leadership in the evolutionary economy at the University of Chicago Graduate School of Business and is a leading authority in the field of change management. Pay attention to what she says, because she is a sought-after adviser to senior corporate leaders around the world for her expertise in fashioning programs that maximize the success and profitability of change efforts.

The Illusion of Control plays a major role in the success or failure of almost every team. It's what can make or break a team, and it more often than not ends up breaking teams. Annunzio has seen pretty much every kind of organizational structure and team dynamic. You'd be hard-pressed to prove that your situation is unique. However, what she's seen—and proven through numerous studies—is that individual greatness plays a huge part in the success of any team.

"Smart people will do a good job at almost anything because they'll figure out how to do it," she says. However, good isn't the same as great. For example, one person who works for her is a natural project manager. As good as Annunzio is, she readily admits that no matter how hard she works at it, she'll never be as good a project manager. It's simply not within her capacity or natural strengths. "People also have patterns of behavior that they're naturally good at," she adds.

Annunzio explains that most companies focus individual development on strengthening weaknesses. That's totally backward, she says. For example, look at any baseball team. You might have someone who's a natural pitcher and say, "This guy has an arm. I'm going to work with him to make him a great pitcher." You wouldn't force him to play second base because he's weak at fielding. This is quite an issue of control, and it emphasizes one aspect of the Illusion of Control.

Annunzio notes, "What I see in a lot of these young people is that they take their strengths for granted." She has observed that many companies, and individuals, don't look to strengthen or build on their natural talents. They don't consider it very important because it comes so naturally. One key way that the Illusion of Control comes up in organizations is to think that we can take anyone and shape him or her into whatever we want, even if it's not in alignment with their unique strengths. "A natural doesn't necessarily become a star," she says. "You can see a kid in a Little League game who's a natural pitcher, but if somebody doesn't identify that and take that on, they'll always be a natural pitcher, but they're never going to be a star."

*This is what I mean when I talk about Living into Greatness as Living into the Greatness of your Capacity.* We try to control things that are outside of our control, and one way we do this is by focusing on fixing our weaknesses instead of developing our strengths. It's a matter, Annunzio says, of "assessing what we can be great at, instead of trying to be great at everything."

High-functioning teams, she says, consist of high-performing individuals. In one research group, for example, she found that the team was very high-performing because they had a knack for "passing the ball." What they did, she says, was to "identify people's functional strengths and their content expertise, as well as their natural talents. Somebody could be in the marketing department and know brand management and would be best at taking charge. Another was a natural at taking charge, while somebody else on the brand management team might be best at seeing patterns. Somehow, you put that team together to make the best decisions for the client by using their content expertise as well as their natural abilities."

In other words, you let go of control over who does what according to job descriptions and allow them to use their natural strengths. This way, everyone lives into his or her greatness, which naturally creates a great team. Says Annunzio: "In today's world, work requires collaboration and collaboration requires making your best effort about which way to go forward."

This applies equally to hiring, she's observed. Some companies, especially entrepreneurs, like to hire a lot of people just like them. "That's why the technology boom bombed," she adds. "You've got to consider the individual strengths and capacity of each individual, and more importantly, let go of trying to control every aspect of the business. You simply can't be great at everything, but there are others who are great in areas you can't touch."

The Illusion of Control arises in other ways as well. Annunzio has seen repeatedly that "If you tell people what to do and how to do it, all you necessarily do is make people hide the truth from you." One glaring example of this was with a focus group she worked with. The company had put in $12 million on a new process to reduce cycle time. It was critical to their success in how quickly they made money. She read the reports about the progress of the program, and they all pointed to a dramatic reduction in cycle time.

When she congratulated the focus group, they simply laughed at her. It turns out that they were never provided a chance to provide any real feedback. They were told what to do by the executives of the company and were never able to provide input into the process. It was all a big joke to them. They lied about the results to look good, just as the company managers tried to control the situation because they didn't trust their employees. Annunzio says, "I don't think they asked anyone's opinion on whether they saw if it was really going to work. By doing that, they were going to lose control. It didn't work."

She has suggestions this for solving problems of control: "First is to identify the natural talents of the people who will work with you. For example, I'm a blue sky-er. I used to think of people who assessed downside risks as naysayers. I used to think that those people got in the way of my success. I now understand that the only thing that got in the way of my success was not listening to people who were able to assess downside risk because I'm not good at it."

One of the clues that you've found this person, she says, is when you get a feeling in the pit of your stomach, and you want to just tune that person out. "That's when you know the person has a natural ability that's different from yours."

Perhaps the most interesting, but obvious, lesson Annunzio has learned is the impact of micro-management. She's found that "the number one killer of performance was short-term thinking followed by micro-management. Micro-management is telling people what to do as well as how to do it. When you tell people what to do and how to do it, you're totally underestimating their ability to think. If there's ever an Illusion of Control, it's micro-management."

It's unfortunate that this happens so frequently. When you try to control employees, she says, they'll hide the truth—hide numbers or other factors—effectively limiting your success. While I talk about the concept of limiting beliefs, Annunzio refers to these as the biases of companies. "Companies have their biases," she says, "that they're not aware of, and these biases severely limit their success."

I couldn't agree more.

## SHIFTING THE BALANCE FROM CONTROL TO SURRENDER

*You don't get to choose how you're going to die or when. You can only decide how you're going to live. Now.*

JOAN BAEZ

When you see the word *Surrender*, do you imagine waving a white flag? We commonly mistake Surrender for failure. Unfortunately, there's a fine line between obsessive control and determination, or between Surrender and giving up. Imagine hanging onto a small branch on the side of a steeply pitched cliff. You'll hold on as tightly as possible to keep from falling to the ground, won't you? You'll grit your teeth with a dogged determination, vowing not to give up until help arrives. The last thing you want to do is Surrender to the inevitable fate of falling.

What if I then tell you that you're actually only two feet from the ground? Are you ready to loosen your grip on the branch? This is Surrender. It's the ability to relax one's grip on life in the face of the illusion of danger. Yes, it's possible that your business might fail. Your wife or husband may divorce you. Your whole city could be wiped out by a natural disaster. This doesn't mean you shouldn't be prepared, and do those things for which you have some control. But, you'll be on the scarcity side of the equation when you try to control things outside of your direct influence.

> Surrender is demonstrated by the willingness to let go of the need to control things outside of your direct influence.

Surrender happens when you're in action, doing all that you *can* do, and letting go of those things outside of your control (see Figure 8.2). Tara, for example, was a well-meaning therapist just starting her practice when her daughter was diagnosed with an eating disorder, which Tara herself had experienced as a teen. She was swept back into old and uncomfortable memories and desperately wanted to protect her daughter from the same pain she had experienced.

Tara provided her daughter with professional help but didn't stop there. She pushed hard to control her daughter's response to and use of the assistance. Her fear of reliving her nightmare through her daughter was too much, so she held tightly to her role as Caretaker, which only pushed her daughter farther into her disorder. Nothing changed until Tara Surrendered to the situation. She'd done what she could, and she had to let go of controlling her daughter. As is usually the case, once she

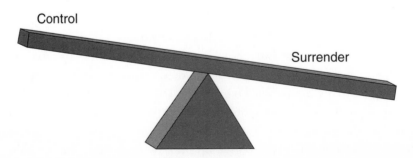

Figure 8.2    Tipping the Balance to Surrender.

Surrendered control, she not only got her own business back on track, but her daughter responded more favorably to treatment.

Surrender is often seen as a weakness, but actually Surrender takes tremendous strength. To stop trying to control a situation and Surrender to the truth of the moment is perhaps the most difficult thing any of us can do. It means seeing things as they are, accepting this truth, and doing what we *can* do, leaving all else to be as it is. There's great freedom in Surrender. Control moves from unconscious patterns to conscious actions. Fear becomes a Catalyst for positive change. Surrender creates life, opening the door to new opportunities.

Here's a way to experience Control versus Surrender for yourself. Clench your fist. Make your hand so tight that nothing can slip through your fingers into your palm. What would you do if I then said I wanted to put $1,000 into the palm of your hand? Would you keep your fist clenched, or would you Surrender your clenched hand to my offering?

*The key action step of Surrender is: Embrace Simplicity.*

## THE CONSCIOUS PATTERNS OF SURRENDER

*As I grow to understand life less and less, I learn to live it more and more.*

JULES RENARD

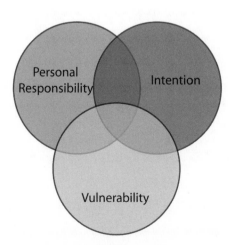

Figure 8.3    The Conscious Pattern of Surrender.

## THE CONSCIOUS PATTERN OF PERSONAL RESPONSIBILITY

*The greatest gift you give others is the example of your own life working.*

SANAYA ROMAN

Caretakers have the weight of the world on their shoulders, but they are often not responsible for their own actions or well-being. The flip side of Caretaking is Personal Responsibility. Often, the best thing we can do for others is to be fully responsible to and for ourselves. We become responsible for our health, our conscious awareness, our results, and our actions. The focus moves from others to self.

---

Personal Responsibility occurs when an individual releases blame and victimization to become fully responsible for his or her life.

---

What you don't have, you cannot give. Personal Responsibility has no room for blame (self or otherwise). By becoming Personally Responsible for our lives we gain the real capacity to care for others. We care for others from a position of strength and abundance, not weakness and scarcity. We can hold others up without crumbling to the ground from the weight of giving. In fact, giving creates a lightness because we understand from experience that we have far more to give than we could have ever imagined.

Put down the weight of the world and shift the focus to the one place we can control—ourselves. The focus and attention starts from within before moving out. This allows us to see opportunities as they develop.

---

DISTINCTION: REACTING VS. RESPONDING

Reacting is a conscious response to external events. There's no room for thinking. Someone yells at you, and you yell back. That's reacting.

Responding requires thought. Someone yells at you, and you respond by quietly ending the conversation and moving away. Responding is a way of taking Personal Responsibility for your thoughts and actions.

---

## CULTIVATING A CONSCIOUS PATTERN OF PERSONAL RESPONSIBILITY

*Life isn't a problem to be solved but a reality to be experienced.*

SÖREN KIERKEGAARD

To cultivate a conscious pattern of Personal Responsibility, you will probably have to alter your self-image. Caretakers often have a poor self-image. They hope that by taking care of others, their status will rise. They need to create a new self-image in which they see themselves as important enough for Personal Responsibility.

Trying to change any unconscious pattern without changing what's inside is like trying to change your reflection in a mirror without changing your true appearance. Caretakers must first create a belief that they are worthy of putting themselves first. Then, they come to understand that they are better able to care for others when they take Personal Responsibility. They must realize that they can't possibly save the world until they've saved themselves. All great leaders have come to this realization in one form or another. They don't sacrifice themselves, but they do become personally responsible for being in good enough mental and physical health to make a difference.

## THE CONSCIOUS PATTERN OF INTENTION

*Happiness sneaks in through a door you didn't know you left open.*

JOHN BARRYMORE

To play a role is to move through life without any clear idea of what you're doing or where you're going. It's the opposite of living an intentional life. In a role, you can't help but see all events and situations as isolated. Nothing is connected because you're too busy protecting yourself from harm.

An intentional life is one that sees all things as connected. You look at the bigger picture and see that there's much that happens completely outside of your control, but within the realm of your Intention. Role-Playing is like living life on autopilot, except that you have no idea where you're going. Intention fixes the destination, but not the course. You may not know *how* you're going to get to your destination, but you do know you'll get there, or somewhere better.

When playing a role, we ignore synchronistic events. If I'm a shy person I will ignore an opportunity that might require me to speak in public. If, however, I'd set the conscious intention to double my business this year, I definitely won't ignore such an opportunity. I'll jump on the chance, doing what I can to overcome my feelings of shyness. There's no role to play—only the Intention of accomplishing a goal or dream.

> Intention is characterized by the ability to set the destination of your life, allowing for flexibility and adaptation in getting there.

*People who play roles allow life to happen around them. People who set Intentions make things happen.* This is an important distinction that you'd do well to remember! In fact, the conscious pattern of Intention is very closely linked to the conscious pattern of Vulnerability. Set the Intention, then stay open to the amazing and colossal synchronicities that will literally come flying your way. Play more roles, and you'll just have to keep learning new variations of the same old role over and over.

I like to talk about the law of reciprocity. When you consciously set an Intention, you're free to give without any need for something in return. You know that by acting authentically in the direction of your Intention, you'll create all that you want. The law of reciprocity states that whatever you put out you will receive back. If you play roles and give from a sense of scarcity, you'll get back more roles and more scarcity. Give with a clear Intention and purpose, and from a sense of abundance, and that's exactly what you'll receive.

## Cultivating a Conscious Pattern of Intention

The key to cultivating a conscious pattern of Intention is to practice focusing on *what* you want to happen, and not *how* it's going to happen. Intention does require new beliefs, but more importantly, it requires specific action. Cultivate the new belief that the world is a safe place for your ideas and dreams. Believe that you're actually safer in the open waters of Intention than in the closed capsule of roles. How can luck ever find you if you're hidden behind a mask?

Intentions must be consciously set, and acted upon. I could hope or wish for more business, but unless I set the clear Intention of increasing my business, and acting upon that Intention, I'll remain in the role of poverty.

## The Conscious Pattern of Vulnerability

*The greatness of a man's power is the measure of his surrender.*

WILLIAM BOOTH

Vulnerability requires developing a great deal of trust: first, by trusting in your own greatness; and, second, by learning to trust others with a keen eye. We've all been used by others. There's not a soul on this planet who hasn't had someone break our trust. Rather than close up shop and create massive defenses, these hurts can create learning opportunities. What are the signs of untrustworthiness? How can I legitimately and honestly protect myself without avoiding many opportunities?

For example, a friend of mine has a written contract with everyone with whom he does business. He maintains a balance between protecting himself and trusting others. He won't do business on a handshake, not because he doesn't trust the other person, but because he *does* trust them. It's those who refuse to work by a contract that he doesn't trust! He shows up abundantly by remaining open to all opportunities and has more freedom to fully express himself because he has reasonable safeguards in place.

You'll notice that most of the highly successful people don't play it safe. They're wide open and very vulnerable. They know they'll be attacked, but they also protect themselves in conscious and reasonable ways, whether by having an unlisted phone number, firm office hours, or solid contracts. This kind of open, honest, vulnerable expression is very attractive. People love this kind of conviction and courage.

> Vulnerability is characterized by possessing the strength to be seen as you are in the world.

I think we should change the definition of Vulnerability. Deepak Chopra says, "Fear is the denial of vulnerability." Fear is a disconnection, or separation, from the truth of who we are. It takes incredible strength of will to face ourselves—both our fears and our inherent greatness. It's not easy to live out loud, but it does require Vulnerability. Vulnerability creates flexibility—you can bend with the wind because you know that who you truly are can never be hurt or destroyed. Thus, you can be vulnerable, first with yourself, and then with others.

Perhaps you've seen the movie *Devil's Advocate* with Al Pacino. I watched it again recently. Al Pacino's character repeatedly says to Keanu Reeves: "Don't let 'em see you coming." When you're vulnerable, you imagine that everyone will come after you. Yes, some will. But you're so present to life that you also know that these attacks are irrelevant. Nothing will sway you from your purpose, as you allow events to unfold through you. Off comes the riot gear, and on goes your humanity.

*Vulnerability is the ability to live into what you already have, as you grow into the greatness that already is.*

### CULTIVATING A CONSCIOUS PATTERN OF VULNERABILITY

Because control isn't something we can fight against, cultivating a conscious pattern of Vulnerability requires a gentle touch. You can't move from a strict regimen of Self-Defense to a life of Vulnerability in one step, nor can you instruct your coachee to "just open up and trust the universe," or some other such drivel. Vulnerability occurs best when it's placed on a solid foundation.

Develop a good foundation of trust by setting Intentions, acting on those Intentions, and observing the results from a neutral place. Then, when you see what worked and what didn't, you'll develop trust for yourself. You can't trust others fully until you trust yourself fully. Even then, you can never control the behavior of others, so cultivate Vulnerability by exercising a belief in the greatness of others, tempered with the awareness of human fallibility.

Believe:

- You're strong and flexible enough to get through anything.
- Reasonable and conscious protection makes room for increased Vulnerability.
- Great contributions require great Vulnerability.

## THE FOUR-STEP PROCESS APPLIED TO THE ILLUSION OF CONTROL

> *"It is not how much we have, but how much we enjoy that makes happiness.*
>
> CHARLES SPURGEON

Remember rich, but terribly unhappy Rita? Maybe it's hard to drum up sympathy for someone who's been successful in business, but what you don't know is that she was also on the verge of losing her wealth as well because of the stress-induced health issues. This happens more than you might imagine. In a sense, Rita was totally out of control because of her need for control. This also happens frequently.

The following sections will apply the Coaching into Greatness four-step process to Rita's situation.

## AWARENESS

By now you should be familiar with the routine. Rita has to first become aware of how, where, and why she's holding on so hard to her Lone Ranger role. What does she get from being in control? What beliefs underlie her need for control? What does she imagine will happen if she relinquishes control of parts of her empire to others who may be better suited to the tasks?

Play out a visual scenario in which Rita hires an assistant. What would the assistant do? What procedures and policies would Rita need to put into place to trust that the assistant would be truly helpful? We're not talking about blind trust here, but trust that's well-founded by having the right documents, policies, and procedures in place. Rita can control what is controllable but let go of the rest. All of this takes a great deal of awareness on Rita's part. Help her to discover:

- What are her deeper fears?
- How can she reasonably protect herself in a way that allows greater Vulnerability?
- What are her best skills?
- What are her strengths, which, if she builds on them, will help her Live into her Greatness?
- What are her weaknesses that can be complemented by someone else who's strong in those areas?

## ACCEPTANCE

Someone beset with physical and emotional troubles like Rita's might tend to hold tighter to her beliefs. Acceptance of the awareness gained is absolutely critical. She's too scared of losing everything to let go, yet letting go is exactly what needs to happen. She needs to accept that her present condition and circumstances are a direct result of her Illusion of Control.

Ask her to take small steps. If she can accept that her need for control has created the stress, find one small area in which she can release control. Perhaps she can hire a bookkeeper or assistant to handle filing. She'll tell you that having an assistant isn't possible because she's always on the go, and it would take longer to tell the assistant what to do than to do it herself.

Don't buy her excuses for a minute. Gain acceptance that her circumstances are her responsibility and are caused by her Illusion of Control, then swiftly move to step 3.

## CONSISTENT ACTION

People under the Illusion of Control won't easily let loose of the reins. Creating and cultivating new beliefs and abundant patterns will take some strategy. In Rita's case, we'll have her take the time to develop very specific plans, policies, and procedures (the three Ps of efficiency) for all the tasks for which she'd hire an assistant. Only then will she hire the assistant. Your coaching is very important in this phase. Ensure that Rita doesn't sabotage the situation by hiring the first person she finds. She needs to develop specific criteria and stick to the criteria.

Then, have her commit to a daily practice of *not* checking up on the assistant. The assistant will provide a weekly status report and no more. I'll tell you up front that this will drive someone like Rita nuts! In fact, the best thing to do would be to have her stay as far away from the office as possible.

Once she feels comfortable with her assistant, move on to the next job, and the next, always coming back through the four-step process.

## AUTHENTICITY

For Rita, her control patterns feel authentic. It feels more like her than giving up control and becoming vulnerable. She'll feel "weak" or "inadequate" by letting go of her control patterns. The authenticity will come through the constant and consistent repetition of the Coaching into Greatness process.

With each new step toward releasing control, Rita will gain awareness of how it affects her body and her relationships. Once she sees that her life actually improves, she'll begin accepting and appreciating her true greatness, which comes directly from Personal Responsibility and Vulnerability. This will take some time, and repeating the cycle is essential.

## CHAPTER SUMMARY

*He who grasps loses.*

LAO TZU

Control is an attempt to line up the world to meet our "shoulds."

You cannot give what you don't have.

Any time we play a role that becomes an excuse for not doing what we *can* do, that role is a conditioned pattern of scarcity.

Surrender happens when you're in action, doing all that you *can* do, and letting go of those things outside of your control.

Vulnerability is the ability to live into what you already have, as you grow into the greatness that already is.

For additional information and chapter resources, visit http://www. coachingintogreatness.com/the_illusion_of_control.

## CHAPTER NINE

# The Illusion of Time

*No snowflake ever falls in the wrong place.*

ZEN SAYING

For two years I watched helplessly as my mom transformed from a vibrant, exuberant human being to a jaundiced, agonizingly thin rack of skin and bones. The cancer had metastasized to her liver. Her eyes were sunken to dull, lightless orbs. She was tired of fighting the disease, and so were the rest of us.

In the final eight months of her life, I found myself wishing she would die. That sounds awful, doesn't it? What kind of a daughter would wish that on her mother? For a long time after her death, I thought of myself as a horrible, unloving person.

People who've lost someone to a slow, debilitating disease like cancer know what I'm talking about. A dying process like that not only strips the health and vitality from someone you love, but also their dignity and grace. It is a heartbreaking experience that feels in the moment never-ending. For eight long months, I wished my mother would simply go, and with her this impenetrable knot of suffering that felt like death for all of us.

I remember the moment she died like it was an hour ago. I was in the study hall, relaxing from our wonderful evening the previous day. We'd watched TV, laughing at the ridiculous sitcoms, just as we had before

161

her illness. I clearly remember a strange feeling, and when I glanced at the clock, I knew what had happened. I just knew she was gone.

Two hours later, I left the school building and saw my dad waiting for me. He almost never came to school, so it wasn't hard to figure out what had happened. I'd already felt the loss—the huge hole that kept expanding with each tick of the clock and nearly knocked me over when I saw him. Even now, 21 years later, I can feel the pain of that moment.

It took me a long time to get over my feelings of guilt for wishing my mother would die. Therapists told me it was a normal reaction to such a traumatic situation. It didn't feel normal to me. Time stood still, and the guilt remained with me for years. Time, in fact, had become my enemy. I raced against it, trying to run from the pain of my loss. But time, as we shall see, plays many tricks.

## THE DYNAMICS OF TIME

*Later never exists.*

ANONYMOUS

When we're born, we don't get an owner's manual for our minds. We create reality through the focus of our attention and by our thoughts. We create stories, one right after the other, about who we are and what we can or can't do. We create stories about time as well. Time is too short. Time is too long. When it comes to time, we're much like the three bears, except that the "just right" time forever eludes us. People who are bored by life will say that time moves too slowly. People who are fearful that they may miss out on something important say that time moves by too quickly. They're all just stories we make up, like I did, to push away what we don't want.

Our perception of time can be a great source of unhappiness or joy, scarcity or abundance. We choose, moment by moment, second by second, whether time will be a prison, or a catapult to doing what we *can* do.

> The Illusion of Time is characterized by focusing on what you don't have instead of on what you *do* have.

162

How is it that we sometimes lose the sense of time, and then in other instances we're acutely aware of it? Has time suddenly changed course, like a car weaving its way through winding streets? Time does not change. We change. That is, our *perception* of time changes according to our thoughts, our moods, and more importantly, whether we're running from or moving with life's events. We will sometimes say that time is relative. That's just another story we tell to avoid the truth of who we are. Time isn't relative, but our relationship to time changes.

> *The sense of time creates stress, pressure, anxiety, fear and endless disgruntlement in a myriad of ways.*

> DAVID HAWKINS

Time becomes a prison when it becomes too little or not enough. We're either rushed by time or, as I was with my mother, cursing the slowness of time. When I refer to the Illusion of Time, I'm not saying that time itself is an illusion. Time simply is what it is, never changing. We create an Illusion of Time by giving time the power to dictate what we can or can't do. We abuse time by focusing on what we don't have instead of what's here and now.

So many people spend their creative energy looking backward in longing or regret or wistfulness, or looking forward with hope, worry, or anxiety. In this way, by focusing on what we don't have, we hold the present hostage. The present is unique because it's the only opportunity we have to do the things we *can* do. Right now. Right here. And yet, we ferry away our precious, unchanging time for a variety of reasons, which I explore in this chapter.

We end up hiding in the past or the future. We venture into the past in a futile attempt to change it or to relive it. We want freedom from the pain, or to hold on to pleasure. Time keeps moving, anyway, and it offers us no handholds. When we can't find relief in the past, we fly into the future. Don't get me wrong here. I totally believe in imagining your future as a way to visualize and clarify what you want to create, but most of us simply fantasize without any real plan or Intention of fulfilling these fantasies.

Time plays tricks with us. On one of my research and development (R&D) calls, someone commented, "When I love something that I'm doing, it seems that time goes by so quickly; and when I'm doing something that bores me to tears or that I hate doing, it takes me forever." We can get lost in daydreams for what seems like hours but takes only a few minutes. A pleasurable job is over in seconds. A laborious task, like scraping ice off your sidewalk, might take hours. Yet, when we check the clock, the same amount of time has passed.

What's going on within our overactive minds? Our relationship to time has everything to do with attitude, beliefs, and focus of attention. When we're worried, scared, or unfocused, time takes forever. When we're excited, positive, and focused, time flies by. Again, the Illusion of Time is the illusion that some sort of magical elixir for feeling better exists either in the past or the future. It's a "magic there" that doesn't actually exist. We look for truth behind us and ahead of us but never look exactly where it is all the time—right here, right now, in us.

It's estimated that we have between 50,000 and 75,000 thoughts a day, and for the majority of people, over 90 percent of these thoughts are repetitive. That's a lot of wasted energy and attention! What would be the impact to your business and your life if you could recapture and redirect even 10 percent of that wasted energy?

Eckhart Tolle, author of *The Power of Now,* says that all the things that truly matter arise from beyond the mind. He's right, and by the end of this chapter, you'll come away understanding how you can recapture a lot of wasted energy—in a sense, recapturing time.

## A STORY OF TIME

Jonathan and Elaine are very busy people. They run their own business, have three school-age children, and are taking care of Elaine's aging mother. They're very challenged to find the time to do it all. One or both missed several consecutive coaching sessions, and it was nearly impossible to gain any momentum in any area in their lives. The simple answer would have been to put coaching off until they could find the time, perhaps after all three kids were in college. However, there's a tremendous opportunity here that I don't want to miss.

While this may seem like a no-win situation, see if you can come up with ways to work with Jonathan and Elaine that will help them shift from the Illusion of Time to the Aptitude of Actualization. That is, from "not enough time" to "everything of importance is handled."

## THE CONDITIONED PATTERNS OF TIME

> *The supreme value is not the future but the present. Whoever builds a house for future happiness builds a prison for the present.*
>
> OCTAVIO PAZ

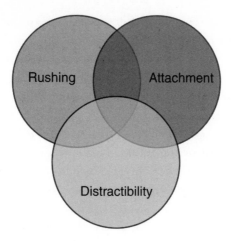

Figure 9.1   The Conditioned Patterns of Time.

## THE CONDITIONED PATTERN OF RUSHING

*What time would it be if all the clocks were stopped?*

ZEN QUESTION

I wasn't exactly sure what to call this conditioned pattern. I toyed with the idea of calling it judgment, or impulsiveness, but neither seemed to hit the mark. We're all conditioned to judge things as good, bad, right, wrong, high, or low. I covered this in great detail in my discussion of the Illusion of Comparisons. We interpret the world based on our past experiences, thus judging situations and people accordingly.

Judgment is, I determined, closely associated with the Illusion of Time. We have to reach into the past to pull out a judgment. A situation is judged as bad or good, depending on past experience. Of course, the situation is neither bad nor good—it's just a situation. But our past experience dictates whether we judge it as good or bad. Shakespeare said (in *Hamlet*), "There is nothing either good or bad, but thinking makes it so."

The same goes for impulsiveness. Sometimes impulsiveness can be a good thing, and sometimes bad. When we act impulsively, though, it's often based on a past experience. "The last time something like this happened, I waited. Not this time! I'm *jumping* on this opportunity!" Or sometimes impulsiveness is based on the future, such as: "You never know what's going to happen, so if I don't act *now*, I may lose out." Both of these scenarios are related to the illusion that time is short.

165

Finally, I realized that, especially in the United States, we're very conditioned to hurry or rush through things. We have rush hour, happy hour, and a lunch hour. Everything must be done ASAP. When do I need it? I need it yesterday, of course. We say that time is of the essence, or that time waits for no one. Everything we do today is rushed, even our TV watching. I don't watch much TV, but when I do I notice that even the commercials seem to be in a hurry to get their message across. Even the way we talk and write is done in shorthand now to save time. Multitasking is revered as an art form.

What's the hurry? Life isn't going anywhere, but we sure think that we're going to miss out if we don't hurry up. Ever hear the phrase "hurry up and wait?" There's nothing worse than rushing down to the store, only to wait in a long checkout line. There's really nothing wrong with doing things quickly. The most successful people in the world are very fast at what they do. But they're not in a hurry. This is a very important distinction.

> Rushing is characterized by the belief that there is a scarcity of time and opportunity, causing people to focus on what they think they *should* do, instead of what they *can* do.

Rushing actually keeps us from doing what we *can* do. We're so concerned about getting there or finishing on time that our quality (of life, of work) suffers. We're not really doing what we *can* do; we're doing what we *should* do.

Consider this: What would happen if you simply stopped—stopped striving, searching, hoping, or trying to become something or someone? Just stop. It may seem like I'm telling you to sit in a corner and wait until life comes to you. No, not at all! Stop striving, but go do what you *can* do. Stop searching, and instead simply do what you *can* do. It's Nike's "Just Do It™" slogan, but done without a need to hurry. There's absolutely no reason to carry the world on your shoulders when you're doing your day's work.

We're simply too scared to stop. Here are a few of the conditioned beliefs that feed the conditioned pattern of Rushing:

- I just have too much to do. I can't possibly slow down.
- If you wait or stop, life will pass you by.

- The world would be nothing but chaos if we all stopped.
- I feel like I'll sink to the bottom and drown if I don't keep going.

Get the point? The idea, as success coach Bob Proctor is fond of saying, is to calm down, not slow down.

## THE CONDITIONED PATTERN OF ATTACHMENT

*Attachment is the great fabricator of illusions; reality can be attained only by someone who is detached.*

SIMONE WEIL

Buddhists say that Attachment is the cause of human suffering. While I think we can argue that Attachment isn't all that bad, they can definitely keep us from doing what we *can* do. You need some Attachment, after all. Your wife or husband wouldn't appreciate it if you ran off with another man or woman simply because you thought that Attachment caused suffering. Like everything else, however, there's a Tipping Point at which Attachment moves us into scarcity thinking instead of abundant thinking.

---

Attachment is characterized by needing something or someone to the extent that it limits our Capacity to be who we are and do what we *can* do.

---

We see our Attachments as facts, when they're actually rooted in our beliefs, fears, and assumptions about what we need in life.

We can have Attachment to:

- People.
- Places.
- Things.
- Patterns/habits.
- How something occurs.
- Past events, situations, feelings, or circumstances.
- Future events, situations, feelings, or circumstances.
- Thinking a particular way.
- Traditions or rituals.
- Opinions—looking for things that support our ideas and opinions.

- The status quo.
- Our scripts/stories.
- Our identity of who we're (shy, clever, talented, a goofball).

Attachment is very time-based. It's like trying to stop the clock in some fixed location because we want to keep things the way they are or the way they were. Attachment is also closely related to struggle—it's an endless searching for how and why. We constantly look for explanations as a way to explain life. Explaining gives us a false sense of security, of knowing.

---

DISTINCTION: NEEDS VS. WANTS

A need is a dependency, and an Attachment. Of course, we need shelter. But, we become attached to needing a particular kind of shelter.

A want, on the other hand is a desire for expansion. A want is not attached to a particular look or feel but is open to any form of manifestation. It is not required to be who we are.

---

Why do we become attached? We're trained to long for what we don't have, or to fear that we'll lose what we do have. That's why advertising is so effective. Good advertising taps into the Illusion of Not Enough to create a need, and then connects to the Illusion of Time to show that you have to act *now*, or you'll miss out. Clever, those advertisers. Better buy now, because time is running out!

Anthony De Mello, in his book *The Way to Love,* says, "Almost every negative emotion you experience is the direct outcome of an attachment. Attachments can only thrive in the darkness of illusion."

## CONDITIONED BELIEFS ABOUT ATTACHMENT

Since this is an illusion, can you see from where it comes? Look to your underlying beliefs, such as:

- I can't live without _____.
- If I let her/him/it go, I just don't know if I can continue on.
- Hold on as if your life depended on it.

- I refuse to look at any alternatives. This is what I've believed all my life.
- There can't possibly be a better way.
- What would I be without _____?

Attachment beliefs are those in which options and possibilities are shut out. Any sign of clinging is a good indication of an Attachment. It's a way of playing very small in what could be a very big game. Attachment is the ultimate form of holding on. How can you possibly move forward if you're holding on to the past?

## THE CONDITIONED PATTERN OF DISTRACTIBILITY

*Nothing is worth more than this day.*

GOETHE

Everything we do is a sound bite. People say they don't have enough time, that they're doing too many things. That's not the real problem. They've simply been conditioned to switch gears every 30 seconds. TV commercials last about 30 seconds, and each scene in a TV show (and many movies today) lasts no more than 30 seconds.

Ring. Ring. It's the phone. Better go get it.
"You've got mail!" Stop whatever you're doing to read it.
Fax coming in? Put your work down to see if it's important.

We've become so distractible that if I sent you an instant message right now, you'd probably jump up to read it. Wouldn't you?

> Distractibility is characterized by allowing people, events, emotions, and fears to conveniently keep us from doing what we *can* do.

We say we don't have enough time, when in reality we're too distracted by everything that's going on around us to pay much attention to time. It's the perfect excuse for procrastination. It's a way to escape change by focusing on other things. "Oh, I can't do *that*. I have to attend to this important thing over here." And, how long does this last? It lasts until the *next* important thing comes up. It's all about convenience, not time.

Here's an equation for you:

$$\text{Distraction} + \text{Justification} = \text{Avoidance}$$

We justify our Distractions as a way of avoiding doing what we *can* do. Why? Failure comes to mind. If we do what we *can* do, there is the possibility of failure. What better reason to avoid failure (or success) than having far too much to do?

It's kind of a strange paradox, isn't it? We don't have enough time to do what we *can* do, so we distract ourselves doing things that we *ought* to do. How much of your day is really effective? I'm not talking about productivity here. You can have a very productive day but effectively not do anything that moves you closer to having the kind of life you want. That's why so many people remain stuck. They stay busy, but not doing things from a sense of abundance. They act from lack or scarcity, doing because they hope that it will someday (Illusion of Time) help them feel good.

I still hear from almost every one of my clients, like clockwork every six months, that they don't have enough time or don't have enough money. Both of these beliefs are Convenient Distractions. They distract my clients from doing what they *can* do, right now, in this moment. This is the real killer about Distractions. A lot of our beliefs are Distractions. Any belief that keeps you from doing what you *can* do and Living into your Greatness is a Distraction.

I've had many clients tell me that they didn't reach their goal because they got distracted by other things. What? Are they afraid of completing the assignment? That may be the case for many people, since, as I've already said, I think many people are terrified of their own greatness. After all, if they don't have the Distractions available, what might happen? Answer: They might actually have to commit to something!

One client said, "When I was building my business, I would always talk about all the prospects I had. I became distracted by getting more prospects, but was afraid that if I actually spoke to any of them, they'd go away. Then, I wouldn't have any more prospects!" What a great example of scarcity thinking and habitual Distraction!

Here's another good example. Laura, a consultant, and I had come up with several powerful business-building strategies. We discussed the benefits of creating strategic alliances, and one in particular caught her eye. She's wanted for ages to create an alliance with one of the largest office-supply chains. We talked strategy; we made an action plan and identified her next steps. Her first action was to call the local store manager.

After reporting three weeks in a row that she hadn't made the call because she was "so busy, and didn't have the time," I decided it was time to do a little exploring. Rather than focus on time management (the most likely option for most people), we dug a little deeper. She finally admitted that lack of time wasn't the issue. In fact, she *looked* for Distractions. She was simply scared of making the call because she was afraid of doing an in-store demonstration, going to the bathroom, and coming out with her skirt tucked into her pantyhose. Ridiculous? No. Just pure, honest fear. After exploring options about her fear, including wearing a pantsuit instead of a skirt to the in-store demo, she was noticeably relieved and in fact got a good laugh out of it. She made that call, ended up doing the in-store demonstration, and the thing she most feared never even happened.

## Conditioned Beliefs about Distractibility

Here's a good one: "I don't have the time." That's a bunch of hooey. It's one of the greatest Distractions of all time. I know a working mom who's always "running out of time" because she works at home. Why? Well, there's always laundry to do, things to pick up, dusting, cleaning, and so on. Her belief is that as a mother, it's her job to do these things—and to work full-time on her business. This is a family that can easily pay for household help, but it doesn't fit their belief system. As a result, she's always distracted.

How you choose to spend your time is a choice. The belief is that we don't have choice, but we do in very many cases. We just tolerate Distractions.

Other beliefs:

- I have to take care of it myself.
- If I don't check e-mails as they arrive, I'll just get overwhelmed later.
- What if I miss an important call (e-mail, fax, etc.)?
- What if someone needs me?

## The Tipping Point of Time

Time is your friend. Really, it is. There's the same amount of time every day. It never changes, unless you're hurtling through space at close to the speed of light. Time flips to scarcity when we imagine that there isn't enough time, so we hurry, attach ourselves to ideas, people, beliefs, or attitudes; or, we distract ourselves with a thousand little things. That is, we become a victim of time.

We also tip toward scarcity when dwelling on the past or hanging out in the future instead of being with what's here, now. We try to rewrite the past, or become so attached to it that we try to recreate it in the present (or the future). It never works because it's scarcity thinking. Time also becomes "scarce" when we allow ourselves to be distracted by people or events instead of staying focused and clear.

Take a good, long look at highly successful people. Do you notice how difficult it is to get an appointment with them? And when you do, you must get there on time and leave on time. They're not doing 10 things at once. They're doing one thing at a time, and they do it very well and to completion. They don't allow others to distract them, and because of that, people honor and respect their time. Time becomes an Illusion of Scarcity only when we fail to respect ourselves and the value of our time and energy.

## PROFILES IN GREATNESS: "MIKE$^2$" OF THE REFERRAL INSTITUTE®

The Illusion of Time can be a slippery critter. We'll always find time for Distractions, but will we find the time to stop, step back, and get really curious about what's real and what's not? Copywriter Dan Kennedy says, "Rich people have big libraries; poor people have big TVs." It's all about where you choose to allocate the time you have that makes the biggest difference. Take, for example, "Mike$^2$" from The Referral Institute®.

You've already heard from Ivan Misner, the founder of BNI. Michael Macedonio and Michael Garrison are partners of The Referral Institute®, which provides referral coaching, consulting, and training programs for individuals and companies. The Referral Institute® is an offshoot of BNI, with similar values and philosophy of building long-term relationships. These are people who are very busy, but not rushed or easily distracted. They're focused and, as a result, have grown the referral business into a very thriving operation. Mike$^2$, as I enjoy calling them, oversee 70 chapters in three states with over 1,500 members, and work with more than 30 groups and 500 individual participants. Busy? You'd better believe it. Rushed? No way.

Part of the reason they can accomplish so much in the same time allotted to all of us is their beliefs about scarcity and abundance. Mike Garrison says, "Abundance is truth and scarcity is the illusion. Truth is grounded in a firm grasp of reality. I think so many people who are in scarcity are not facing reality."

Macedonio agrees, adding, "Scarcity leads to desperation and a scarcity mentality. Sometimes people have such a narrow view of the business that's out there that they think they have to capture all the business and be open to anyone who might possibly need them. They end up becoming the marketing version of Wal-Mart, with the lowest prices and one of everything. As such, they don't have any industry value."

Nor do they have much time. Everything seems rushed and they're far too easily distracted. Macedonio commented that many of the people he works with come in very afraid of their competition, and this keeps them being overly busy competing. Instead, he suggests they can see these as opportunities for collaboration, where they can work together and both can profit. He says that, "Coming from scarcity, they think they have to have or do it all, or somebody else is going to get it. To me, that communicates desperation. That's one of the things you have to learn about marketing, whether it comes out of your mouth or out in your behavior or your actions, when people see desperation they usually go the other way. Desperation isn't referable."

I love that line—*desperation isn't referable.* Even when we look at the partnership of these two men, we can see how they can step back and be truthful with themselves and each other. At one point, Garrison was going through a rough time due to a big personal loss. He wasn't being effective at work, and rather than sweep it under the table, Macedonio suggested Garrison drop back and not do something he had agreed to do because of his general ineffectiveness. This is evidence of trust, and it requires facing reality in a big way.

The real truth, they say, is that if "people are in scarcity mode, they tend not to depend on relationships, and unless you're positive and you're focused on abundance, it's really hard to maintain those rewarding relationships. The scarcity people who run around are the ones who destroy social capital."

The Referral Institute® helps people do good business that ends up in long, lasting, stable relationships. It's what Garrison says is "the process of abundance that leads to endurance." When people get pressed for time, they tend to give up on these relationships, when that's *exactly* when they should be including the relationships. Especially, both Mikes added, when you make mistakes. Macedonio emphasizes that when you have a relationship of abundance, you can recover from almost anything.

While these two will joke around with each other, prodding and kidding each other about their personal quirks, it's quite evident that they have a very close relationship. I think part of the reason they work so well together is that they see no problem with time. As far as they're concerned, they've all the time in the world to do what's most important—to be authentically themselves, as much as possible, while they focus on building lasting relationships. It's a lesson I think we can all learn from.

## SHIFTING THE BALANCE FROM TIME TO ACTUALIZATION

Most people think of Abraham Maslow in relation to the word *Actualization*. He emphasized in his famous hierarchy of needs pyramid that "self-actualization was at the top." Here's how the dictionary defines actualization: "To realize in action or to make real." This definition may help shed some light on why I chose this word to depict the abundance aptitude related to the Illusion of Time (see Figure 9.2).

| |
|---|
| Actualization is characterized by consistent and authentic action. |

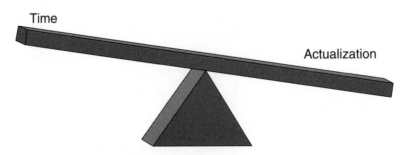

Figure 9.2   Tipping the Balance to Actualization.

In other words, Actualization is what's realized through consistent and authentic action. See the difference? The Illusion of Time focuses on how, and the aptitude of Actualization focuses on when. There is no talk of not enough time when you are focused on actualizing what you want through consistent and authentic action. You drop into the Illusion of Time only when you think you can't do what you want to do because you don't have the time.

*The idea is to move from problem to solution.* The Illusion of Time only points at the problem. The aptitude of Actualization moves toward the solution. Notice that I didn't say "looks for the solution." The belief that a solution must be looked for is a trap that brings us back into the Illusion of Time. Inevitably, you're faced with a time crunch in which you have to *find the solution* within an ever-shortening time frame. Instead, we simply *move toward* a solution, taking consistent and authentic action in the direction of a solution. It's a subtle but important difference.

*Another way to look at it is that Actualization is a way to maximize the present and create the future.* The Illusion of Time never even looks at the present—it's either stuck in the past or looking to the future. An important point here is that we don't just act for the sake of acting. It's all about acting authentically, which means you hold beliefs that are in alignment with your inherent greatness, and act accordingly.

I know that my successes have come because I let my passion lead, and I did whatever I could, not knowing the exact outcome. I focused on doing things *when* they could be done, instead of getting stuck trying to figure out *how* to do the things I thought I needed to do. This doesn't mean I didn't have a plan, or didn't pay attention to the details. I did, *but I paid attention to what I could do right now.*

For example, when I was a senior in college, the school asked me to create a volunteer organization. Having never done this before, I was naturally unsure. But I had a strong conviction of helping people, and I loved bringing people together to do cool, interesting things. I just started acting right from where I was, doing whatever I could in the moment. With each consistent action, the next step was magically revealed. I worked with other people and tapped into resources and knowledge, and most of all, I believed in myself. I let my environment inspire me and I learned by doing. By the time I graduated from college, my organization had recruited over 250 volunteers (students, faculty, and staff) to contribute over 1,200 volunteer hours during the school year. I left a legacy that's still helping that community to this day.

Then, when I became a VISTA volunteer, I was charged with creating a grant-writing process for the homelessness agency into which I was placed. Again, I had no experience with writing grants, so I just did what I could in each moment. By the time I completed my two-year stint, we'd raised over $125,000. What was the catch? Getting out of my own way and reaching out for help. None of that would have been possible, or ever happened, if I hadn't believed that I could do it and that there was purpose for my doing it. Nor would any of it have happened if I'd believed that I didn't have the time to figure it out. I let go of the how and started from where I was. I acted in the present.

*The key action step of Actualization is: Not how, but when.*

## THE CONSCIOUS PATTERNS OF ACTUALIZATION

*Self-actualizing people must be what they can be.*

ABRAHAM MASLOW

*What lies behind us and what lies before us are tiny matters compared to what lies within us.*

OLIVER WENDELL HOLMES

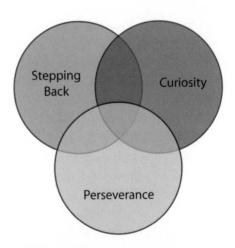

Figure 9.3   The Conscious Patterns of Actualization.

176

## THE CONSCIOUS PATTERN OF STEPPING BACK

Eckhart Tolle, whom I mentioned earlier, says, "You are not your mind. Thoughts are just thoughts. They are not who you are." Your identity, your greatness isn't what you think. It is a combination of thinking, feeling, and acting.

> Stepping Back is characterized by the ability to see what is and respond accordingly instead of reacting to a situation based on judgments and assumptions.

Essentially, what Tolle is saying is that we all have the ability to Step Back from not only the events of our lives, but also our thoughts. One way I've come to understand this concept is by asking a simple question: If you're having a thought, and become aware that you're having a thought, then *who* is it that's aware of the thought? See the point? If you can step back and observe yourself having a thought, then that thought can't possibly be "you." You are the observer of the thought.

If this is really true, then doesn't it make sense that there's no rush? At any time, you can step back and observe your own thoughts. Calm down, don't slow down. This is a big responsibility that most people aren't willing to take. We'd rather respond to what's happening than step back and observe before thinking or taking action. To make this work, you have to take Personal Responsibility for your own thoughts, as well as your actions.

Thoughts come and go all the time. It's up to each of us to then *choose* the thoughts to which we want to give attention. At any time, you can step back and see these thoughts, very much like watching the words scroll across your TV set or during a movie with subtitles. And if you think that it's not possible to watch your thoughts and stay in motion, go ahead and observe yourself the next time you *do* watch a subtitled movie. You'll read the subtitles and not miss a beat with what's on the screen.

We can play piano with both hands (at least some people can). We drive and listen to a book or talk on our cell phones at the same time. Our minds are absolutely amazing. So, yes, you *can* step back, observe your thoughts, and simultaneously stay in consistent and authentic action.

Stepping back moves us from "what if" time to "what is" time. Instead of reacting to a situation based on judgments and presumptions, we can step back, see what is, and respond accordingly. Imagine what your life would be like if, instead of automatically reacting to situations, you could step back and respond in terms of what's really there.

A colleague recently related to me what is unfortunately a common e-mail event. Because he used exclamation points to emphasize his *excitement,* and a client of his saw these same exclamation points as a form of *yelling,* she thought he was angry and frustrated with her. She was ready to give up the project and walk away. He stepped back, saw that it was a simple misunderstanding, and calmly clarified the situation. Had he reacted, he could have accused her of being irrational and also walked away.

The interesting point is that all of this took place in an instant. That's how quick our minds are. I'm not talking about spending two hours in meditation every time something happens. But cultivate the habit of Stepping Back—for an instant—instead of Rushing toward a reaction.

The trick is to see the possibility in what might otherwise be interpreted as a difficulty. Earlier I gave you the example of Tara, the therapist whose daughter had an eating disorder. Through coaching, Tara saw the possibility of growth for her daughter, *because* she had to go through the difficulty of dealing with the disease. Tara saw that trying to solve or fix her daughter's disease could actually prevent her daughter from growing as a result of life's challenges.

## CULTIVATING A CONSCIOUS PATTERN OF STEPPING BACK

You know those awkward moments of silence in the midst of an intense conversation? Most people can't handle these silences, so they fill them with chitchat. It's an emptiness that feels very uncomfortable. Often, we interpret this emptiness as something bad that has to be fixed. The first step in cultivating a conscious pattern of Stepping Back is to become friendly with silence and emptiness.

Emptiness doesn't mean you have nothing left; it means you don't have the emotional charge around life's ups and downs, and you can experience the full face of life without being swept away.

Here are a few thoughts you can entertain:

- Silence is golden (trite, but useful).
- It takes less time and energy to respond than to clean up the mess from a reaction.

- Remember Lincoln's lesson: If you have eight hours to cut wood, spend six of them sharpening your saw (Stepping Back).

## THE CONSCIOUS PATTERN OF CURIOSITY

Is detachment the opposite of Attachment? In my mind, detachment is something else entirely. I've seen a lot of people become detached from uncomfortable situations, and it's more like they've stepped off the ride because they got a little woozy. They usually just walk away because they were hurt in some way by the intense attachment to an idea or feeling.

To me, such a reaction is still a condition of lack or scarcity. Instead, I propose that the opposite of Attachment is Curiosity. Attachment makes the assumption that we can keep things from changing. Once you can accept the impermanence of things, it's easy to then become very curious about life.

> Curiosity is characterized by the ability to embrace wonder and appreciate all of something—not just one opportunity, but many opportunities.

What else is possible? If you aren't attached to a particular outcome, then you're more flexible and can conceive of different ways to do what you've always done but in ways that are no longer working. If, for example, you were building a new Web site to promote your services or products, you might be very attached to having it look just like your brochure. What if, instead, you became very curious about what else might be possible? You might discover that you have enough information to create a subscription-based Web portal; or, that you can make additional income by selling noncompeting products on your Web site.

Curiosity cures the endless thinking and worrying that happens when ideas or beliefs are rigidly held. You learn to appreciate more of what life has to offer, and the abundance of opportunities.

Learn to appreciate not just one of something, but all of something. Not just one opportunity, but many opportunities. If you are focused on just one of something, you are excluding the beauty and opportunity that exist in all the others. If you are convinced this is the one job or person to make you happy, you will exclude all other possibilities.

I'll give you an example. My friends and many colleagues know that I love trees. A couple of years ago, I noticed that someone was cutting down two of my favorite trees in my neighborhood. Yes, I was attached to those trees being there, and I was angry that they were cutting them down. Did this change the fact that "my" trees were gone? No, not in the least. While I can definitely appreciate the beauty of nature and love all trees equally, these felt special to me. See, I could feel angry about what was happening, realize my Attachment, and become curious. I could change my route, help plant new trees, or befriend new trees. It was my Attachment to the trees that caused me pain, not the cutting down of the trees. For all I know, they may have been dead inside and would have come down in the next storm.

## CULTIVATING A CONSCIOUS PATTERN OF CURIOSITY

> *The lure of the distant and the difficult is deceptive. The great opportunity is where you are.*

> JOHN BURROUGHS

Curiosity can be taught, but it's often stifled, and at an early age. Coaches are generally taught to be curious. Asking questions will usually give you a lot more information than dictating answers. The Illusion of Time makes us think that we don't have time to be curious. Does a four-year-old child ever consider that there might not be enough time to have his questions answered?

One of the easiest ways to cultivate Curiosity is to preface every statement with, "I wonder if. . . ." How can any of us ever be absolutely certain about anything? After all, nothing is permanent. No thoughts, ideas, or even objects are permanent. Everything changes, and it's Curiosity that has enabled humans to evolve. Where would we be if the Wright brothers and others had not been curious about flying?

Thoughts that might help are:

- Only by letting go of what I have can I make room for something better.
- To let go is to truly enjoy.
- By letting go, I'm not giving up or depriving myself. I'm positioned to receive more of the great things coming my way.

## THE CONSCIOUS PATTERN OF PERSEVERANCE

> *The best way to predict the future is to create it.*

> PETER DRUCKER

Many time-management books and techniques would have you focus on what you do with your time. They're all missing the point. Instead, focus on your activities. You have exactly the same amount of time as everyone else — 24 hours a day. It's what you *do* with that time that counts, so the focus should be on energy management, not time management.

> Perseverance is characterized by focusing on what you *can* do in the present as part of the process of Living into Greatness. It is doing the thing you *can* do even when it is not easy, convenient, or proven.

The flip side of Distractibility is Perseverance. It's not focus, because if you're focused on the wrong activities, you'll still end up in the wrong place. Besides, Perseverance is a requirement of focus. It's one thing to focus your attention on something for 15 minutes. It's an entirely different thing to remain focused when things turn sour. That takes Perseverance.

I think that people remain distracted not because they can't focus. They can certainly focus on the Distractions! They remain distracted because they don't persevere. You have to have a clear picture of where you're going, and then cultivate the Perseverance to get there.

There's something wonderful that happens when we persevere. We become increasingly present. The past is gone, and the future is being made right now. Perseverance is like a field of immense power that forms around a person. It's directed energy that's reinforced by Intention and desire. You can't live in the past or the future (which is what happens with Distractions) when you're moving forward with Perseverance. Perseverance enables you to do the thing that often isn't convenient, popular, easy, affordable, proven, certain, or understood.

CULTIVATING A CONSCIOUS PATTERN OF PERSEVERANCE

Perseverance is both a practice and an art. It's an art because it requires having a vision that's filled with Intention and desire. You simply can't persevere toward something for which you have no desire. It's a practice because we're not trained to persevere. We're trained to be distracted (roughly every 30 seconds).

The caveat here is that to be effective, Perseverance must be innerdirected, in alignment with who you are. Perseverance can actually become a form of scarcity if it's abused to push us to strive unnaturally, to kill ourselves to become something we're not, or when it creates an unhealthy Attachment. Perseverance in its best form helps us to stay on the path of being who we are. It energizes us to be abundant.

Practice this:

- No e-mail, phone call, or even a live person is more important than Living into my Greatness and doing what I *can* do.
- I'll manage my energy more closely than I manage my time.

## The Four-Step Process Applied to the Illusion of Time

*Time is what keeps the light from reaching us.*

MEISTER ECKHART

Jonathan and Elaine have no time. Running a business can be an all-consuming affair for anyone. Top that with children and an aging mother, and you have the perfect ingredients for the "no time" illusion. Let's run through the four step process.

### AWARENESS

We don't tell Jonathan and Elaine that they have plenty of time. It's not a matter of enough time, but a matter of gaining more awareness of how the time they have is allocated. You can't convince people as busy as these two that they have plenty of time. They'll ditch you pretty quickly, saying, "We don't have time for this nonsense."

They need to become aware of how their feelings, beliefs, and thoughts about time are impacting their ability to manage their activities. While it's difficult at best to manage activities with school-age kids, it's not impossible. The whole idea that they need to rush through everything because there isn't enough time to get it all done is of major concern. We can ask them to stop, if only for a moment, and Step Back in their situation. They can't change the fact that they have a business, children, and a mother to take care of, but they can become aware of how their decisions are influenced by their attitude and beliefs about time.

Are all the Distractions necessary? Where can they implement greater discipline? Are they attached to certain beliefs or habits? What if they investigated other ways to manage their activities, enlisting the whole family in moving toward solutions? Sure there's a lot to do, but what can be done more calmly, without losing speed?

## ACCEPTANCE

Jonathan and Elaine will be quite hesitant to accept that anything can be different. Acceptance begins with awareness. Once they become aware of *how* their beliefs have influenced the results they're getting, and become aware of their Attachments and Distractibility, they will be more likely to accept that there are alternate approaches. This step is critical, because if they haven't accepted the possibility of alternate approaches, no amount of action will change their results.

## CONSISTENT ACTION

For Jonathan and Elaine, consistent action means consistently managing their activities. What are the three most important activities each day? What's their vision for their family and business? Which activities will most likely move them closer to this vision? It really will take a certain amount of Perseverance for them to eliminate Convenient Distractions, but this is a necessary ingredient for consistent action.

Can they eliminate TV watching? Arrange car pools for the kids? Set realistic schedules for focusing on the business? Hire a part-time caretaker for Mom? They need to break the habit and the cycle of Distractibility and release any Attachments to doing things the same way they've always done it. You simply can't continue down the same road you started when your life circumstances have changed.

## AUTHENTICITY

What is authenticity to a family like this? Authenticity has a lot to do with the family vision and values. Busy families will often find themselves fighting against their own values. They know that family time is necessary, but they can't seem to pull it off. This is the perfect time for Jonathan and Elaine to revisit (or create for the first time) the vision and values for their family. Then, they can reflect on their behaviors and actions to see if these behaviors and actions are in alignment with their vision and values. If not, they've gained some new awareness, from which they can create new consistent actions.

## CHAPTER SUMMARY

*The next message you need is right where you are.*

BABA RAM DASS

We don't experience life by thinking about it.

Time becomes a prison when it becomes too little or not enough.

Time is a choice.

Desperation isn't referable.

Actualization is a way to maximize the present and create the future.

What happens to us in life doesn't hurt us; how we think about it does.

For additional information and chapter resources, visit http://www.coachingintogreatness.com/the_illusion_of_time.

## CHAPTER TEN

# The Illusion of Hope

*If we continue to pursue hope, then we had best become a producer of it, rather than a consumer of it.*

PETER BLOCK

I remember sitting in the chair in the corner of the hospital room, holding the newspaper up in front of me like a makeshift paper wall, attempting to block out the pain and fear of what was happening on the other side of the room. I heard the hospital bed shaking as if we'd suddenly been hit by an earthquake. My mom was having a bad reaction from her chemotherapy, and her platelet count was dangerously low. It was causing her entire body to shake uncontrollably. I couldn't bear to watch it, and I couldn't bear to say anything to her. I might fall apart, and she would know exactly how terrified I was. I couldn't damage my reputation as *The Rock*.

Funny thing about cancer—it's the certainty of the uncertainty that does the most damage. All that time during the two years of her illness, I was desperate with hope. Hope that she would go into remission, hope that she would come home from the hospital, hope that she could be the mom she used to be, hope that I would somehow be able to be me, unchanged . . . just a kid.

It's taken me years to get over the guilt and shame of sitting in that corner and doing nothing. I could have held her hand and talked with her. I could have told her a stupid joke to make her laugh. Instead, I just sat in the corner and hoped that it would all go away.

Hope. We all do it. I did, and I still do. I hope I'll stay healthy. I hope that somebody in our government will finally get his or her act together. I even hoped that the Red Sox would win the World Series again.

Is hope really an illusion—a source of scarcity? Read on, and see for yourself if hope helps you to do or hinders you from doing what you *can* and want to do.

## THE DYNAMICS OF HOPE

> *A man will sometimes devote all his life to the development of one part of his body—the wishbone.*
>
> ROBERT FROST

Take a moment and reread the opening quote for this chapter. It's taken from Peter Block's amazing book, *The Answer to How Is Yes*, featured in my recommended reading list.

What does it mean to be a consumer of hope? To me, it gives us a taste of how hope can be a form of scarcity. I recently read the cover article in *Fortune* about Michelle Wie, the phenomenal 16-year-old female golfer. She dreams of not only competing, but *winning* on the *men's* pro golf tour. She sees Tiger Woods as her competitor, and not necessarily the women on the women's tour. Does this anger the women pros? You can bet your golf handicap on it.

Michelle Wie is a producer of hope. She doesn't *hope* to win golf tournaments. She *plans* on winning on the pro tour—men's and women's. She produces hope for every young girl who's thinking of taking up golf, or virtually any other sport for that matter. Hope doesn't stop her from doing what she *can* do. It propels her into doing exactly what she *can* do—every day.

What does it mean to be a producer of hope? People who produce hope are creators, activators, and change agents; they are doing what they *can* and want to do. In the process, they are virtual hope factories for sometimes millions of people worldwide.

Doing what you *can* do. Read that phrase again and again until it's firmly planted in your consciousness. It has become my main mantra. Am I doing what I *can* do? Or am I being held back or limited in some way by my thinking?

Hope can be one such limiting factor. It can also be a beautiful thing. Hope enabled my mom to live two years with cancer when the doctors gave her six months. It enables the entrepreneur to take that big leap from having a job to creating a business. Hope is essential—without it, life is a daunting task.

Even so, there is a side of hope that few people talk about. Hope works when it keeps people engaged. I'm sure Michelle Wie has hopes. Those hopes, though, never stop her from improving her game. Hope doesn't work when it takes people out of the game, whether that game is a business venture, a game of golf, or the game of life.

Hope, when it becomes an excuse to avoid the necessary steps that will create forward movement, is an illusion. Michelle Wie can see millions of dollars in her future. She even admitted that she's motivated by the $5 she gets for every birdie during practice. But this is very different from hoping for a raise, hoping for a boyfriend or girlfriend, or hoping to create a successful business.

The difference is in what we do or don't do with the hope. The producers of hope do what they *can* do, with or without hope. Those under the Illusion of Hope play a waiting game. They wait for the right opportunity, the helpful hand, or the lucky break. Producers create their own luck. Consumers hope for luck to happen.

> The Illusion of Hope is characterized by waiting for other people or events to solve our uneasiness about who we are.

In this respect, hope is like the dark side of positive thinking. Positive thinking alone rarely brings about lasting change because it's a passive activity.

We might as well get this out on the table. I have a confession to make. I have a problem with affirmations.

Don't get me wrong, it's not a bad thing to focus on the positive. It's just that, when I hear affirmations, I can't help thinking of Stuart Smalley on *Saturday Night Live:* "I'm good enough, I'm smart enough, and doggone it, people like me." Affirmations and hope both fall short when they enable us to live passively. As long as we're telling ourselves we're abundant and successful, and that money will come our way, we fail to take action. I've heard many a coach affirm, "I'm a great coach, and people will hire me." Then, they sit back and *hope* those clients will start calling. As I said, hope becomes a waiting game.

The Illusion of Hope is similar to the "Field of Dreams" mentality. If you build it, they will come. Hope is only one small part of the equation. Without action, hope is the linchpin in a negative reinforcing cycle of expectations, disappointment, and stagnation.

When hope is passive, it allows us to escape a discomfort around the uncertainties in our life. Yet, this is such a paradox. We hope because we're uncertain of the future, and our hope often keeps us from doing what we *can* do. Yet doing what we *can* do is the only thing that can give us a measure of certainty.

*Hope is the longing and wishing for things we think we don't have.* In its worst form, it's a negation of our greatness and what we *do* have. The energy we put into wishing and waiting actually prevents us from receiving what we want.

Hope as an immobilizer. It enables us to think we're out of choices, and that we don't have enough, or can't be enough. It encourages us to wait and see, to be acted upon. The Illusion of Hope portrays us as buoys in a hurricane, completely out of control and at the whim of the storm of life.

Hope keeps us doing things longer than we might otherwise if we felt empowered. Hope keeps us hanging on, when our intuition tells us we could have let go a long time ago.

Hope is a prison. It's a conditioned belief that there is nothing we can do, other than sit back and hope for the best.


## A STORY OF HOPE

*Few people have the imagination for reality.*

GOETHE

I was coaching the owners of a newly formed small business to help them create a good, solid team. They had a great concept, the enthusiasm to back it up, and what I interpreted as the willingness to push through whatever obstacles arose. The problems they encountered were almost identical to many small businesses and entrepreneurs: They hate selling.

I noticed the Illusion of Hope slithering in, quite slyly I might add, about three months into our coaching. We'd gone through their marketing plan in detail, identifying exactly who they needed on the team to get their idea launched and ready to fly. We'd even gone so far as to identify the particular skill set needed by each new person.

However, they were more focused on building a "family" than on building a business. They hired a sales manager who shared their philosophy of life but unfortunately also shared their distaste for sales. They claimed, "We don't need to sell, at least not in the usual sense. We want to attract customers because of who we are as people and as a company."

In other words, they were running their business on a hope and a prayer. They hoped that business would come to them, and expected clients to knock down their door because of their life philosophy. This may work well if you're a spiritual guru, but even they have to do a little marketing and sales (even if they don't call it sales). Eckhart Tolle (author of the very popular *The Power of Now*) would have remained an obscure though enlightened man without a little old-fashioned marketing and sales.

What's a good-hearted company to do?

## THE CONDITIONED PATTERNS OF HOPE

### THE CONDITIONED PATTERN OF EXPECTATIONS

*Life's under no obligation to give us what we expect.*

MARGARET MITCHELL

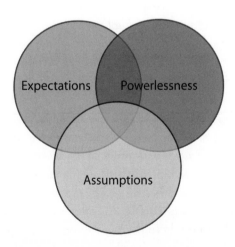

Figure 10.1   The Conditioned Patterns of Hope.

The dictionary defines hope as a desire for something to happen, while expecting or being confident that it will come true. I wondered if I should call this the conditioned pattern of "the waiting game," instead of Expectations. Expectation is a prerequisite of hope. When we hope, we do so fully expecting a certain outcome.

> Expectation is characterized by the belief that life is supposed to go according to our version of happiness.

Many people create a dream, and then wait for a sign from heaven that they're on the right track. When that sign fails to come, they split. Whoosh! Off they go onto some new adventure, again waiting for a sign that this is finally "it."

We're conditioned to wait. We wait for the bus. We raise our hands and wait to be called upon. We even have to "hold it" until recess, if you know what I mean. We wait until our parents, teacher, or some other adult tells us that it's okay to do what we want to do. How are any of us going to learn how to think on our own?

Bob Proctor talks about raising his children differently. When they asked him what he thought they should do, he responded, "What do *you* think?" Because we learned to wait, we also learned the passive (scarcity) form of Expectations. We want something. We really, really, really hope for it, and because we're supposed to wait (for a sign, a signal, or approval), we can't help but then "expect" it to finally come about.

This is a very passive form of having Expectations. And, unfortunately, it's also the most common. On the flip side are active Expectations. These are the kind held by people like Michelle Wie. She absolutely expects to make it on the men's pro golf tour. But she's not waiting around for a sign, signal, or approval from anyone.

In fact, Michelle's situation offers a good clue as to which side of the scarcity/abundance teeter-totter one's Expectations might lie. Not only is she not likely to get approval, she's more likely to get disapproval and even condemnation (from men and women). She doesn't care. She expects to proceed, and to win. And, most importantly, she takes consistent action to fulfill her Expectations.

The scarcity side says, "Wait until the coast is clear." The abundance side says, "Do what you *can* do, regardless of external events or people."

We also have Expectations of ourselves. Of course, we're often our own worst critics. We're also often the worst critics of those around us. Expectation without action (often, communication) always leads to trouble ahead. Expectations of ourselves or others is a perfect setup for disappointment and disillusionment.

What are the indicators of the scarcity side of Expectation? As I said, seeking approval is one. Another is rigidity—an unwillingness to evaluate reality or make changes. For example, one client had to face an angry information technology (IT) manager who was upset that a facilities manager had called his team to task for not following through with their commitments. The IT manager expects (waits for) others to resolve his team's problems. My client expected (waited for) the IT department to do their job. Both are rigidly stuck in a scarcity cycle of Expectations.

A third indicator of the scarcity side is a sense of entitlement. Any time you or one of your coachees feels entitled to a particular outcome, you can bet that it's a conditioned pattern of Expectations at work. Best to nip it in the bud quickly.

It's like we're born with a certain number of chips we can cash in, but at the same time we deserve to be happy and have a fulfilling life. Is it really true that we're entitled to happiness?

One of my clients decided to leave her boss after eight years of loyal service. She complained over and over that her boss never "got her." She couldn't figure out why he hadn't begged her to stay, and she really resented it. On the surface, she felt wronged, invisible, and powerless. When we explored the situation through coaching, she found that she had an underlying Expectation. She expected that her boss would figure out all the sacrifices she made. She expected her boss to be a mind reader. After all, didn't he owe her for all the times she had gone above and beyond—stayed late, taken work home? When he didn't respond the way she hoped, she got angry and left. A year later, she still carried that anger with her, and the old pattern of Expectation was beginning to surface in her new consulting business.

The cycle of hope that leads to Expectation is often this kind of entitlement. When we don't get the thing that we want, we get frustrated. We become disconnected. We want things to be different, but we don't want to do anything to become different or to cause our circumstances to become different.

<br>

DISTINCTION: DESERVING VS. RECEIVING

Do we ever really deserve anything? Karma aside, the idea that we deserve a particular outcome is silly. It's a completely external focus, and it's a perfect recipe for suffering.

Receiving is an active state. It's something we do as a result of having taken some action. I actively receive money from my work. I don't deserve it, but I do receive it.

## CONDITIONED BELIEFS OF EXPECTATION

- I've worked hard, and I deserve to (get a raise, promotion, better job. . . .)
- As long as I stay on the up-and-up, I'll be treated well.
- I'm an honest (kind) person, so I expect others to be honest (kind) with me.
- Just stay the course, and everything will work out.
- Of course, life should be fair.

## THE CONDITIONED PATTERN OF POWERLESSNESS

*Our greatest fear is not that we are powerless. Our greatest fear is that we are powerful beyond measure.*

MARIANNE WILLIAMSON

I can't stand whiners. I have little tolerance and patience for people who feel the need to complain and whine when things don't go their way. Maybe it's a part of my own conditioned pattern related to control and the Illusion of Struggle, but the truth is that they drive me nuts.

The conditioned pattern of Powerlessness is at the heart of whining, and it's one of the more visible patterns of the Illusion of Hope. You see it all the time: Sally and Jim hope they can buy a new home in a nicer neighborhood. But, the real estate market changed, they had a "bad realtor," or they were simply too busy to move fast enough to get the house of their dreams. Then, they blame everyone and everything else for their inability to get their new home. They are "powerless" in the face of all these huge external forces.

> Powerlessness is characterized by a person feeling trapped, victimized, and out of choices in the face of external forces.

Powerlessness is a conditioned pattern. Why is it that we can read about people who overcame great odds to accomplish some fantastic feat, but we can't for the life of us manage to get to an appointment on time? We're powerless because of heavy traffic, kids who won't cooperate, or some other such excuse. If we really faced the truth of the situation, we'd see that this supposed Powerlessness is a clever ruse to keep us resisting doing what we *can* do.

Why? Well, we might fail! If you get right down to the core of it, you'll see that people act powerless because it's far easier to blame circumstances than to go ahead and do it anyway, and maybe look really stupid in the process. So we give our power away to others. It's like we're saying, "No, please, *you* take my power. This way, I can blame *you* if things don't work out right."

The Illusion of Hope attempts to prove that we're powerless. In reality, it's avoidance—an avoidance of responsibility and an avoidance of making decisions. People say Yes when they mean No. They forget that it's okay to set boundaries. They're nice people who feel it's their duty to get trampled, and then they complain that "there was nothing else I could do." They unquestionably conform to what's expected of them, because that is far easier than making a decision for themselves that just might turn out badly.

Some conditioned thoughts of Powerlessness:

- I'm not the one in charge here, so there's really nothing I can do.
- I believe that my fate is in God's hands (it may be, but that's no excuse to avoid responsibility).
- "They" won't let me (government, rich people, or anyone who appears to have more power).
- What's the use of trying? The odds are clearly stacked against me.

## THE CONDITIONED PATTERN OF ASSUMPTIONS

*Tomorrow is often the busiest day of the week.*

SPANISH PROVERB

You know that saying, "To *assume* is to make an ass out of u and me"? It's cute, and there's a lot of truth to it. We all make Assumptions on a daily basis. Of course we assume that the sun will rise in the morning and set in the evening (unless you happen to be living at the North or South Pole). We assume that the car will start when we turn the ignition, and that it will move forward when we put it in gear and apply a little pressure on the gas pedal.

There's absolutely nothing wrong with assuming these things. Why shouldn't you assume that everyone will obey the traffic signals? Or that everyone you meet has your best interests in mind? Making Assumptions about everyday life events is natural and healthy. I certainly wouldn't care to be surrounded by people who feared or questioned everything. It's important to be discerning, but to assume nothing at all in life would leave you walking forward by looking over your shoulder the whole way. It's not a good way to live.

However, sometimes we make Assumptions as a matter of habit (a conditioned pattern) that keep us from doing what we *can* do. For example, if, after reading the profiles of the more experienced coaches on the CoachVille site, I made the Assumption that there weren't enough clients to support all of us, I would have opted to do something else. My Assumptions that (1) I could never reach their level of expertise, and (2) I would therefore fail to find clients, would've kept me from doing what I *can* do.

This could have been a conditioned response for me. Fortunately, it wasn't. *It's when we make Assumptions that are based on other people's views of the world that we run into problems.* It totally ignores the fact that life is uncertain and constantly changing. We hear someone say when we consider introducing ourselves to an influential person, "Oh, he *never* talks with people he doesn't know," and we back away. That is someone else's Assumption about how life operates. It isn't reality, and it isn't hardwired into the fabric of the universe.

> Assumptions are characterized by the habit of taking for granted that our view of the world is everyone else's view.

Nothing is hardwired. The key is to catch when an Assumption is keeping you or your coachee from doing what you *can* do. If it is, then it's a good time to start asking questions. Is the Assumption reasonable or unreasonable? What proof or evidence do you have about the Assumption? And, the question I absolutely love: If you were to accomplish something that others thought impossible, how would it fundamentally change the nature of your life?

Think of this in terms of your return on investment (ROI). In business, we focus heavily on ROI, but we forget about using the concept in our lives. When we fail to do the thing we want to do because of an Assumption, we're forgetting about the concept of ROI. What would be the ROI for doing it anyway, even if someone, somewhere holds the Assumption that it's impossible? If all any of us ever did was follow Assumptions, we'd all still be afraid of falling off the edge of the earth.

## CONDITIONED BELIEFS OF ASSUMPTIONS

- He (she) is the expert, so who am I to question his (her) Assumptions?
- I work hard, and I assume I'll be well-rewarded.
- I've never tried anything like this before, and I always mess up the first time.

Each of these conditioned beliefs leads down the path of scarcity thinking. We fail to take action because we assume we'll fail or it won't work. It might not work the first time. So what? Flip the Assumption around and assume that no matter what, the *experience* will lead to a better life.

## THE TIPPING POINT OF HOPE

Is it wrong to hope, to have Expectations? Absolutely not. As I said earlier, hope is essential. But just as with everything else in life, there's a balance. As with all the illusions, to find the Tipping Point where hope becomes scarcity, we must identify when hoping keeps us from doing what we *can* do.

When does hoping become a Convenient Distraction, a crutch, an excuse for not Living into Greatness? Often, hope alone can't do for you what you can do for yourself.

When we believe that hope doesn't require action, we're left holding the proverbial bag. We'll still get an outcome, but it's rarely the desired outcome. It's a small game that's played, and it's called the waiting game.

If we live our lives with hope as our key strategy and we need to hope to keep going, it's almost like we're walking in a maze. Worse yet, we're stuck in the maze and hope that someone will come rescue us. We begin assuming that there's no way out but still expect to be saved. Hope can be a death sentence when it tips to scarcity, but it can be inspiring when it tips toward abundance.

Are you held hostage by hope?

## PROFILES IN GREATNESS: JOE VITALE

Joe Vitale is known as Mr. Fire. He's one of the best and most dynamic copywriters (and writers) around today, with several best-selling books. He lives, as he says, "a luxurious lifestyle, with all the cars and things you can imagine." But he wasn't born rich. And he certainly wasn't born with an abundance mentality, not more than anyone else. He struggled growing up. At one point, he was homeless, living in poverty in Houston for a full 15 years. He struggled, complained, and was never sure if he'd ever dig his way out of the hole. He hoped and prayed for a change but knew on some level that he'd have to get rid of the programming and scarcity beliefs to make any dent in his poverty lifestyle.

Thirty years ago, as the story goes, he "sat on the steps of the post office, hoping I could find some money for something to eat and hoping I could find a place to live." Today, he says he feels as though he's tapped into a never-ending flow from the universe. He looks the same on the outside, but now the hope is gone, replaced with an abundance mindset.

The amazing thing about Joe is that he's really no different from you or me, except maybe in how he thinks. Scarcity and abundance, he says, are perceptions. "We are in a belief-driven universe. This is one of the things that I claim in my book *The Attractor Factor;* that the beliefs we have, most of which are unconscious, determine what we see." If this were coming from anyone else, I might pass it off as more wishful thinking. But Joe has proven these concepts in his own life. He adds, "We are interpreting everything around us through this lens that we call our perception, but it's really our filter of belief. Once we become aware of our filter and beliefs and we change them, we see an abundance of everything we were looking for to begin with that was there all along."

The whole concept of hope, Joe says, is comforting; yet, it has a razor's edge to it. "You can end up falling to the other side and not doing anything. One side of hope is very positive and very feel-good; it's very illuminating and very comforting. The other side of hope is that you may not do anything because you're simply hoping things will work out." There are a number people who get into this kind of hopeful state and miss the other side, which Joe refers to as "taking inspired action." That is, when you want something, you take the action to make it happen, ensuring all the while to pay attention to your intuition. According to Joe's experience, it's been his intuition that's nudged him into action, doing things he's never before considered. When you get this kind of nudge, he says, "your job is to act on it."

This has made the difference for Joe, and with other members of his family who have taken his advice to take inspired action immediately toward their dreams. When you want to achieve or create something, he says, you can either remain hopeful, or you can take inspired action, which completes the formula for manifesting what you want. "Hope with inspired action will equal the desired result. Hope without action is still missing the rest of the formula."

Hope is the perception that there's only so much to go around. "Abundance," Joe says, "is the realization that everything you want is already out there in the world, and we don't see it until we turn on that perception that allows us to see it." It is, he appropriately adds, determined by our beliefs.

I love Joe's view of the world. He equates it to a giant mail-order catalog, or to a giant candy store. It's absolutely chock-full of products, people, and experiences. Any time, you can walk though and say, "I'd like to have this experience, that product, or to meet this person." It becomes, he says, "a wonderful wish-land where the wishes turn into reality." Scarcity and hope, on the other hand, keep you thinking that you can't order anything because you don't have the money for the stamp. You have to wait until the money comes in to buy the stamp. That's all backward.

Hope keeps us inside a negative reinforcing cycle. The way out, Joe claims, is to follow our natural calling (what I call Living into your Greatness). "I believe we come into this world with some sort of calling," he says. "We can be anything we want to be within certain physical limitations. I remember as a kid wanting to be a number of different things, from an actor to a reporter to an attorney, and what felt the most comfortable to me when I started to role-play each one as a teenager, was being an author." What Joe did was simply follow his calling, paying attention to the nudges to take action. When he got a nudge, he immediately took action, without bothering to hope for an outcome. He had no idea where it was going to take him.

Clearly, though, it's taken him to some pretty amazing places. Today, when he feels one of these nudges, he drops everything and goes for it. Now, it's your turn, he says.

## SHIFTING THE BALANCE FROM HOPE TO SIGNIFICANCE

One definition of the word significance is that it's a "meaning that is not expressly stated, but is inferred." While Hope is based on the conscious or unconscious evaluation of external factors, Significance is an internal affair. True Significance isn't won, earned, or fought for. Others won't bestow Significance upon you (see Figure 10.2).

> Significance is characterized by shifting from external Expectation to internal realization by embracing and acting upon your Greatness Capacity.

Every human on this planet is significant in his or her unique way. Significance is an Abundance Aptitude because it's a natural by-product of abundant thinking. Feigned Significance is more like arrogance. It's put on like a fine set of clothes but merely hides the scarcity thinking that lives underneath.

*Real Significance is knowing who you are, knowing your place in the world, and Living into that Greatness every day.* In that sense, the scarcity thinker will hope for the best, but the abundant thinker will take action because he or she *knows* the Significance of every action. *We* are who and what we've been waiting for—not some knight in shining armor.

Put another way, if you've been waiting for proof of your Significance, you're stuck in the Illusion of Hope. *You are the Significance you've been*

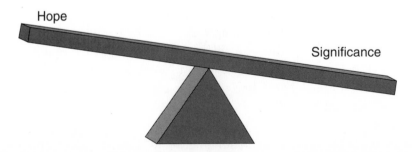

Figure 10.2    Tipping the Balance to Significance.

*waiting for.* It's a matter of shifting from external expectations to an internal strength. Become mobilized through the awareness and acceptance of your Significance. To hope, on the other hand, is to become immobilized.

The abundance aptitude of Significance moves you from hope to reality, and from potential to actualization. What good is an idea if it never gets out of your head? Hope causes us to hold onto the idea until we get a sign to move forward. Significance moves forward without the sign because we understand that every action is significant and in some small way moves us closer to our goals.

*The key action step of Significance is: Think positively and act accordingly.*

## THE CONSCIOUS PATTERNS OF SIGNIFICANCE

### THE CONSCIOUS PATTERN OF ENGAGEMENT—DOING WHAT YOU *CAN* DO

> *Most of the shadows of this life are caused by standing in one's own sunshine.*
>
> RALPH WALDO EMERSON

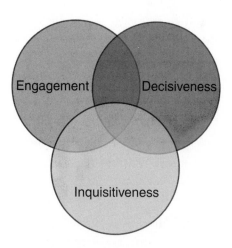

Figure 10.3  The Conscious Patterns of Significance.

I talked earlier in the book about the feeling of dread I had when I first found the CoachVille page and compared myself to all those great coaches. What helped me make the shift from scarcity (Not Enough) to being a great coach was a combination of experience and conviction. I was determined to be a coach, and I did everything I could to learn and build the right relationships and get the training I needed. My willingness to go beyond the fear and become fully engaged in the coaching world made the difference.

Our society is rapidly becoming one of entitlement, which is a nasty strain of the Expectation virus. I hear some of my clients complain that they're just as good, talented, knowledgeable, or experienced as someone who's very successful in their field. They feel entitled to more success and expect that simply by being good, they'll reap the rewards.

The problem is that they're not engaged in the active pursuit of that success. Successful people are fully engaged. They'll read one new book a week, take classes, experiment, and take action daily.

Ask any entrepreneur if he or she is taking some action daily to bring in new business, and most will say, "I don't have the time." And yet, they *expect* their businesses to grow, simply because they're doing a good job. That's Entitlement, not Engagement. Successful entrepreneurs will be *engaged* in the daily pursuit of growing their businesses.

How can they do this? First, they accept who they are (their Significance), and what they have to offer, and apply what they *know* daily to their lives and businesses. Then, they *express* this love for self and love for life through action. It's the perfect combination of authenticity and action. They're engaged in the daily pursuit of greatness because they're not at all assuming happiness will be handed to them on a silver platter.

---

Engagement is characterized by hope manifesting into action. The more frequently we are authentic, the more we are engaged in the world around us and in us.

---

To be engaged is to be fully in the game. Who wants to sit on the sidelines and watch all the action? The scarcity side of hope creates resignation and complacency, while Significance encourages being fully engaged — not watching the roller coaster, but being in the roller coaster as it screams up and down and around.

Complete Engagement is a combination of using your mental, emotional, spiritual, and physical faculties. Remember a time when you felt fully engaged in an activity? Every part of you was there. Exciting,? Well, there's absolutely no reason you can't have this kind of Engagement on a daily basis. Begin cultivating the conscious patterns described below, and you'll soon be having the ride of your life.

## Cultivating a Conscious Pattern of Engagement

To cultivate a conscious pattern of Engagement is fairly straightforward. When the ad firm of Weiden and Kennedy coined Nike's famous slogan, they understood the power of Engagement. "Just Do It!™" they exclaimed.

Don't think about getting on the ride. Get *on* the ride. Don't think about getting into the game. Get *into* the game. Don't hope for or think about expanding your business. Become fully engaged in the process of expanding your business. The conscious beliefs aren't as you might think, either. They're not positive affirmations, like "I know I can." *You're not the little engine that could. You're the little engine that does.*

Conscious thoughts:

- I am.
- I do.
- I enjoy.

---

### Distinction: Activity vs. Action

An activity is often an individual act that may or may not be part of a larger vision or strategy. Activity is often equivalent to Busyness. It's only an Illusion of Progress. Most people engage in activities (even our time management systems call them activities). They keep us busy but usually don't keep us engaged.

Action is a grouping of consistent, strategic activities that together produce a desired result. We become engaged in actions—they *mean* something; and, they produce the results we want.

---

## The Conscious Pattern of Decisiveness

*Your spark can become a flame and change everything.*

E. D. Nixon

201

People who feel powerless are generally very hesitant to make decisions. Often, none of the choices feel right, and the decision is usually to make no decision at all. They feel powerless to do anything but hope for the best (and expect the worst).

> Decisiveness is characterized by your ability to hold yourself accountable for the results in your life by moving through fear to do what you *can* do.

To cultivate a conscious pattern of Decisiveness, you have to suffer the paradox of choice. There's never a right or a wrong choice. There's only choice itself. However, the decision makers know that whatever happens, they can (and will) adjust course as necessary and even make new choices if required.

Napoleon Hill described successful people as those who make decisions quickly and stick with those decisions. Sure, they might experience some fear that the decision won't pan out, but they never let the fear stop them from making decisions. And, just as important, they stick to those decisions. They see the decisions through to the end, until they're certain of the outcome of the decision and can then adjust course as needed.

Earl Nightingale talked about the power of circumstances over most people's lives. He said that we can either let circumstances rule us, or we can take charge and rule our lives from within. The present moment is the only place we have, and it provides the only source of opportunity for making decisions. To be powerless is to be a victim of circumstance. To be Decisive is to *leverage* current circumstances.

The powerless person will tell you that we're in a recession and that's why his business is failing. The Decisive person will see and seize the opportunity of the current business climate and will create a successful business in spite of the recession.

This is really a shift from blame to accountability. Decisive people hold themselves accountable for the results in their lives. Powerless people blame others for their results. To cultivate a habit of Decisiveness, you first have to drop all blame. There's nobody to blame—for anything. Even the habit of blaming yourself must be dropped. Sometimes decisions don't work out. Sometimes they do. There's no blame—only learning.

<br>

> ### DISTINCTION: ACCOUNTABILITY VS. BLAME
>
> Accountability is an active process. It's about taking action and being responsible for the results of those actions. Accountability doesn't judge something as good/bad, or right/wrong. Accountability learns from every action, regardless of the positive or negative nature of the results.
>
> Blame is passive. There's no action, and no forward progress. Blame looks for the problem, while accountability looks for the solution.

Ask what worked and why, and what didn't work and why. Then, make a new decision and stick to it. Hold yourself accountable for follow-through, and accountable for your results.

Decisiveness is about moving forward, while blame and Powerlessness look back. There was a recent news broadcast about a couple of people wrongfully convicted of crimes and put into prison for life. DNA testing showed their innocence, and after 15 to 20 years in prison, they were just released. How awful! You'd think that they'd be so angry they'd be gunning for everyone. Quite the opposite happened. One of the men interviewed showed no bitterness. I counted the number of times he said he was "thankful"—seven times in a 10-minute interview! I was so blown away by his ability to forgive and allow his greatness and power to come forth in what must have been an unimaginable life experience. Amazing! What power that comes from this kind of Decisiveness!

### CULTIVATING A CONSCIOUS PATTERN OF DECISIVENESS

I've found that the key to cultivating a pattern of Decisiveness isn't to force a decision, as many of my clients believe. They think that they'll "just make a decision." The real power of decision is in conviction and desire. Had I not had both the conviction and desire to be a coach, I never would have followed through with my decision.

Most people run from a decision at the first sign of a problem because they are not clear enough about what they want and why they want it. To cultivate a conscious pattern of Decisiveness, you have to work on your underlying belief systems. Try the following (or variations more appropriate to yourself and your coachee):

- I can decide what I want.
- I'm completely independent of the positive or negative opinions of others when it comes to the decisions I make.
- I trust that I can handle whatever results from my decisions, and I'll end up stronger and better.
- The fear of the consequences is always worse than the consequences themselves, and so I'll decide to move forward.
- There's no testing the waters here. I'm either in the water, or out. I choose to be in the water.

Find the balance between believing that things will get better on their own and doing nothing, and seeing how actualizing who you are will create a better world.

## THE CONSCIOUS PATTERN OF INQUISITIVENESS

*We don't see things as they are, we see things as we are.*

ANAÏS NIN

You know how annoying it can be when your five-year-old asks "Why?" to every answer you provide? Eventually, most adults will say something like, "Just because, and stop asking questions!"

Oops. Well, if we can't ask questions, what's the alternative? The alternative is to make Assumptions. I can't tell you how many coaching clients I've worked with who go on and on about a situation, unclear about what to do. Inevitably, the decision hinges on an Assumption about what some other person thinks or believes. John, for example, can't decide if the new job will offer him the kind of opportunity for growth he wants. He makes Assumptions about the job, some of them positive, and some negative. He wavers in his decision and feels quite powerless in the process. He hopes for a miraculous sign from God about which direction to turn.

Why doesn't he just ask someone? This is the conscious pattern of Inquisitiveness. It's the excited little five-year-old who keeps asking, "Why?" until he's fully satisfied that he understands the situation. John, for example, can ask people who've had the job what it was like for them. He can ask the hiring manager or human resources director, or even go straight to the head of the organization. The amusing part about this is that I'll often have my clients come back with news that by being inquisitive, they uncovered an even better job that wasn't being advertised.

> Inquisitiveness is characterized by the commitment to unearth and examine a person's Assumptions about his life, his business, and the world.

We talk a lot about clarity in the coaching world. We say that clarity is a way of excavating your Assumptions. It's a commitment to unearth, and bring into the light of day these Assumptions about life, business, and the world. The four-step process is definitely an excavation tool. And, at the heart of the tool is the conditioned pattern of Inquisitiveness. Through Inquisitiveness, we gain clarity. Through clarity, we make decisions and take action.

Inquisitiveness doesn't assume there are many choices available. Inquisitiveness *knows* there are many choices. These are choices in how you run your business, to what you say yes or no, and how you view yourself in relation to those around you.

I get really irritated when I encounter what I assume is an inconsiderate driver—someone, for example, who cuts me off in traffic. I make Assumptions about the person, few of which have a positive spin. How dare that person *not* think about *me?* What an inconsiderate jerk! (Of course, all the time, I'm thinking only about my point of view, as if I'm the center of the universe.)

The same thing happens in conversation. I have a therapist friend who says that the number one cure for a failing relationship is simple communication. People don't talk enough, she says. They make Assumptions that what they said was heard, or heard in a certain way. That's almost never the case. So, they stop talking. Or, more importantly, they stop being inquisitive.

"What did you hear me say just now?" "What is your understanding about our plans?" My therapist friend says that once she gets the couple asking each other questions, they start communicating; and, once they start communicating, they start getting along again. It's really not that complicated.

### Cultivating a Conscious Pattern of Inquisitiveness

Ask clarifying questions. Okay, maybe that's not so easy for most people. We've had the concept of asking questions so drilled out of us that most of us are terrified to "ask a stupid question." Here's an example of asking clarifying questions.

One of the partners of a telecommunications business I was coaching was getting more and more frustrated with another partner's perceived lack of follow-through. Jennifer couldn't figure out why her partner Sara failed to do what she was "supposed" to do. It was a point of contention that festered until there was a big explosion. In the coaching session, we examined the situation in depth. What we discovered is that Sara had no idea Jennifer was expecting her to perform the task. When she and Sara had discussed the topic, she thought it was taken care of. Jennifer thought she had communicated her Expectation to Sara but discovered that the way she phrased the request wasn't interpreted the way she initially intended. Jennifer and Sara learned that by asking clarifying questions, neither had to assume the other was understood.

Here are a few conscious beliefs to cultivate:

- What's stupider than a stupid question? An incorrect Assumption.
- I'd rather be informed than look foolish later by saying, "well, I *assumed*. . . ."
- It's far better to ask and listen than to speak without knowing.
- There's a reason I have two ears and one mouth.

## THE FOUR-STEP PROCESS APPLIED TO THE ILLUSION OF HOPE

*Your own self-realization is the greatest service you can render the world.*

SIR RAMANA MAHARSHI

Let's get back to our enlightened small-business owners with the brilliant idea, strong values, and a hatred of sales. Now, I'm not saying that you can't (or shouldn't) run a business on the basis of strong values and high ideals. But you can't run a business on hope, especially if that hope keeps you from doing what you *can* do to generate business. Any business owner owes it to herself, her clients, her family, and her community to be successful. What good is a fabulous idea if you fail to do what you *can* do to get the idea out there?

The following sections will apply the Coaching into Greatness four-step process to the small-business owners' situation.

## AWARENESS

Awareness begins for our intrepid business owners with their results, which were far less than they had "hoped" for. It's not my purpose to teach you how to read a P&L (profit and loss) statement, but it's often a very good means of getting a reality check for a small business. Are you doing what you want to do, financially speaking?

A good look at the P&L showed that more money was going out than going in, and that their sales manager, however compatible, wasn't doing his job. We examined their original financial goals and compared them to the actual goals. Only by seeing the results could they see that what they had hoped for wasn't occurring. This created an awareness that they had swung the teeter-totter to the scarcity side of hope. Something needed to be done. (By the way, this is known as a gap analysis.)

## ACCEPTANCE

Acceptance may be the toughest pill to swallow when it comes to the Illusion of Hope. We all have a great love affair with hope. It feels so good! Ever notice how people put their hands over their hearts when they talk about their hopes and dreams? Hopes often start from the heart, but when that's all that happens, those hopes never become reality.

Our business owners had to accept the facts as they were. This required a tremendous amount of ego deflation. People who try to run a business on the hope that by being good, honest people they will succeed are deceiving themselves. It's a way of inflating their egos and self-importance, instead of acting on the basis of their inherent Significance and the Significance of their idea. They had to accept and believe that their idea was so significant that they couldn't do anything other than sell it with authority and confidence.

Also, the scarcity side of hope often stems from a *lack* of confidence. They had to accept that they could only build their confidence by taking consistent and authentic action.

## CONSISTENT ACTION

Here, we see just how closely the four steps are tied together. They didn't want to take consistent action that was, in their minds, out of integrity with their values and principles. But they still had to do some real marketing and sales. So, we focused on developing a sales action plan that remained consistent with their values.

I won't go into the details of their plan, since that's not our primary purpose here. The key point is that they did develop a plan and followed through with the plan, step-by-step, day-by-day. Oh, and they had to fire their sales manager and hire a new one who not only shared their values and interest in their ideas but also knew a thing or two about selling (and happened to like the process).

## AUTHENTICITY

The interesting thing about this story is that (as often happens), by selling and marketing authentically, my clients realized that they actually *enjoyed* selling. They'd been so conditioned to think of sales in a very specific way that they made all kinds of erroneous Assumptions and thought themselves powerless in the face of having to market their idea.

They learned how to market and sell, taking only those steps and actions that aligned with their values. I'll give you one example just to illustrate the point. They assumed that "selling" meant convincing people who neither needed nor wanted the product to purchase it anyway. They wanted their product only in the hands of those who would value and use the product. All of their marketing materials clearly stated who would or wouldn't benefit from their product. This not only allowed them to market with authenticity, it also dramatically increased their sales.

Every step they took gave them a clearer picture of hope versus Significance and allowed them to move more fully into authentic and powerful action.

## CHAPTER SUMMARY

> *How many joys are crushed underfoot because people look up at the sky and disregard what is at their feet?*
>
> UNKNOWN

Hope is the longing and wishing for things we think we don't have.
You are the Significance you've been waiting for.
Hope is not a strategy.
The ROI of life is to be who you are.

For additional information and chapter resources visit: http://www.coachingintogreatness.com/the_illusion_of_hope.

# CHAPTER ELEVEN

# The Illusion of Certainty

*Greatness is a road leading towards the unknown.*

CHARLES DE GAULLE

One of the most interesting, but not surprising, things about writing this book has been what I experienced as I wrote. With each chapter, the illusion on which I'm focused seems to stand up, tap me on the shoulder, and say, "Hey, here I am! Here's something to write about!"

This was the case on a recent trip to visit my dad. As I mentioned earlier, we've been getting along great in the past few years. I've enjoyed listening to him and meeting him where he's at. I've begun to realize the many gifts he has given me, including my knack for building social capital and my love of trees.

Recently, with growing health concerns, my dad has been talking about his death. We talked about his wish to donate his body to science and the various details of his funeral. His next statement came out of left field. He mentioned that he was leaving everything to his current wife. Ouch!

My first reaction was "What about me?"

He stared at me blankly, replying, "Well, what do you mean?"

My jaw dropped. He really didn't get where I was coming from. I could feel my heart clenching into a tight ball. "You know, aren't you going to leave me anything?"

This question may sound materialistic or cold. Here's the point. I didn't have a hidden vendetta against his third wife. I love her and she's a wonderful woman. I didn't even care about the money. What I yearned for was to matter enough as his daughter that he'd consider me in his will. I wanted him to say that he understood, and yes, of course he would include me.

Instead, the whole situation fell apart. My dad said nothing, and I flipped into an old pattern of anger. In an instant, we were back to our old ways. He defended his position, and from my perspective, I was once again faced with the old familiar wall. I felt once more like the 15-year-old kid who'd been abandoned as I sat alone, crying in the living room.

It was downright ugly, and it hurt. Five years ago, I would have remained the hurt child, and he would have held his ground. Today it's a different story. When we pulled ourselves together enough to talk, he presented me with a beautiful gift. He apologized. He recognized that he had hurt me. Perhaps for the first time, I truly felt seen and heard by my father.

His apology gave me the emotional freedom to step back and examine the entire situation more closely. I realized that it was my need for certainty that had a great deal to do with my anger and hurt feelings. Unconsciously, I reasoned that if I was in the will, I'd have proof that I mattered and that he loved me. Only then would I feel certain that he cared. My certainty, or need for certainty, was an illusion.

I already know my dad loves me. It's obvious in his broad smile and open arms as he greets me at the train station. His eyes sparkle with delight when we talk about my becoming a published author. The evidence is everywhere. But, even if it weren't—even if he didn't give me bear hugs or say he loves me—I would cherish our relationship. I don't need his assurances, in writing or in person. Most importantly, I don't need to feel certain about his love for me. That, for me, is the ultimate freedom. Certainty without the need for certainty.

Once again, I have come full circle, through the pain and fear of loss to the joy and relief of feeling things fully. I know that my dad loves me, and of that I can be certain.

## THE DYNAMICS OF CERTAINTY

*To be surprised, to wonder, is to begin to understand.*

JOSE ORTEGA Y GASSET

# The Illusion of Certainty

Life doesn't come with a money-back guarantee, and yet many of us live like it does. People are certain that they'll keep their jobs. They're certain of living a long, healthy life. Others might be certain that they'll lose their jobs, or get sick and die young. Certainty comes in many forms, and it rarely corresponds to the truth.

The truth, as I see it, is that nothing is certain, except, as they say, death and taxes. Even then, many wealthy people have figured out how to avoid taxes. Is death next?

I receive many arguments in favor of certainty. Isn't it healthy to believe in God, the goodness of other humans, and that maintaining positive thinking will get us what we want? Belief and certainty are very different. While I might believe in the goodness of other humans, I can't always be certain that this goodness will show up in all my encounters.

The need for certainty is a need for safety. Some might say that if nothing can be counted on, then why bother trying? In order to proceed, these people need to have a sense of certainty about the outcome. But this kind of certainty is an illusion. They're the first to complain when life doesn't go according to plan. Unfortunately, they'll also attract more of the same.

The media does its part to push us toward developing a sense of entitlement to certainty. We want to feel certain that we won't be hit by a natural disaster or terrorist attack, and if something like that does happen, we will be absolutely cared for. We can hope, pray, and even plan for certainty, but certainty won't be found.

> The Illusion of Certainty occurs when the need to know an outcome keeps you from acting, making authentic decisions, and doing what you *can* do.

Certainty is a form of disconnection—from truth and from ourselves. When we feel certain about something, whether it be a paycheck, our family, or a loved one, we're disconnected from the natural flow of life. In a sense, we're stuck, not because of any apparent fears, but because of an avoidance of fear. Fear is distasteful.

The real downside of the Illusion of Certainty comes when our certainty keeps us playing small. Since everything is okay as it is, we don't feel any need for change and, in fact, will avoid change until it's thrust upon us.

Few people will consciously adapt to their changing environment. Most will adapt only when forced to by a major or traumatic event.

The Illusion of Certainty makes you believe that nothing else is possible. It causes us to put on blinders to any other possibilities. Certainty keeps us closed. Why take risks when the outcome is certain? Most people would sooner jump out of a plane than change jobs, for example. What makes one risk greater than another? What makes one risk more possible than another?

## A STORY OF CERTAINTY

*It is better to know some of the questions than all of the answers.*

JAMES THURBER

Matt's story is, unfortunately, a typical one that many managers and coaches have encountered. He's in his 50s and very set in his ways. Yet, he's lost three jobs in the past five years. According to Matt, he lost these jobs because of a combination of management ignorance and the horrible practice of outsourcing work to less expensive workers overseas. He's absolutely certain of these facts, just as he's absolutely certain that he can't change how he thinks or acts in his jobs.

The truth is never just one fact or another. While it's true that many jobs have been shipped overseas, and that the pointy-haired boss of Dilbert™ fame isn't necessarily too far from reality in many organizations, Matt's certainty has been the root of his problems. What was Matt so certain about? Let me count the ways. Matt was certain that:

- His way of thinking wasn't related to his difficulties.
- Management didn't appreciate his most useful skills.
- He would lose his jobs if he didn't do everything perfectly the first time.
- His thoroughness was a part of his personality and couldn't be changed.
- His family would hate him if he didn't stay up and watch TV at night with them.
- He couldn't change his work habits.
- All he had to do was figure out a step-by-step system, and he'd have no more problems.

And the list went on. Matt was a tough one. It's easy to give up on someone who's given up on himself, and this was often the case with Matt. As you'll see in this chapter, Matt was definitely under the illusion that certainty was the answer to his problems. He was under the illusion that his certainty was unchangeable, and that it was his certainty that would save the day for him. He was wrong on both counts, and it was only getting worse as time went on. He became increasingly complacent about changing and more entrenched in Tactical Thinking, and he refused to release his hold on his Perfectionism. Was Matt a hopeless case?

## THE CONDITIONED PATTERNS OF CERTAINTY

*To the dull mind all nature is leaden. To the illumined mind the whole world burns and sparkles with light.*

RALPH WALDO EMERSON

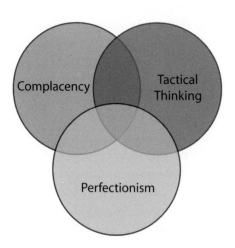

Figure 11.1    The Conditioned Patterns of Certainty.

### THE CONDITIONED PATTERN OF COMPLACENCY

*Suffering makes you feel safe because you know it so well.*

DON MIGUEL RUIZ

Complacency may not at first seem to be a conditioned pattern. Isn't it natural for us to become complacent when things are going well? Actually, it's not.

Complacency is a choice; it's a way of giving up, of stopping, and of avoiding taking the risk of Living into Greatness. It's not that there's anything wrong with taking a breather. We go through natural rhythms of activity and rest. We need rest periods to continuously function at our best—like sharpening the saw. Complacency arises when these rest periods extend far beyond what is really necessary for replenishment. Complacency then becomes a habit—a conditioned pattern of avoiding doing what you *can* do because it's easier to do nothing.

Is Complacency the same thing as laziness? Perhaps. I think there are definite similarities. Complacency is a resignation, which in turn arises because of a certain resistance to change. Complacency in this form is a survival mechanism that comes into play when change feels a bit too frightening. What's dastardly about Complacency is its closeness to ease. I'll have coachees who avoid taking any bold new steps because they've worked hard to get to where they are and now deserve a rest. It becomes like an extended vacation in which consistent action is put on the back burner until the need arises to do something different. It's scarcity thinking, pure and simple.

> Complacency is characterized by desiring the status quo more than improvement.

Complacency causes people to live half a life. They'll tolerate many small annoyances just to maintain the current comfort. All the while, opportunities for more—much more—stream by at an amazing clip. Thomas Leonard said that people do what they do because they have nothing better to do. I agree—to a point. Rather than not having anything better to do, they choose to ignore opportunity, even when it smacks them upside the head, because opportunity equals danger, and danger is a bad place to go when you're comfortably complacent. That is, comfortably complacent in your satin-lined coffin!

In one of my earlier side projects, I collaborated with coaches Andrea Shea Hudson and John Satta on a project called minkholes. Minkholes are the seductive, fur-lined traps where our best intentions languish; the comfort zones we know all too well. Complacency is a big component of being in a minkhole.

There's no itch—no burning desire for a worthy goal—with Complacency. I've heard that 97 percent of the Western population have no real goals. Buying a new car or high definition TV isn't a worthy goal. Yet, that's how we're conditioned to think today. Goals are equated with owning things, and it's hard to avoid Complacency when all you have to look forward to is a new TV.

There's a paradox of Complacency that is very ironic. The place we think is safest is often the least safe. Think about it.


## CONDITIONED BELIEFS OF COMPLACENCY

See if any of these conditioned beliefs look familiar:

- Better safe than sorry.
- The devil you know is better than the devil you don't know.
- You deserve . . . (a break, a reward, etc.).


## THE CONDITIONED PATTERN OF TACTICAL THINKING

*The great individual is the one who does a thing for the first time.*

ALEXANDER SMITH

We often hear that people like General Patton or Napoleon were great tacticians. I disagree. I think they were amazing strategists who also had a tremendous amount of discipline in tactically implementing their strategies. It's often the great tacticians who lose the battles because they can't see what's not right in front of their faces.

Tactical Thinking can be a hazardous trap. We are taught to be tactical, not strategic. We plot out straight-line courses throughout our lives, using tactics we've learned from others to do our jobs, find relationships, or even launch a new business. Most business plans, for that matter, are very Tactical. They spell out in excruciating detail the goals and specific steps that will enable you to meet those goals. You know what happens to most business plans? Once written, they sit on the shelf, never to again see the light of day. They're Tactical, but they lack emotion or feeling.

---

Tactical Thinking is characterized by plotting out straight-line courses through life often using tactics we've learned from others. This frequently results in excluding other possibilities and options.

---

217

Tactical Thinking is black-and-white thinking. There's always a sense of certainty that if you do "A," you will get a result of "B." There's often little or no choice in Tactical Thinking, and no room for changing course if something goes awry. Tactical Thinking is necessary and important, but it can also become a crutch and a way of avoiding living greatly.

For example, there was the coaching client I mentioned earlier who had a home office for a business that was growing by leaps and bounds. He wanted to expand and move into an outside office, but to do so, he needed more revenue. The catch was that to generate more revenue, he had to be out delivering business instead of staying inside running the office. In short, he needed help.

Thinking Tactically, he saw that he needed to hire an assistant and get out into the field more. But he couldn't bring an assistant into his home. It was "unprofessional." Tactical Thinking couldn't get him past this conundrum. This is black-and-white thinking. He couldn't do what he knew he *could* do because of this one Tactical problem. He was *certain* that there was no logical way around this, short of "reducing his standards."

He was stuck until he gained awareness of how his certainty and Tactical Thinking were holding him back. He had to switch to Strategic Thinking in which the vision of what he wanted to create drove the tactics, instead of the tactics driving the strategy. By thinking strategically, he found ways to hire not one, but two people to help him, both of them in his home. It only took him three months to generate enough revenue to move into an outside office. That's Strategic Thinking—an abundant way to live. His Tactical thinking kept him in scarcity, unable to see what else might be possible.

Can you see how Tactical thinking creates exclusions, or black-and-white thinking, and how limiting this way of thinking can be? We exclude other ideas, other interpretations, other viewpoints, and other

---

DISTINCTION: CLARITY VS. CERTAINTY

Certainty leaves no room for other considerations. If I am certain of something, I believe it to be absolutely true. It is "your final answer."

Clarity about something, on the other hand, implies that some understanding has been achieved or revealed, and yet there is room for additional or further consideration.

possibilities about life. It's the worst kind of certainty because it's so inherently limiting.

You might have heard the story about six blind men standing around an elephant trying to figure out what it's like. The one standing by the leg pats the leg and says an elephant is very much like a tree. The man standing near the side says it's like a wall. The man standing in the back near the tail says an elephant is like a rope. The man standing in the front holding on to the trunk says an elephant is very like a snake, and the last man standing by the ears says an elephant is like a fan—and they're all right but still missing the big picture. They're thinking Tactically, and with that they have blind certainty.

## THE CONDITIONED BELIEFS OF TACTICAL THINKING

Tactical thinkers are what we often call "left-brained" thinkers. They prefer logic over emotion. For example, they might believe:

- I won't do it if I can't logically conclude that it will work.
- I've spelled out our plan in great detail, so it's bound to be successful.
- Emotion only gets in the way of real decision making.
- I've included all possible variables.

## THE CONDITIONED PATTERN OF PERFECTIONISM

*The thing that is important is the thing that is not seen.*

ANTOINE DE SAINT-EXUPERY

I've already written quite extensively about Perfectionism in Chapter 7, on the Illusion of Struggle. For our purposes here, I'll relate how Perfectionism is a conditioned pattern of the Illusion of Certainty.

Perfectionists are always in search of the perfect external approval of their actions. They try to force an outcome and, if in doubt, will leave a wake of ready-made excuses as to why the situation wasn't ideal to success. They're never satisfied, and yet they're almost always certain. It's a strange combination. For the perfectionist, the Illusion of Certainty lies in the belief that "if only" they could get everything just so, they would then be certain of having the outcome they want.

Perfectionism is characterized by an inability to reach completion due to an endless search for the external approval of one's actions.

Certainty is the perpetual elusive dream of perfectionists. They're not satisfied until it's all in place, and only then can they be certain. They're in a constant mode of playing catch-up, never meeting their own unrealistic expectations, and setting themselves up for struggle and procrastination.

Perfectionists have a hard time admitting they're wrong. You see, *they're* not wrong—they just didn't have enough time (resources, information, etc.) to get it done properly. How could they ever be certain if there were so many external factors to control? Since they have a high need to prove they're right, they remain attached to the Illusion of Certainty. Someday, some way, they'll finally have all they need to be certain.

Is anything ever really perfect? Perfection is relative. As a little girl, I used to imagine a world where all the houses were "perfect"—white, with perfectly manicured lawns and white picket fences, and lush flower boxes. I realized eventually that this vision of the world was impossible, simply because it was *my* version of perfection. Someone in the green movement (organic living) might imagine a perfect world as having nothing but straw hay-bale homes with rooftop gardens.

A great question to ask yourself or your coachee is—what is your version of perfect?

Conditioned beliefs of the perfectionist might include:

- I'm sorry. That's just not possible.
- I have to. I'm just a perfectionist at heart.
- People always point the finger at me when things go wrong.
- Just one more try and I can make it perfect.

## THE TIPPING POINT OF CERTAINTY

*Few among men are they who cross over to the further shore. The others merely run up and down the bank on this side.*

DHAMMAPADA

Certainty tips toward scarcity when we play small, missing opportunities because we're too comfortable to move. The Opportunity Cost exists because we refuse to see what's right in front of us.

When the need for certainty becomes so big that you don't do the thing you want to do and end up tolerating a bunch of natty little inconsistencies, you're giving up your greatness. Then, certainty keeps you loving the satin-lined coffin of safety and the Illusion of Security.

Certainty leans toward scarcity when the perfectionist, with his ultra-high standards, holds back from taking risks and doing what he *can* do. He becomes distracted or compiles a long list of excuses to hide his insecurity and fears. His world becomes scarce because he thinks that he can only take consistent action when, and if, he is certain.

## PROFILES IN GREATNESS: YASMIN DAVIDDS

Nothing is certain, especially for Latina women struggling to find their voice, their power, and a place in Western culture. Yasmin Davidds, highlighted as one of the top leading Latinas by *Hispanic Magazine*, and author of the groundbreaking book *Empowering Latinas: Breaking Boundaries, Freeing Lives*, understands this quite well.

First in her work to empower Latinas, and then in her own efforts to get published and become an inspiration for other Latinas, she had numerous barriers to overcome. She could never be certain of the results or the impact of her work, but she knew it had to be done. "People will only treat you the way you allow yourself to be treated," she says. "If you want others to respect you, begin by respecting yourself first. That means standing up for yourself and not allowing anyone to mistreat you in any way."

In Yasmin's eyes, Latinas all over the world have unique, untapped talents, which have gone unrecognized for too long. Her mission is to teach them to embrace their worth and their talent so that they can improve their quality of life. A daughter of Latino immigrants, and raised in a predominantly Hispanic neighborhood east of Los Angeles, Yasmin had her share of stereotypes and opinions from others to overcome. She believes in people, and she's in no way complacent in her beliefs. She has a willingness to learn and grow, always "living into the core of her truth."

She describes Living into your Greatness as "living in a place inside yourself where you feel completely one with the world. You live in a place where you did the best that you could, and even if you do something wrong, you take responsibility for it, and that's truth."

She faced herself and uncertainty when her investors and financial backers wanted her to create a particular "public persona" that simply wasn't who she is. Yasmin adds, "I wasn't certain if it was the right thing to do, but I felt I had to go with my instinct and my instinct told me 'No, this isn't you' so I didn't do it. I've learned that if I block everybody else out and listen to my gut, I never, ever go wrong. When I have detoured from my truth, *I've always found my way back to myself.*"

The Illusion of Certainty brings with it a belief that there's a right way and a wrong way. Yasmin realized that "there's no right way, there's just my way. I know I'm going to fall on my face once in a while, but that's okay. I'm the only expert of me—and I've been looking for the expert outside of me. I remember when my investors wanted me to be like Anthony Robbins." Clearly, she's not Anthony Robbins. She's incredibly inspirational, but her inspiration comes from being herself. "Connecting with people is the core of my work," she says.

Like many who face the Illusion of Certainty, Yasmin had to face her own illusions, and her humanity. Perfectionists will attempt to hide the past. When Yasmin was writing her first book, for example, she was also contemplating running for the U.S. Congress within five years. As we know, with politics comes mudslinging. In her book she planned on telling her life story about the drug addiction and mental illness in her family, among other things that you don't want to discuss when running for office.

"I had to make a decision," she says. "I remember feeling this was so unfair, but I knew I had to decide on a path to take. I was married at that time and I asked my husband what he thought I should do. He said I should follow who I was and that I should say the truth." It wasn't an easy decision. That is the challenge of cultivating the habits of Inquiry. She had to look hard at everything she was doing, and everything that she stood for before making a decision. It took her almost five months to decide.

Yasmin decided that she needed to do what she needed to do. She emphasizes that "I will always be politically involved, but I will not be ashamed about what I went through." These were brave words, and with that decision, she put her full story into her book. Later, she says, women e-mailed her to say that they were close to killing themselves before reading her book, but the book gave them the hope to go on. "It was a phenomenal feeling," she says.

While she can never be certain about how people will react to her or what she says, she continues to care for herself emotionally, and to do what she *can* do. "If people have issues with me," she says, "it's their issue, not mine. I am good and respectful to all people." This sense of adventure about life, and a willingness to Live into her own Greatness (not someone else's) isn't only appealing, it's downright inspiring

## SHIFTING THE BALANCE FROM CERTAINTY TO INQUIRY

*We have to move from the illusion of certainty to the certainty of illusion.*

SAM KEEN

The story goes that a well-regarded professor of psychology decided to enrich his learned resume with a trip to an equally well-known Zen master. The professor was so full of himself (and his certainty about life and the human mind), that he didn't hesitate to reveal his wisdom to the Zen master. For his part, the Zen master simply poured the professor a cup of tea. And he poured, and poured, until the cup was overflowing. Observing this for several seconds, the professor interrupted his monologue to ask, "Why are you not stopping?"

The Zen master replied, "Your mind is like this cup. It is so full, that there is no room for anything else. Until you can empty your mind, there's nothing for me to say."

Eric Hoffer said, "In times of change the learners will inherit the earth, while the learned will find themselves beautifully equipped to deal with a world that no longer exists." What does he mean by this? The learned are like the professor. They are *certain* of and in their knowledge. They are stuck, either through Complacency, a strict adherence to established tactics, or Perfectionism. The learners, on the other hand, are inquirers. They know that everything changes, so they constantly ask, "What else?" They inquire into everything, regardless of whatever certainty they may possess at the time (see Figure 11.2).

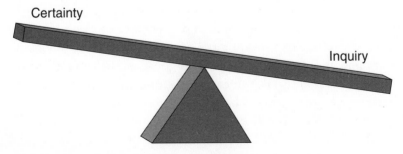

Figure 11.2   Tipping the Balance to Inquiry.

A key to Inquiry, however, is to remain in consistent action. Inquiry is not an excuse for holding back. Inquiring *while* you're in action is not the same as asking questions to avoid action. Inquiry is an abundant aptitude characterized by a person's ability to question their answers, consistently and continuously.

> Inquiry occurs when a person questions their answers consistently.

What in life is certain? There is a part of you (consciousness) that is unchanging. This pure consciousness is certain, while everything else is uncertain, impermanent, and an illusion. But how do you discover or experience this pure, unchanging, certain consciousness?

Through Inquiry, greatness is not contingent upon other things; it simply is. Certainty, on the other hand, is dependent on other things. With certainty, there's a right and a wrong, an up and a down. With certainty, up and down, right and wrong can't simultaneously exist. Inquiry allows all possibilities at once, independent of any concept you have of right, wrong, big, small, good, bad. Inquiry doesn't depend on proof for its existence. Certainty does, and yet certainty can only be found when it is fully discarded.

That is, if you're certain about something—anything, for that matter—you've immediately placed a lid on that thing. It can't change. You won't let it change, because if you do, you'll be wrong in your certainty. But all things, except one thing, do change. The one thing that doesn't change is what is commonly called consciousness, or pure consciousness. Consciousness is what remains when all concepts, ideas, beliefs, habits, and ways of thinking are stripped away. In other words, all of your ideas, concepts, beliefs, and so on will change over time. If this is true, then doesn't it make sense to practice the art of Inquiry?

This is how you can form new conscious patterns. By inquiring into how and why you get certain results in your life, you learn about the beliefs and patterns that create those results. Then, through the power of your mind, you can willfully form new conscious beliefs and patterns. It's really quite a miracle! You can move from an unconscious pattern that requires certainty, but is based on uncertainty ("I'm not sure, but when I am sure, I can finally do something"), to adopt new beliefs (reinforced through consistent and authentic action) in which the need for certainty is replaced by a relaxed "learner" pattern of Inquiry.

By practicing Inquiry, we demonstrate the courage to move from being an expert to being a student. All of life, all experiences, everyone and everything is our teacher. This doesn't mean that we are influenced to the point of losing ourselves and our identity for the sake of others. But we can focus on our authenticity, and not our conditioning.

Inquiry is inclusive. It is a choice to develop conscious patterns instead of following conditioned patterns. Inquiry finds the continuous thread of revelation in life. There's no "one point" at which we find peace, find happiness, or find success. The irony is that peace, happiness, and success are always right here. Inquiry is how we learn to experience these things, and it requires as much stopping as it does action.

If we continually accept reality based on what we see, feel, taste, touch, and hear, and we fail to explore and examine (inquire about) life, we'll get more of the same. Can you imagine a world in which nothing changes? It would be absolutely miserable. Inquiry is the aptitude that leads us out of that misery.

*The key action step of Inquiry is: Risk life and Live into Greatness*

## THE CONSCIOUS PATTERNS OF INQUIRY

*Social stagnation results not from a lack of answers but from the absence of the impulse to ask questions.*

ERIC HOFFER

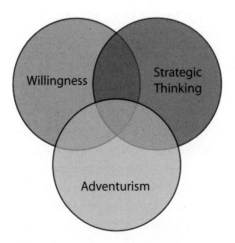

Figure 11.3   The Conscious Pattern of Inquiry.

225

## THE CONSCIOUS PATTERN OF WILLINGNESS

*It isn't enough to be very good if you have the ability to be great.*

ALBERTA LEE COX

There's one question many managers and coaches forget to ask others: Are you *willing?* Are you willing to change? Are you willing to do whatever it takes to succeed? Are you willing to say what needs to be said, or do what you *can* do?

---

Willingness is characterized by the degree of Self-Inquiry, openness, and exploration an individual demonstrates.

---

We often launch into a new adventure with tons of enthusiasm, but without a true Willingness to keep moving forward, no matter what. Without a conscious decision of Willingness, Complacency is always right around the corner when trouble hits. Willingness isn't something that just happens. You have to be brutally honest with yourself when considering the matter of Willingness.

Say, for example (this really happens) you attend a conference, getting totally enthused about implementing a new technique or strategy. Everything goes well for, maybe, a few weeks. Then, life gets in the way. Other priorities arise, creating conflicts with your new program. Soon, the new program falters and dies a slow, painful death. What was missing? The Willingness to change. We become very complacent with the old ways of doing things, even when we're struck by the lightning flash of a brilliant idea. Willingness is critical to Living into your Greatness.

## CULTIVATING A CONSCIOUS PATTERN OF WILLINGNESS

Step one: Question your answers. It sounds odd, but if you can practice questioning the answers you have about life, your business, and especially your Assumptions, you'll understand where and how you've become complacent. There's no shame in Complacency. We all become complacent, some more than others. Try cultivating some of the following beliefs:

- Since everything changes, I might as well change at the same time.
- Where there's a Will(ingness), there's a way.

- Without a good dose of Willingness in the world, I'd be riding my horse to work.
- I am much more attractive because of my Willingness to change.

## THE CONSCIOUS PATTERN OF STRATEGIC THINKING

*We should find perfect existence through imperfect existence.*

SHUNRYU SUZUKI

Thinking strategically takes practice. We're taught not to think strategically, but to follow an ordered set of rules and patterns developed by those who "know better." Strategic Thinking is what enables inventors to invent and entrepreneurs to succeed in business. It's what enabled Apple to so successfully sell the iPOD, and Dell to almost create a monopoly in the personal computer market. Dell didn't necessarily have a better computer, but they definitely had a much better strategy to sell their computer.

> Strategic Thinking is characterized by an ability to do new and different things by engaging possibilities that often can't be seen, heard, or measured.

When we focus on Tactical Thinking, we're focused on doing better what we already do well. That will only take you so far, until the degrees of improvement are so tiny that there's hardly any change. When you focus on Strategic Thinking, you're focused on doing different things. It's a very conscious choice to do different things first, and only then to do those different things better (Tactical Thinking).

There is always uncertainty with Strategic Thinking. You can't possibly know how it will turn out, but you trust that you can handle whatever happens in the process. In fact, the Strategic thinker *appreciates* divergences in the plan. These divergences to the plan are what will often spell the difference between being just good and being great. When you're riding a big old wave of uncertainty, you've got a wonderful opportunity to be unique, and to ride that wave all the way to success.

Earl Nightingale used to say that if you're going to follow anyone, don't follow the crowd. Follow the one or two who are going *against* the crowd. They are the strategic thinkers who lead the way because they're Living into their Greatness through their openness to new ideas. This is the ability to engage possibilities that often can't be seen, heard, or measured. That is a conscious choice. When we can be open to possibility, to things that we can't see or measure, then living can really begin.

If you're going to stay complacent and stay in the middle, you're also going to cut off your access to the joys and the real beauty in life. There's this challenge in being open to feeling things that are scary, uncertain, and really painful. In my own life, what I found is that the anticipation of feeling the emotion is far worse than what it's ever like to really feel it.

## CULTIVATING A CONSCIOUS PATTERN OF STRATEGIC THINKING

Perhaps the best way to cultivate a conscious pattern of Strategic Thinking is to emulate other strategic thinkers. Select at least three people whom you consider to be strategic thinkers. Most business people would consider Tom Peters to be a strategic thinker. What about in other industries or professions? How about Oprah Winfrey, Steve Jobs, Nelson Mandela, or others?

Then, think about the qualities that make these people strategic thinkers. What beliefs do they hold? What are they willing or not willing to consider? Success always leaves a track, and in the case of Strategic Thinking, that track will be the way in which these people think about the world. Are they open or closed to new ideas? Do they think about the past or the future? If so, how?

You'll find that they're always looking for new ways to do things. They are independent thinkers, but they don't stand alone. See what other qualities you can find, then begin emulating them, but in your own unique way. Think in terms of what you're going to do differently first, and then how you'll do it differently. *What* always comes before *how* with Strategic Thinking.

## THE CONSCIOUS PATTERN OF ADVENTURISM

*To not take a risk is to risk being ignored.*

DREW NEISSER

When I think about the opposite of the perfectionist, I imagine the great risk-taking adventurers. When Thomas Leonard said that the present is always perfect, he was thinking of the adventure that's always available. It doesn't mean that things won't, or shouldn't, change. He knew that everything changes all the time, but he also understood that the perfection of the moment opens us to tremendous opportunities for new adventures in the next moment.

Thomas was a constant creator. Knowing that the present was perfect gave him the freedom to create his future. He wasn't concerned about fixing the past or even fixing the present. Since the present is perfect, all we have is the adventure of the moment. Again, it may not be perfect in the way that we want it to be or expect it to be. *It is ideal in the opportunity it presents to us.*

> Adventurism is characterized by the ability to take educated risks and embrace the adventure and uncertainty of life.

Sure, I'm a bit of a perfectionist myself. I can really get down on myself for not doing things just right. I used to wish that everything was perfect all the time, but I've learned that none of the wonderful opportunities I've come across in the past few years would have happened if I'd stuck to my Perfectionism. It's only because I've taken some risks to jump into the adventure (of coaching, and of writing) that I'm having these successes. It's really the adventure that's given me life and helped me to Live into my Greatness.

Perfectionism kills. It kills dreams, goals, happiness, spontaneity, and wonder. It kept me in a satin-lined coffin of safe living. I didn't have to risk because I had to have things perfect before I did anything. I don't want to live that way any more. I like the perfection of the moment and the freedom it gives me to open myself to new adventures. The perfection is in life showing us the way. We don't have to figure it out ahead of time. That is what's so great about this perfect adventure.

Trust is a big part of the equation with perfection. We trust that we can't miss out on what's coming for us—we're already creating it, attracting it, and manifesting it. Trust comes from not being able to see it in tangible form yet, but believing it is coming.

## THE FOUR-STEP PROCESS APPLIED TO THE ILLUSION OF CERTAINTY

*Everyone has talent. What is rare is the courage to follow the talent to the dark places where it leads.*

ERICA JONG

I asked the question earlier if Matt was a hopeless case. What do you think now? Is he hopeless? Can he change? More importantly, how would *you* work with Matt to help him shift from Certainty to Inquiry?

The following sections will apply the Coaching into Greatness four-step process to Matt's situation.

### AWARENESS

Awareness is the most critical step for someone like Matt. His Certainty about himself, his situation, and his habits are tough nuts to crack. The only way to break the cycle is to start with an awareness of his current results. You can't simply put Matt through a series of consistent actions and hope for the best. His lifelong thinking, beliefs, and behavior patterns will prevail every time.

The first step is to help him review his current circumstances. The goal is to keep him very far away from judgment, criticism, or black-and-white thinking. For now, he has to stay out of action, which will be both crucial and challenging. He feels like he has to do something and will push for suggestions on what he should do to change his situation. He'll balk at the suggestion that he change his beliefs, saying that his beliefs have nothing to do with what's happening.

You have to carefully go through his current situation, layer by layer, simply pointing to what is, without getting into the details of how he got there. He has to first understand and accept his situation for what it is. He's lost three jobs in five years, all for very similar reasons. He gets into work at 10 A.M., spends an hour or more reviewing e-mails, and then takes lunch. He's late on his current project. See how we're just listing the facts about his life and work situation. There's no judgment or rationalization, or even any suggestions as to why these things are happening. They just are.

That's the first stage of awareness. The second stage of awareness is for Matt to understand that it's what *he* does that creates his results. You have to take each piece and break it down into steps. Ask, "When you spend ten hours researching a situation before starting your work, what do you think happens to your project schedule?" He has to understand first that he's responsible for the results he gets.

The third stage of awareness is to tie habits to beliefs. What belief makes Matt take three times longer to research a situation than his peers? Does he think he's not as smart? Not likely. More likely, he believes that he's simply more thorough, and if only they'd give him more time, he'd do a much better job than his peers. This process will take some digging, but the key is to keep up with the investigation until you can find the underlying beliefs that hold his habit patterns in place.

## ACCEPTANCE

Acceptance is often difficult. It's perhaps hardest with people under the Illusion of Certainty. Can Matt really accept that his way of thinking and his beliefs about himself aren't accurate? He has to if he wants his situation to improve. For some time, Matt has to express a Willingness to change, and to act as if his new beliefs are right. You have to take the time to lay the foundation for these new beliefs. What might Matt change about his beliefs?

He might decide to believe that he doesn't have to get all the details in place before proceeding. He can change his beliefs about his family, his TV watching, or his habits at work. He can change his belief that his problems are simply the result of bad management and decide to take responsibility for creating his own future. In fact, he can change his belief from "I'm a victim" to "I can create my own future."

Then, acceptance of these beliefs will take time and will come only as a matter of cycling through the four-step process several times. He has to experience different results before he'll really believe that it's possible for him to change himself and his situation.

## CONSISTENT ACTION

For Matt, consistent action must be strategic, not tactical. His tendency will be to lay out a tactical plan and try to follow it without understanding why he's doing what he's doing. He'll want to simply revert to the old patterns and blame his failure on the plan. You'll have to develop a thorough strategy with Matt, carefully describing the objective goals, the purpose, the intention, and the values that are maintained.

Your strategy will identify the specific points of failure—the thoughts, beliefs, and behaviors that will most likely cause Matt to become complacent in his actions. And you should devise strategies to help Matt reinforce new beliefs and behaviors. These are strategies, and not tactics. For example, you might develop a strategy to help Matt take more risks with his work. The strategy might consist of having Matt act first and think second. He'll have to let go of any concept of what might happen. The strategy would also consist of ideas of how Matt will deal with the inevitable mistakes that will be made. Again, these aren't specific tactics, but strategies that leave room for adaptation.

It's important for Matt to follow through with these consistent strategic actions. If the strategy, for example, is to limit research time to two hours, he should follow through, and report back on what happened as a result. No hedging can be allowed, because Matt will easily shift back to old patterns.

## AUTHENTICITY

What is authentic for someone like Matt, who's so certain about everything? You'll know you're getting close to authenticity when Matt can say something like, "I'm not sure what's going to happen when I try this, but I'm excited about the possibilities." Matt's typical, nonauthentic response would have been more like, "Yeah. I'll try it. But I can't see how it's going to make a difference." Not much willingness or openness in that statement, is there?

Authentic action admits that there's uncertainty in the results. Yet, Living into Greatness means reveling in this uncertainty. Sure, there's fear involved. But the fear becomes a signal that you are on track instead of a sign to stop.

It will take time with certain people like Matt. Matt is still working hard on moving through the four-step process. He's at it daily, in fact. He's catching himself when he slips back into Certainty, sometimes before he acts on the Certainty, but mostly still after the fact. That's okay. Over time, he'll learn more how to question his Certainty and develop the aptitude of Inquiry. Soon, I think, his bosses *will* appreciate Matt's skills, but not because his skills have changed.

## Chapter Summary

*Atop a 100-foot pole, how do you step forward?*

Shishuang

We expect life to come with a guarantee, but that very expectation is
the Illusion of Certainty.
Inquiry is moving from expert to student.
Insanity = applying your "fixed reality" to an ever-changing world.
Question your answers.
The perfection is in life showing us the way.

For additional information and chapter resources, visit http://www.
coachingintogreatness.com/the_illusion_of_certainty.

## CHAPTER TWELVE

# Creating Abundance Intelligence™

*The longer I live the more beautiful life becomes.*

FRANK LLOYD WRIGHT

*I'm 36 years old as I write this. Life handed me a lot of early loss, pain, and challenges. I looked at them as barriers, obstacles, and things to over-come. But as my awareness grows, I see them as gifts. All that has hap-pened has been a blessing—in ways still yet to be revealed. About a year ago, a friend asked me if I would change anything about my life. I paused before I answered, and at first I couldn't figure out why.*

*It's not that the pain is completely gone. When you lose someone, it always stays with you. But for me, that pain has moved from a source of tremendous anger and emptiness, to a source of self-definition and awakening. The anonymous "they" say what doesn't kill you only makes you stronger, but I think that's only part of the picture. The experiences I've gone through didn't kill me, although they could have. There were many times I thought about dying. They did make me stronger, but most importantly, the experiences introduced me to myself. That's what life does. If we're willing and open and flexible, we can learn something, we can rediscover our great-ness. Sadly, for many people, the illusions keep them in a box, often comfortable, but mediocre at best, just getting by. That's why you're reading this book. It is my fervent hope that you and the people you coach and work with don't become any of those casualties.*

*No, I would not change anything that has happened in my life. Of course I would love to have my mother here with me right now, but she's not. The time for looking back and wishing things to be different has come and gone. My mom continues to teach me and love me in countless ways after her death. She is with me always. She has written this book.*

*One of her greatest ongoing lessons is to love what's here with us now, to love who we are now. Today, I can love my dad for who he is, and he is great. Equally important, I can begin to love myself for who I am, and I am great.*

*You are great, too. Now go out and be your great self and help others to be great!*

*It takes courage to grow up and turn out to be who you really are.*

E. E. CUMMINGS

Abundance is greatness, and a whole lot more. In the first chapter, I introduced the concept of the AQ (Abundance Quotient) system. Throughout the book, we've explored the definitions of abundance and scarcity, the illusions and aptitudes that make up their pattern language, and how this shows up in business and life. We've learned that the Tipping Point is the point at which the patterns in our lives are no longer useful—they actually keep us from doing what we *can* do. We've learned

Figure 12.1   The Abundance Quotient System.

that with every conditioned pattern there is an Opportunity Cost. For every illusion we practice, the price is living in scarcity. For every conscious choice we practice, the reward is living in abundance and being who we are.

The four-step Coaching Into Greatness process (see Figure 12.1) is what moves us from the illusions to the abundance aptitudes. In doing so, we reduce and, in many cases, eliminate the bottom-line impact of scarcity and we then experience greatness. Put all of these elements together, and you have the beginnings of the AQ System.

## Doing What You *Can* Do

*If the world is cold, build fires.*

HORACE TRAUBEL

Abundance is much more than the belief that there is enough to go around. Likewise, scarcity is much more than the belief that there isn't enough. These two topics are really about choice and how our choices profoundly impact our lives—the choice to consciously live in abundance or unconsciously exist in scarcity.

When I first envisioned this book, it was all about helping people Live into their Greatness. As a coach, this is what I help my clients do every day. And yet, something bigger quickly began to emerge. On this journey, I've realized greatness is one aspect of this work. Abundance is like a multifaceted diamond, revealing a kaleidoscope of riches when we have the courage to flood it with light.

I have always been fascinated by stories of ordinary people who did amazing things—unknown people who responded in the moment and changed the world. Even if it was just one person's world, they had a positive impact—they created something that mattered. Each individual action created a ripple effect. Stories of people jumping into the water to save a drowning person, individuals starting grassroots organizations to solve a community problem, and entrepreneurs who found a way to make a profit and be socially responsible always caught my attention. *These people were doing something.* They weren't looking the other way like so many others, and that made them very different.

Throughout my life, my interest in people doing what they *can* do has grown. I admire the entrepreneurs who start businesses on no more than a dream—heck, I became one. I heard the story of Julia Butterfly Hill and her famous tree sit-in and I marveled at her courage and compassion. I reflected on the recent passing of Rosa Parks—how her simple, yet profoundly authentic act of refusing to give up her seat on a segregated bus became the passionate cry of a nation.

I found myself wondering, how are some people able to do what they *can* do more than others? I've come to call this phenomenon *The Difference of One*, and it is intimately connected to my concept of abundance. People who practice *The Difference of One* distinguish themselves in many ways, but there's one of critical importance. *They are different in how they respond to life.*

People who do what they *can* do have an Authentic Abundant Response to life. What does this mean? People who demonstrate this kind of response have the ability to be who they are in the world, *when it matters most.* They consistently display the abundance aptitudes we've explored in this book. They rush into a crumbling World Trade Center when everybody else rushes out. They speak their minds, they stand up, they act on what is authentic for them, even when it's not convenient, and sometimes when it's downright terrifying. But they do it anyway. Being inauthentic is not an option. They can't *not* be who they are. They can't *not* do what they *can* do. They have left excuses, blame, justification, and trying at the door.

There's no better widespread example than the rescue stories coming out of New Orleans in connection with the devastation of Hurricane Katrina. Amid the death, despair, and incompetence of many, these people restored our faith in humanity. These rescuers demonstrated an Authentic Abundant Response by doing what they could do. They had an attitude of action.

You may have heard the story of Jabbor Gibson, an 18-year-old who stole a bus in downtown New Orleans to drive 100 desperate people, most of them strangers, out of the city to safety. His bus actually beat all the other sanctioned government buses arriving at the Houston Astrodome by hours. Jabbor had never driven a bus before, let alone stolen one. When asked how he felt about the possibility officials may prosecute him for the theft, he replied, "I don't care if I get blamed for it, as long as I saved my people."

There are stories of fishermen in the surrounding states just showing up with their boats, pulling stranded people off of roofs and out of trees. They did what they could do. They were *The Difference of One,* multiplied. Then, there were the thousands of animal rescuers who flew, drove, and walked into the city in response to the forgotten animals for which an overwhelmed government had no time or compassion.

## PROFILES IN GREATNESS: ERIC RICE

Eric Rice was one such individual. From the moment he heard about the disaster taking place from Hurricane Katrina in New Orleans, Eric Rice was on the message boards and Internet chat rooms. He was in constant contact with many people who were already there or on their way, keeping track of who was doing what. He knew he was going, too. It was just a matter of time. But, even two weeks before he left, he was connecting rescuers with people searching for their pets. Eric knew he couldn't sit back and watch all the innocent animals suffer without helping.

"Whenever I've been needed, I've acted," Eric says. He went on his planned vacation to Mexico but used his time there to further plan his trip to New Orleans. By the time he returned from Mexico, the trip was planned, and his fiancée had arranged for Eric to receive $500 in shots before he headed to the contaminated streets of New Orleans. He rented a box truck, which as it turned out very few people bothered to do. He rented a generator and had everything he needed lined up before he left.

"I don't think there was any doubt in my mind that I was going," he said. "I didn't know exactly what I was going to do when I got there, but I figured it out pretty quickly. I went in with the knowing that I was going to make a difference. I think that was true of everybody I met."

How is it that someone like Eric can focus so strategically, go into such a situation not knowing what would happen, but be confident that he would figure it out when he got there? Eric is a very good example of someone with a very high Abundance Quotient. Nobody was surprised he went. His fiancée said to him before he'd even mentioned his plans, "You're going there, aren't you?" People who know Eric know that he's highly involved in whatever he does, and when he does act, it's after he's put a lot of thought and attention into his strategy.

Eric was in New Orleans for 23 days. He faced tense situations, where he had to break into houses, search for missing animals, face the possibility of attack (by dogs *and* people), and worst of all, deal with the contamination. It wasn't easy, and he spent over $2,000 on cell phone charges; but none of this ever entered his mind as a possible excuse or deterrent.

He slept in the back of his truck, only occasionally leaving the city to shower and clean up. He surrounded himself with a team, knowing he couldn't do it alone. He won't say that he's a hero, because there were so many people helping, mostly without the safety equipment that was promised but was unavailable. He received calls from people he didn't know who were on the fence about going and told them where they could help. He didn't say, "I'm going to be an organizer." He simply did what he could do.

"I was drawn to this like nothing I've ever been," Eric said. For him, there were no excuses. "I think I was planning it from the second I heard about it. I knew I was going. I was just trying to educate myself as much as possible about what I was going to do there. I was amazed that I was able to get into the city after dark when I got there."

One thing it taught him was that he cares about animals more than he'd ever known. But perhaps the most important lesson from Eric's experience is expressed by these words: "I said *just show up;* you're going to make a difference. That's all it took for some. It wasn't going to be hard to be a hero; it was about getting off the couch and getting there."

If we look at the stories of these rescuers, we find that they are classic examples of individuals with a high AQ. With Eric Rice as an example, we find the prevalence of the Abundance Aptitudes:

1. *Self-Worth:* Eric recognized his ability to contribute. He didn't doubt what he could do, even though he had never before rescued animals and had no training in disaster relief. He had an absence of the Illusion of Not Enough.
2. *Empathy:* It was Eric's ability to empathize with the animal victims and their suffering that prompted him to act. He also displayed the Capacity to empathize with his personal call to be part of the solution, and to make a difference. He did not compare himself to others and what they could do or what he should do.
3. *Self-Expression:* Eric's actions demonstrate his Self-Expression. Not only did he rescue animals, his ability to tell the world about it through www.ericsdogblog.com has brought untold additional resources and support to the cause. Eric did not struggle with whether he should go to New Orleans. He listened to his intuition.
4. *Surrender:* Unlike some, Eric didn't get caught up in the red tape of regulations and requirements. He identified and worked around the

barriers, safely and legally finding alternative ways to get results. His and other rescuers' ability to adapt and let go of control of the situation allowed them to be much more effective.

5. *Actualization:* Eric didn't get stuck in the past or worry about the future. He thoughtfully and strategically prepared for what it would take to be involved in rescue operations, and he focused on what he had, not what he didn't have.

6. *Significance:* Eric recognized the Significance of his actions and the difference he could make. He didn't wait for others to respond. He didn't stand by and hope that the government would solve the problem. He didn't hope for the best, he *created* the best.

7. *Inquiry:* Eric had no idea what would happen when he arrived in New Orleans. He didn't allow a need for Certainty, for safety, for knowing the outcome to keep him from Living into his Greatness. He jumped in with everything he had, and that was more than enough.

Does this mean that Eric Rice had no challenges or second thoughts, or that he was totally fearless? Of course not. *The critical thing to remember is that those fears and uncertainties did not keep him from doing what he could do.* He responded abundantly, which made his contribution possible.

You may read this example and say, well, that's a great story, Kim, but I couldn't be like that. I couldn't drop everything to go and save lives. There are two caveats here:

1. Remember that someone else's definition of abundance and greatness will most likely be different from yours. I am not advocating that everyone go to the extreme of jumping into burning buildings, exposing themselves to toxic sludge, or other types of heroism. Living into Greatness is about exploring your abundance, reconnecting with who you are, and acting upon it in your unique way. Greatness is personal. It doesn't matter what your definition of greatness is, only that you live into it. So don't fall into the Illusion of Not Enough because you have greatness envy. Focus on what you *can* do and live into that.

2. When I refer to doing what you *can* do, *can* is intimately linked to your Authentic Abundant Response. I'm not talking about what you have the *potential* to do. All of us have the potential to

do millions of different things, but remember, abundance is not about potential. Abundance is all about Capacity, and Capacity is all about what you already have. Therefore, just as the illusions have Tipping Points, so does doing what you *can* do. The Tipping Point is the moment your awareness about who you are causes you to shift, causes you to realize that the way you have been living in the past has not been an Authentic Abundant Response to life. The Tipping Point is all about that moment when you realize you have a choice to live differently, to live greatly, to embrace conscious choices versus conditioned choices.

## ABUNDANCE INTELLIGENCE™

*A rock pile ceases to be a rock pile the moment a single man contemplates it, bearing within him the image of a cathedral.*

ANTOINE DE SAINT-EXUPERY

What if we could put a language to this thing called doing what you *can* do? That's the purpose of Abundance Intelligence™. AQ is a pioneering way of identifying a new standard of intelligence — identifying what lies beyond IQ and EQ. AQ is made up of aptitudes, conscious patterns, and beliefs that enable us to do what we *can* do consistently and authentically. The higher our AQ, the more likely it is that an individual has an Authentic Abundant Response to life. AQ is much bigger than greatness. Someone can pursue greatness for money or power and yet never be truly abundant because they are not being who they are.

---

Abundance Intelligence™ (AQ) is the study of doing what you *can* do. It is the process of identifying and giving language to people's Authentic Abundant Response to life.

---

With every abundant person I interviewed for this book, not one of them could fully articulate how they did what they did. Yet, they all clearly demonstrated the prevalence of the abundance aptitudes. How can this be? My thought is that they are so busy living who they are, and that abundance is such a way of life for them, the possibility of living in scarcity isn't even an option. Did the Katrina rescuers know that they were living abundantly? Would they know that they have a high AQ?

They probably wouldn't be able to articulate it, as was the case when I interviewed Eric Rice. He couldn't describe what made him different from everyone else and able to respond to the tragedy; he was too close to it, and that is exactly the point.

Imagine what could happen if people had an access point to their abundance? What if people had an understanding of AQ and could recognize it in their lives and the world around them? What would be possible?

> *Celebrate what you want to see more of.*
>
> TOM PETERS

By creating a language for abundance and the AQ System, we will be able to exponentially increase people's understanding of what it means to be abundant, to Live into Greatness. We have a means to study AQ and celebrate its existence in many situations that go unrecognized. The abundance we identify, study, and celebrate we can create more of. AQ gives a voice to the courageous rescuers and so many others that live like them. AQ is my Authentic Abundant Response to life, and the next phase of Living into Greatness.

## THE OPPORTUNITY BEFORE US

> *The creation of a thousand forests is in one acorn.*
>
> RALPH WALDO EMERSON

I have one more question for you: *Are you doing what you* can *do today?*

Are your clients and employees doing what they *can* do today? It sounds a bit simplistic, doesn't it? Through our exploration of the illusions and the conditioned patterns of scarcity, we know that's far from the truth. The concept may be simple, but putting it into consistent practice is not easy. That's where the guidance of a great coach is instrumental. Living abundantly is a life's work. The AQ System is the guidebook.

*The Difference of One* — one choice, one person, one thought, one action — this is the beginning of the ripple effect. As Cicero said, "It is not enough to acquire wisdom, it is necessary to employ it." You've read this book and something has awakened in you. Go out and share what you've learned with a client, an employee, a loved one, a friend. You'll make a difference in their life, their business. Doing what you *can* do is truly abundance in action. Join me in bringing this work to the world.

## CHAPTER SUMMARY

The four-step Coaching into Greatness process moves us from the illusions to the abundance aptitudes.

People with a high AQ have an Authentic Abundant Response to life—they have the ability to be who they are in the world when it matters most.

*The Difference of One* is the profound impact one individual, idea, or event can have on the world when embraced abundantly.

Abundance Intelligence™ (AQ) is a pioneering new form of intelligence that enables people to do what they *can* do.

For interviews and highlights of people and organizations with high AQ, visit http://www.coachingintogreatness.com/aq_in_action.

# The AQ System at a Glance

See Figure A.1 for an illustration of the balance between the illusion of scarcity and the aptitude of abundance.

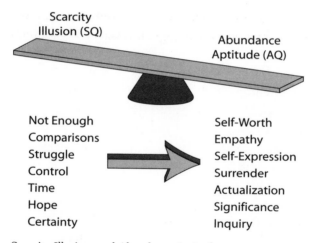

Figure A.1    Scarcity Illusions and Abundance Aptitudes.

| **The Illusions** | **The Abundance Aptitudes** |
|---|---|
| Illusion of Not Enough | Self-Worth |
|    Conditioned Patterns: |    Conscious Patterns: |
|       More |       Capacity |
|       Scriptwriting |       Greatfulness |
|       Contingency |       Catalyst |

Illusion of Comparisons
    Conditioned Patterns:
        External Drivers
        Personalization
        Busyness
Illusion of Struggle
    Conditioned Patterns:
        Resisting
        Complexity
        Overachieving
Illusion of Control
    Conditioned Patterns:
        Caretaking
        Role-Playing
        Self-Defense
Illusion of Time
    Conditioned Patterns:
        Rushing
        Attachment
        Distractibility
Illusion of Hope
    Conditioned Patterns:
        Expectation
        Powerlessness
        Assumption
Illusion of Certainty
    Conditioned Patterns:
        Complacency
        Tactical Thinking
        Perfectionism

Empathy
    Conscious Patterns:
        Internal Drivers
        Discernment
        Effectiveness
Self-Expression
    Conscious Patterns:
        Receiving
        Simplicity
        Flow
Surrender
    Conscious Patterns:
        Personal Responsibility
        Intention
        Vulnerability
Actualization
    Conscious Patterns:
        Stepping Back
        Curiosity
        Perseverance
Significance
    Conscious Patterns:
        Engagement
        Decisiveness
        Inquisitiveness
Inquiry
    Conscious Patterns:
        Willingness
        Strategic Thinking
        Adventurism

# Recommended Reading

Annunzio, Susan Lucia. (2004). *Contagious Success: Spreading High Performance Throughout Your Organization*. New York: Portfolio.

Block, Peter. (2002). *The Answer to How Is Yes: Acting on What Matters*. San Francisco: Berrett-Koehler.

Chodron, Pema. (1997). *When Things Fall Apart: Heart Advice for Difficult Times*. Boston: Shambala.

Chopra, Deepak. (2004). *The Book of Secrets*. New York: Harmony.

Dyer, Dr. Wayne W. (2004). *The Power of Intention: Learning to Co-create Your World Your Way*. Carlsbad, CA: Hay House.

Ferrazzi, Keith. (2005). *Never Eat Alone and Other Secrets to Success, One Relationship at a Time*. New York: Currency.

Giono, Jean. (1999). *The Man Who Planted Trees*. Boston: Shambala.

Hill, Julia Butterfly. (2000). *The Legacy of Luna: The Story of a Tree, a Woman, and the Struggle to Save the Redwoods*. San Francisco: HarperCollins.

Keen, Sam. (1999). *Learning to Fly: Trapeze-Reflections on Fear, Trust, and the Joy of Letting Go*. New York: Broadway Books.

Loehr, Jim, & Schwartz, Tony. (2003). *The Power of Full Engagement: Managing Energy, Not Time, Is the Key to High Performance and Personal Renewal*. New York: Free Press.

Markova, Dawna. (2000). *I Will Not Die an Unlived Life: Reclaiming Purpose and Passion*. Berkeley, CA: Conari Press.

Misner, Ivan, & Morgan, Don. (2004). *Masters of Success: Proven Techniques for Achieving Success in Business and Life*. New York: Entrepreneur Press.

Pink, Daniel. (2005). *A Whole New Mind*. New York: Penguin.

Richo, David. (2005). *The Five Things We Cannot Change . . . and the Happiness We Find by Embracing Them*. Boston: Shambala.

Ruiz, Don Miguel. (1997). *The Four Agreements*. San Rafael, CA: Amber Allen.

———. (2004). *The Voice of Knowledge*. San Rafael, CA: Amber Allen.

Sanders, Tim. (2002). *Love Is the Killer App*. New York: Crown.

Schwartz, Barry. (2004). *The Paradox of Choice: Why More Is Less*. New York: Ecco Press.

Secretan, Lance. (2004). *Inspire! What Great Leaders Do*. New York: John Wiley & Sons.

Tolle, Eckhart. (1999). *The Power of Now: A Guide to Spiritual Enlightenment*. Navato, CA: New World Library.

Vitale, Joe. (2005). *The Attractor Factor: 5 Easy Steps for Creating Wealth (or Anything Else) from the Inside Out*. New York: John Wiley & Sons.

Williams, Margery. (1985). *The Velveteen Rabbit*. New York: Random House.

# Glossary

**Abundance:**   State of mind in which an individual exercises the freedom to be who they are.

**Abundance Aptitude:**   Essential ability inherent in being who you are.

**Abundance Intelligence™:**   A form of intelligence that is made up of aptitudes, conscious patterns, and beliefs that enable us to do what we *can* do consistently and authentically.

**Abundance Quotient (AQ):**   A number resulting from the AQ assessment that gives you a snapshot of the amount of Abundance Intelligence™ you are exercising on a regular basis.

**Acceptance:**   Step 2 in the Living into Greatness process; owning who you are.

**Actualization:**   The abundance aptitude characterized by consistent and authentic action.

**Adventurism:**   Conscious pattern of Inquiry characterized by the ability to take educated risks and embrace the adventure and uncertainty of life.

**Aptitude:**   Inherent ability.

**Assumption:**   Conditioned pattern of the Illusion of Hope characterized by the habit of taking for granted that our view of the world is everyone else's view.

**Attachment:**   Conditioned pattern of the Illusion of Time in which our need for something or someone limits our Capacity to be who we are.

**Authentic Abundant Response:**   The ability to be who you are in the world when it matters most.

**Authenticity:**   Step 4 in the Living into Greatness process in which the alignment of thoughts and actions with who you are occurs; showing up as your true self even when it is difficult, scary, uncertain, or unpopular; being in alignment with your greatness, your vision, and your values.

**Awareness:**   Step 1 in the Living into Greatness process; remembering who you are.

**Busyness:**   Conditioned pattern of the Illusion of Comparisons, characterized by the belief that our worth is tied to how much we accomplish that can be seen by others.

**Capacity:**   Conscious pattern of Self-Worth characterized by the belief that you already have within you all that you want, need, and choose.

**Caretaking:**   Conditioned pattern of the Illusion of Control where an individual derives their identity from transforming others to fit their view.

**Catalyst:**   Conscious pattern of Self-Worth in which you choose to build around you what's essential to Living into your Greatness.

**Certainty (Illusion of):**   When the need to know an outcome keeps you from acting, making authentic decisions, and doing what you can do.

**Comparisons (Illusion of):**   Consistently comparing ourselves to the external world to validate our belief of who we are.

**Complacency:**   Conditioned pattern of the Illusion of Certainty in which the ease of the status quo is greater than the desire for improvement.

**Complexity:**   Conditioned pattern of the Illusion of Struggle characterized by making things more difficult than they have to be as a way to avoid doing what we can do.

**Conditioned beliefs:**   Beliefs we have internalized from sources outside ourselves—our parents, society, school, our culture. They are not the beliefs of our true selves—they are beliefs of External Drivers and they make up the Conditioned patterns.

**Conditioned patterns:**   The culmination of a repeated series of actions and reactions based on and reinforced by Conditioned beliefs. They are the primary evidence of the illusions at play in our lives, keeping us from being who we are.

**Conditioning:**   The process of living someone else's answers about life.

**Conscious beliefs:**   The Self-Actualizing beliefs we choose freely and consciously that reinforce the conscious patterns of the Abundance Aptitudes.

# Glossary

**Conscious patterns:**   The repeated and consistent authentic actions in alignment with our true nature, reinforced by conscious beliefs. They are the primary evidence of the Abundance Aptitudes at play in our lives.

**Consistent action:**   Step 3 in the Living into Greatness process; living who you are.

**Contingency:**   Conditioned pattern of the Illusion of Not Enough, characterized by the need for a condition outside of ourselves to happen for us to do or be something.

**Control (Illusion of):**   When a person's happiness depends on rearranging the world to fit their idea of how things should be.

**Convenient Distraction:**   Conditioned pattern of the Illusion of Time, in which people, places, things, and events serve our need to remain stuck; also called Distractibility.

**Core fears:**   The subconscious reactionary expressions around who we perceive ourselves to be.

**Creative energy:**   The amount of energy you have to creatively express who you are, stretch yourself, go outside your comfort zone.

**Cup:**   Analogy illustrating the concept of Capacity; when you are "the Cup" you realize greatness is inside of you, not to be achieved through outside sources.

**Curiosity:**   Conscious pattern of Actualization characterized by the ability to embrace wonder and appreciate all of something—not just one opportunity, but many opportunities.

**Decisiveness:**   Conscious pattern of Significance characterized by an individual's ability to hold themselves accountable for the results in their life by moving through fear to action.

**Declaration:**   Public promise of your greatness actualized; your statement of truth.

***Difference of One:***   The profound contribution and impact to the world one individual, idea, or event can have when embraced abundantly.

**Discernment:**   Conscious pattern of Empathy characterized by the process of chipping away everything that isn't the truth in order to reveal what is true for you.

**Distractibility:**   Conditioned pattern of the Illusion of Time characterized by allowing people, events, emotions, and fears to conveniently keep us from doing what we *can* do.

**Doing what you *can* do:**   Abundance in action; greatness actualized.

**Effectiveness:** Conscious pattern of Empathy characterized by doing what's most effective without compromising who you are being in the process.

**Empathy:** Abundance aptitude of compassionate internal awareness; the degree to which an individual consciously directs his or her awareness inward, with the same amount of compassion that might be directed toward others.

**Engagement:** Conditioned pattern of Significance in which hope is manifested into action; the more frequently we are authentic, the more we are engaged.

**Expectation:** Conditioned pattern of the Illusion of Hope characterized by the belief that life is supposed to go according to our version of happiness.

**External Drivers:** Conditioned pattern of the Illusion of Comparisons characterized by the interpretation that who you are is dependent on sources outside of yourself (people, circumstances, or events).

**Flow:** Conscious pattern of Self-Expression; allowing life to unfold through you, not because of you or in spite of you.

**Freedom:** Your ability to actualize who you are.

**Greatfulness:** Conscious pattern of Self-Worth that combines the elements of gratitude, appreciation, and capacity; the internal knowing that you are the Cup.

**Greatness:** Living your life reflecting the belief that you already have everything you need.

**Greatness Capacity:** Understanding that you already have within you everything you want, need, and choose to be who you are; potential holds that you need to strive to acquire something outside of yourself and Greatness Capacity holds that it already exists within you.

**Hope (Illusion of):** Waiting for other people or events to solve our uneasiness about who we are.

**Illusion:** A layer of conditioning that provides evidence we are living in scarcity.

**Inquiry:** The abundance aptitude characterized by a person's ability to question their answers consistently.

**Inquisitiveness:** Conscious pattern of Significance characterized by the commitment to unearth and examine a person's assumptions about their life, their business, and the world.

**Intention:** Conscious pattern of Surrender characterized by the ability to set the destination of your life, not the course.

**Internal Drivers:** Conscious pattern of Empathy characterized by beliefs, thoughts, and attitudes that are of your design and making, not external sources.

**Living into Greatness:** The four-step process of remembering so that we become more like ourselves than we've ever been.

**More:** Conditioned pattern of the Illusion of Not Enough characterized by the belief that something or someone outside ourselves will complete us.

**Not Enough (Illusion of):** Illusion in which the belief that you can't trust who you are results in feeling incomplete.

**Opportunity Cost:** The tangible and intangible costs to the individual or business when a person is operating in scarcity; the higher the scarcity quotient, the higher the Opportunity Cost.

**Overachieving:** Conditioned pattern of the Illusion of Struggle characterized by being driven to meet unrealistic expectations that reinforce a false identity.

**Pattern Language:** A way to describe a series of patterns that identify a recurring problem. It gives language to, and allows people to relate to, a problem in accessible, understandable terms.

**Perfectionism:** Conditioned pattern of the Illusion of Certainty characterized by an inability to reach completion due to an endless search for the external approval of one's actions.

**Perseverance:** Conscious pattern of actualization characterized by focusing on what you *can* do in the present as part of the process of Living into Greatness; it is doing the thing you *can* do even when it is not easy, convenient, or proven.

**Personalization:** Conditioned pattern of the Illusion of Comparisons characterized by consistently taking on the opinions and beliefs of others as the ultimate truth, even when those beliefs feel contradictory to our inner knowing.

**Personal RAM:** The amount of energy an individual has to live their authentic life.

**Personal Responsibility:** Conscious pattern of Surrender in which an individual releases blame and victimization to become fully responsible for their life.

**Powerlessness:** Conditioned pattern of the Illusion of Hope characterized by a person feeling trapped, victimized, and out of choices in the face of external forces.

**Quotient:** The measurement of your degree of scarcity mentality or abundance mentality.

**Receiving:**   Conscious pattern of Self-Expression characterized by the ability to consciously choose to receive the opportunity before us, especially when it is not expected, planned, or thought out.

**Resisting:**   Conditioned pattern of the Illusion of Struggle characterized by rejecting things that are not "our way" in life; the ultimate resistance is resisting who you are.

**Role-Playing:**   Conditioned pattern of the Illusion of Control characterized by the persistent obligation to be something you're not—who you think the world should see.

**Rushing:**   Conditioned pattern of the Illusion of Time characterized by the belief that there is a scarcity of time and opportunity, causing people to focus on what they think they should do, instead of what they *can* do.

**Scarcity:**   State of mind in which an individual resists who they are.

**Scarcity Quotient:**   A number resulting from the AQ assessment that gives you a snapshot of the amount of scarcity you are exercising on a regular basis.

**Scriptwriting:**   Conditioned pattern of the Illusion of Not Enough characterized by projecting an image of ourselves that is not real.

**Self-Defense:**   Conditioned pattern of the Illusion of Control characterized by the need to protect oneself from perceived fearful situations and individuals; inherently tied to the belief that good things do not come your way.

**Self-Expression:**   The abundance aptitude with the ability to consistently give voice to who you are.

**Self-Worth:**   Abundance aptitude that you are complete, that you are more than enough exactly as you are.

**Significance:**   Abundance aptitude characterized by shifting from external expectation to internal realization by embracing and acting upon your Greatness Capacity; a shift from external expectation to internal realization.

**Simplicity:**   Conscious pattern of Self-Expression characterized by the ability to let things be as they are and let ourselves be as we are.

**Stepping Back:**   Conscious pattern of Actualization characterized by the ability to see what is and respond accordingly instead of reacting to a situation based on judgments and presumptions.

**Strategic Thinking:**   Conscious pattern of Inquiry characterized by an ability to do new and different things by engaging in possibilities that often can't be seen, heard, or measured.

**Struggle (Illusion of):**   The cycle of resistance, striving, and complexity that keeps people from doing what they *can* do.

**Surface dweller:**   A person who exists at the surface of life — primarily comfortable dealing with the symptoms of unhappiness versus the root causes.

**Surrender:**   Abundance aptitude demonstrated by the Willingness to let go of the need to control things outside your direct influence.

**Tactical Thinking:**   Conditioned pattern of the Illusion of Certainty characterized by plotting out straight-line courses through life, often using tactics we've learned from others, excluding other possibilities and opportunities.

**Time (Illusion of):**   Focusing on what you don't have instead of what you do have.

**Tipping Point:**   The moment when thinking a certain way keeps us from doing what we *can* do.

**Vulnerability:**   Conscious pattern of Surrender characterized by possessing the strength to be seen as you are in the world.

**Willingness:**   Conscious pattern of Inquiry characterized by the degree of Inquiry, openness, and exploration an individual demonstrates.

# About the Author

Kim George is the founder and CEO of The AQ Institute, a coaching, consulting, and training company focused on bringing Abundance Intelligence™ to the world. To find out more, visit www.AQInstitute.com.

Networking and marketing are Kim's other passions. She is a dean of the Collaborative Coaching School for The Referral Institute® (www.referralinstitute.com), a coaching, training, and consulting company focused on referral marketing. As pioneer coach for the Social Capital & Networking community, Kim collaborated with Dr. Ivan Misner, founder and chairman of Business Network International (BNI) in developing a 25-hour curriculum that she coleads with Dr. Misner. For more information and free networking resources, visit www.networkingcommunity.com and www.abundantnetworker.com.

Prior to becoming an author, Kim was vice president of strategic alliances for CoachVille, the world's largest coaching organization. Kim founded the Western Mass Coaching Alliance in her community of Springfield, Massachusetts, and also conducted a radio show, *Coach Live*, for two years on WARE 1250 AM.

Kim's diverse background includes a B.S. in paralegal studies, two years as a VISTA volunteer, and nearly 12 years in the health-care industry in various marketing, volunteer management, fund-raising, and public relations capacities. Kim lives in Springfield, Massachusetts, with her husband, two dogs, two cats, and a cockatiel named Mr. Bird.

# Interested in Learning More about Abundance Intelligence™?

Visit www.CoachingIntoGreatness.com to:

- Take the online AQ assessment for a snapshot of your AQ score.
- Visit the Doing What You *Can* Do blog where you can interact with the author and other AQ pioneers.
- Sign up for our newsletter, *AQ Matters,* jam-packed with interviews, tips, and strategies from the most abundant minds in business and life today.
- Discover how you can participate in free classes, coaching, and community through The AQ Institute (www.aqinstitute.com).
- Find out how The AQ Institute can help you, your clients, and your organization Live into Greatness through one-on-one coaching, group coaching, and consulting services.
- Join the growing ranks of professionals all over the world who are becoming Certified AQ Coaches.
- Hire Kim to inspire your next conference or event to be truly great.

You can also get a sneak peek at the next phase of Abundance Intelligence™: *The Coaching into Greatness Field Guide*—the how-to manual for professionals who want to apply the principles of Coaching into Greatness.

Kim can be reached at Kim@CoachingIntoGreatness.com.

# Index

Abundance
    in action, stories of, 34–35, 36, 67–70,
        239–241
    authentic response, 238, 241, 242,
        243, 244
    external, 19
    as freedom, 20–21
    as it applies to relationships, 34
    living in, 1–2
    mentality, 3, 4, 19–20, 23, 24
    pattern language of, 45–46, 48
    *vs.* scarcity, 16, 19, 20, 21–22, 25
Abundance aptitudes
    Actualization, 174–182
    defined, 26–27
    Inquiry, 223–229
    Self-Empathy, 97–99, 101, 106, 107
    Self-Expression, 123–130
    Self-Worth, 70–78
    Significance, 199–206
    Surrender, 149–156
Abundance Intelligence™, 26–27, 28,
    242, 244
Abundance Quotient (AQ), 26–27, 45,
    237, 242, 243
Acceptance, step 2
    Illusion of Certainty, applied to, 231

Illusion of Comparisons, applied to,
    106–107
    defined, 6, 55, 131
Illusion of Hope,
    applied to, 207
Illusion of Not Enough, applied to,
    80
    process of, 55–56
Illusion of Struggle, applied to,
    131–132
Illusion of Time,
    applied to, 183
Accountability, defined, 203
*Achieving Success Through Social Capital*
    (Baker), 110
Acorn theory, 29, 31, 71
Act intuitively, action step, 99
Action
    as a conscious choice, 56
    defined, 201
    as the key to Living into Greatness, 5
    steps (*See individual step listings*)
Activity, defined, 201
Actualization, abundance aptitude
    conscious patterns of
        Curiosity, 179–180
        Perseverance, 180–182
                                    *(Continued)*

Actualization, abundance aptitude
  (continued)
    Stepping Back, 177–179
  defined, 174–175, 184
  example of, 241
Adventurism, 228–229
Alexander, Christopher, 45
Allen, Woody, 39
Annunzio, Susan, 146–149
AQ. See Abundance Quotient (AQ)
A Return to Love (Williamson), 37
Armstrong, Lance, 117–118
Assumptions, 193–195, 204, 205
Attachment, 167–169
The Attractor Factor (Vitale), 196
Authenticity, step 4
  Illusion of Certainty, applied to, 232
  Illusion of Comparisons,
    applied to, 107–108
  Illusion of Control,
    applied to, 158–159
  defined, 6, 57
  Illusion of Hope,
    applied to, 208
  Illusion of Not Enough,
    applied to, 81
  process of, 57–58
  Illusion of Struggle, applied to, 133
  Illusion of Time,
    applied to, 183
Awareness, step 1
  Illusion of Certainty, applied to,
    230–231
  Illusion of Comparisons, applied to,
    106
  Illusion of Control,
    applied to, 157–158
  defined, 6, 53
  Illusion of Hope,
    applied to, 207
  Illusion of Not Enough,
    applied to, 79–80
  process of, 54
  Illusion of Struggle,
    applied to, 130–131
  Illusion of Time, applied to, 182–183

Baez, Joan, 149
Baker, Wayne, 110

Ballantyne, Sheila, 21
Barrymore, John, 153
Beecher, Henry Ward, 35
Being, defined, 112
Beliefs, 15, 45
  conditioned, 50, 55, 58
    of Assumptions, 195
    of Attachment, 168–169
    of Busyness, 92–93
    of Caretaking, 141–142
    of Complacency, 217
    of Complexity, 116
    of Contingency, 65
    of Distractibility, 171
    of Expectations, 192
    of More, 63
    of Overachieving, 119
    of Perfectionism, 220
    of Powerlessness, 193
    of Resisting, 115
    of Role-Playing, 144
    of Rushing, 166–167
    of Scriptwriting, 64–65
    of Self-Defense, 145
    of Tactical Thinking, 219
  conscious
    of Inquisitiveness, 206
  identifying, 54
Believing, paradox of, 22–23
Berkus, Rusty, 54
Blame, defined, 203
Block, Peter, 185
The Book of Secrets (Chopra), 116
Booth, William, 154
Breakdowns, 57–58
Bruce, Lenny, 107
Buck, Pearl S., 59
Burroughs, John, 180
Business, soft side of, 15
The Business Development Guide
  (Reardon), 119
Business Network International (BNI),
  94, 127
Busyness, 90–93, 103–104

Campbell, Joseph, 135
Capacity, 31, 74–76, 77, 242
Caretaking, 140–142, 152, 153
Carlin, George, 71

# Index

Carlyle, Thomas, 35
Carré, John Le, 144
Carver, George Washington, 99
Catalyst, 78–79, 81
Certainty, Illusion of. *See also* Inquiry
  conditioned patterns of
    Complacency, 215–217
    Perfectionism, 219–220
    Tactical Thinking, 217–219
  defined, 9, 213, 224
  dynamics of, 213–214
  four-step process, applied to, 230–232
  living in, stories of, 214–215, 221–223
  Tipping Point of, 220–221
Ching, Tao Te, 79, 159
Chopra, Deepak, 47, 116, 155
Cicero, 243
Clarity, defined, 218
Coach, defined, 11, 22
Coachee, defined, 11
Coaching into Greatness, 14, 24, 30, 31,
  32–33, 44
Coachingintogreatness.com, 27, 81, 108,
  134, 159, 184, 209, 233, 244
CoachVille, 84, 122
*Coach Yourself to Success* (Miedaner), 83–84
Comparisons, Illusion of. *See also*
  Self-Empathy
  conditioned patterns of
    Busyness, 90–93, 103–104
    External Drivers, 86–88
    Personalization, 88–90, 102
  defined, 7, 85
  four-step process applied to, 105–108
  living in, stories of, 84–86, 94–95
  process of, 84–85
  solutions to, 95
  Tipping Point of, 93
Complacency, 215–217
Complexity, 115–117, 127
Conditioned patterns, 47–48, 49, 56, 57
  Illusion of Certainty
    Complacency, 215–217
    Perfectionism, 219–220
    Tactical Thinking, 217–219
  Illusion of Comparisons
    Busyness, 90–93, 103–104
    External Drivers, 86–88
    Personalization, 88–90, 102

Illusion of Control
  Caretaking, 140–142
  Role-Playing, 142–144
  Self-Defense, 144–145
Illusion of Hope
  Assumptions, 193–195
  Expectations, 189–192
  Powerlessness, 192–193
Illusion of Not Enough
  Contingency, 65–66, 67
  More, 62–64, 67, 73, 75
  Scriptwriting, 64–65, 73, 76–77
Illusion of Struggle
  Complexity, 115–117
  Overachieving, 117–118
  Resisting, 114–115
Illusion of Time
  Attachment, 167–169
  Distractibility, 169–171
  Rushing, 165–167
Conditioning, 41–44. *See also individual*
  *stage listings*
Conscious patterns, 47, 48, 56, 57
  of Actualization
    Curiosity, 179–180
    Perseverance, 180–182
    Stepping Back, 177–179
  of Inquiry
    Adventurism, 228–229
    Strategic Thinking, 227–228
    Willingness, 226–227
  of Self-Empathy
    Discernment, 102–103
    Effectiveness, 103–105
    Internal Drivers, 99–101
  of Self-Expression
    Flow, 128–130
    Receiving, 125–127
    Simplicity, 127–128
  of Self-Worth
    Capacity, 74–76, 77
    Catalyst, 78–79, 81
    Gratefulness, 76–78
  of Significance
    Decisiveness, 201–204
    Engagement, 199–201
    Inquisitiveness, 204–206
  of Surrender
    Intention, 153–154

*(Continued)*

Conscious patterns *(continued)*
    Personal responsibility, 152–153
    Vulnerability, 154–156
Consistent Action, step 3
    Illusion of Certainty, applied to,
        231–232
    Illusion of Comparisons,
        applied to, 107
    Illusion of Control, applied to, 158
    defined, 6, 56
    Illusion of Hope, applied to, 207–208
    Illusion of Not Enough, applied to,
        80–81
    process of, 56–57
    Illusion of Struggle,
        applied to, 132–133
    Illusion of Time, applied to, 183
*Contagious Success* (Annunzio), 146
Contingency, 65–66, 67, 73
Control, Illusion of. *See also* Surrender
    conditioned patterns of
        Caretaking, 140–142
        Role-Playing, 142–144
        Self-Defense, 144–145
    defined, 8, 137, 159
    development of, 136–137
    forms of, 137–138
    four-step process,
        applied to, 156–159
    living in, stories of, 138–139, 146–149
    Tipping Point of, 146
A Course in Miracles®, 74
Cousins, Norman, 32
Covey, Stephen, 16
Cox, Alberta Lee, 226
Csikszentmihalyi, Mihaly, 128
Cummings, E. E., 236
Curiosity, 179–180

D'Angelo, Anthony J., 99
Dass, Baba Ram, 184
Davidds, Yasmin, 221–223
Decisiveness, 201–204
Declaration of truth,
    step 0, 51–52, 58
*Devil's Advocate*, 154
*The Dhammapada*, 220
The Difference of One, phenomenon,
    238, 243, 244

Discernment, 102–103
Distractibility, 169–171
DNA, of greatness, 31, 41
Doubt, defined, 72
Droku, Korrahn, 121–123
Drucker, Peter, 180
Dulles, John Foster, 56

Eckhart, Meister, 182
The Eden Alternative™, 66
Edison, Thomas, 113
Effectiveness, 92, 104–105
Efficiency, defined, 92
Einstein, Albert, 56
Eliot, T. S., 124
Embrace synchronicity,
    action step, 151
Emerson, Ralph Waldo, 29, 199, 215,
    243
Emotional quotient (EQ), 26
Empathy, 96, 97, 98, 141, 240. *See also*
    Self-Empathy
*Empowering Latinas:
    Breaking Boundaries, Freeing Lives*
    (Davidds), 221
Emulation, 43
Engagement, 199–201
Evaluation, defined, 85
Expectations, 189–192
External drivers
    defined, 87, 108
    examples of, 87–88
    *vs.* Internal Drivers, 100, 101

Fach, Ferdinand, 102
Failure, 9, 37
Family, influence of, 21, 41, 42
Fear, defined, 81, 154
Ferrazzi, Keith, 3–4
Field, Sally, 19
Field of Dreams mentality, 188
Flow, 117, 128–130
*Flow: The Psychology of
    Optimal Experience*
    (Csikszentmihalyi), 128
Ford, Henry, 22
Forgetting, stage of, 42–43, 51
Four-step process, 6, 9, 49, 51–53. *See
    also individual step listings*

# Index

Freedom, 20–21, 23, 103, 108
Frost, Robert, 186

Gable, Clark, 142
Garrison, Michael, 172–174
Gasset, Jose Ortega y, 212
Gates, Bill, 17
Gaulle, Charles De, 211
George, Kim (author)
  as an overachiever, 118–119
  on Attachment, 179–180
  as a coach, 2, 10, 83–84
  on death of mother, 39–40, 59–60,
    109, 161–162,
    185–186, 235–236
  The Eden Alternative™,
    involvement in, 66
  on relationship with father, 135–136,
    211–12
  as a VISTA volunteer, 23–24, 33–34,
    175–176
Gibson, Jabbor, 238
*The Gift of Change* (Williamson), 130
Giono, Jean, 36
Giver's gain, 94
Giving, 3, 95
Glascow, Arnold, 139
GoDaddy.com, 111, 112
Goethe, Johann Woflgang von, 169, 188
Graduate School of Coaching, 84
Gratitude, 77–78
Greatfulness, 76–78
Greatness
  arguments against, 32–35
  defined, 5, 29, 30, 41, 108, 122
  external measures of, 19, 23
  in hierarchical terms, 33
  as unique to
    each individual, 33, 78
Green Belt Movement, 36

*Hamlet*, 165
Harris, Marilyn, 109
Hawkins, David, 163
Herrigel, Eugen, 105
High achiever, 116, 117, 118
Hill, Julia "Butterfly," 67–70, 100,
  237–238
Hill, Napoleon, 202

Hillman, James, 31
Hoffer, Eric, 57, 70, 83, 223, 225
Holmes, Oliver Wendell, 176
Hope, Illusion of. *See also* Significance
  conditioned patterns of
    Assumptions, 193–195
    Expectations, 189–192
    Powerlessness, 192–193
  defined, 8–9, 26, 187, 188, 190, 209
  dynamics of, 186–188
  four-step process, applied
    to, 206–208
  living in, stories of, 188–189,
    196–198
  Tipping Point of, 195–196
Houston, Jean, 31
Hubbard, Elbert, 45

Illusion
  defined, 18–19
  negative effects of, 30–31, 32
Impulsiveness, 165
Individualism, myth of, 110
Inquiry, abundance aptitude
  conscious patterns of
    Adventurism, 228–229
    Strategic Thinking, 227–228
    Willingness, 226–227
  defined, 224, 233
  dynamics of, 223–225
  example of, 241
Inquisitiveness, 204–206
Insanity, defined, 233
Insisting, stage of, 43, 51
Inspiration, defined, 67
Intellectualization, 50
Intelligence quotient (IQ), 26
Intention, 153–154
Interdependence, 41–42
Internal Drivers, 99–101
Internalization, 50, 55
Intuition, 100–101

Jong, Erica, 136, 230
Judgment, 165

Keen, Sam, 223
Keillor, Garrison, 111

Kennedy, Dan, 172
Kierkegaard, Sören, 152

Lack, perception/sense of, 60–61, 62, 63, 64, 67
L'Amour, Louis, 52
Langer, Susanne K., 47
Larouche, Lorretta, 64
Law of Reciprocity, 95, 154
Lawrence, D. H., 73
Leonard, Thomas, 84, 97, 122, 229
Leonard's Laws of Attraction, 122
*The Likeability Factor* (Sanders), 101
Lincoln, Abraham, 35
Link, Henry, 65
*The Little Shop of Horrors*, 62
Living into Greatness, defined, 14, 24
Loehr, Jim, 66
Lone Ranger syndrome, 138–139
Long-term gain, defined, 92
*Love is the Killer App* (Sanders), 101

Maathai, Wangari, 36
Macedonio, Michael, 172–174
Maharshi, Sir Ramana, 206
*The Man Who Planted Trees* (Giono), 36
Maslow, Abraham, 174
Mason, John, 48
*Masters of Networking* (Misner), 94
*Masters of Success* (Misner), 94
Materialism, 19
*The Matrix*, 41
Mello, Anthony De, 168
Meyer, Joyce, 98
Miedaner, Talane, 83–84
Misner, Ivan, 11, 94–95, 101, 127, 172
Mitchell, Margaret, 189
More, 62–64, 67, 73, 75
Mother Teresa, 33
Motivation, defined, 67
Muir, John, 20

Need, defined, 168
Neisser, Drew, 228

*Never Eat Alone* (Ferrazzi), 3
*New York Times*, 94
Nightingale, Earl, 17, 57, 90, 202, 227
Nin, Anaïs, 204
Nixon, E. D., 201
Not Enough, Illusion of. *See also* Self-Worth
 conditioned patterns of
  Contingency, 65–66, 67
  more, 62–64, 67, 73, 75
  scriptwriting, 64–65, 73, 76–77
 defined, 7, 60–61
 fears associated with, 61
 four-step process, applied to, 79–81
 living in, stories of, 59–60, 61–62, 67–70
 Tipping Point of, 67
Not how, but *when*, action step, 176

Opportunity cost, 24–26, 28, 121
Opposites, 14–15
Overachieving, 117–119

Parks, Rosa, 238
Parsons, Bob, 111–112
Parsons Technology, 111
Pattern language, 45–47, 48
Paz, Octavio, 164
Perfectionism, 219–220
Perseverance, 180–182
Personalization, 88–90, 102
Personal responsibility, 152–153
Peters, Tom, 243
Philips Electronics, 44
Pink, Daniel, 19, 97
Potential, defined, 31
Powerlessness, 192–193
*The Power of Full Engagement* (Loehr and Schwartz), 66
*The Power of Now* (Tolle), 164, 189
*Prairie Home Companion*, 111
Pretending, stage of, 43, 51
Procrastination, 7
Proctor, Bob, 90, 93, 167, 190
Proust, Marcel, 53

Reacting, defined, 152
Reardon, Richard, 119

# Index

Receiving, 125–127, 192
Referral Institute, 172–174
Renard, Jules, 151
Replicate Simplicity, action step, 124
Resistance, defined, 114–115
Resisting, stage of, 44, 51
Responding, defined, 152
Return on investment (ROI), 195, 209
Rice, Eric, 239–241, 243
Risk Life and Live into Greatness, action step, 225
Role-playing, 142–144, 153, 154
Roman, Sanaya, 152
Ruiz, Don Miguel, 88, 215
Rumi, Jalaluddin, 13
Rushing, 165–167

Saint-Exupery, Antoine, 219, 242
Sanders, Tim, 101
Satin-lined coffin, 4, 5, 9, 14, 17, 83, 139
Saying, Zen, 161
Scarcity
    external, 16, 17
    living in, 1–2, 4, 6, 22
    mentality, 4, 5, 16–18, 21
        effects of, 18, 25, 36–37
        sources of (*See* The Seven Illusions)
    pattern language of, 45, 46, 48
    *vs.* abundance, 16, 19, 20, 21–22, 25
Scarcity quotient (SQ), 45
Schwartz, Tony, 66
Scriptwriting, 64–65, 73, 76–77
Seeking, defined, 112
Self-Defense, 144–145
Self-Empathy, abundance aptitude
    conscious patterns of
        Discernment, 102–103
        Effectiveness, 103–105
        Internal Drivers, 99–101
    defined, 97–99
Self-Expression, abundance aptitude
    conscious patterns of
        Flow, 128–130
        Receiving, 125–127
        Simplicity, 127–128
    defined, 123–124, 134
    example of, 240

Self-help programs, 70–71, 72
Self-Worth, abundance aptitude
    conscious patterns of
        Capacity, 74–76, 77
        Catalyst, 78–79, 81
        Greatfulness, 76–78
    defined, 70–72, 73, 81, 92
    example of, 240
    *vs.* self-help, 72
*The 7 Habits of Highly Effective People* (Covey), 16
The Seven Illusions, 6–9, 18, 37. *See also individual listings*
Shakespeare, William, 165
Shaw, George Bernard, 102
Sheehy, Gail, 142
Shishuang, 233
Short-term reward, defined, 92
Significance, abundance aptitude
    conscious patterns of
        Decisiveness, 201–204
        Engagement, 199–201
        Inquisitiveness, 204–206
    defined, 198–199
    example of, 241
Simplicity, 127–128
Slip 'N Slide®, comparison to life, 17, 50–51, 52, 56
Smalley, Stuart, 187
Smith, Alexander, 217
*The Soul's Code* (Hillman), 31
Spurgeon, Charles, 156
Stein, Gertrude, 93
Stepping Back, 177–179
Stop searching, and start doing, action step, 7
Strategic Thinking, 227–228
Striving, defined, 114
Struggle, Illusion of. *See also* Self-Expression in the business world, 119–120
    conditioned patterns of
        Complexity, 115–117
        Overachieving, 117–119
        Resisting, 114–115
    defined, 8, 110, 119, 122
    four-step process, applied to, 130–133
    living in, stories of, 111–113, 121–123

*(Continued)*

Struggle, Illusion of *(continued)*
  nature of, 110–112, 113, 117
  Tipping Point of, 120–121
Success, 11, 36, 202
Surface dwellers, 17, 32
Surrender, abundance aptitude
  conscious patterns of
    Intention, 153–154
    Personal Responsibility, 152–153
    Vulnerability, 154–156
  defined, 150–151, 159
  example of, 240–241
  living in, story of, 150–151
Suzuki, Shunryu, 227
Sympathy, defined, 98

Tactical Thinking, 217–219, 227
*Tashi deley*, 31
Think positively and *act* accordingly,
  action step, 199
Thomas, Bill, 66
Thriving, defined, 114
Thurber, James, 214
Thurman, Howard, 45
Time, Illusion of. *See also*
  Actualization
  conditioned patterns of
    Attachment, 167–169
    Distractibility, 169–171
    Rushing, 165–167
  defined, 8, 162
  dynamics of, 162–164
  four-step process, applied to, 182–183
  living in, stories of, 164, 172–174
  Tipping Point of, 171–172
*A Timeless Way of Building*
  (Alexander), 45
Tipping Point
  Illusion of Certainty, 220–221

Illusion of Comparisons, 93
Illusion of Control, 146
  defined, 25, 26, 27, 236, 242
Illusion of Hope, 195–196
Illusion of Not Enough, 67
Illusion of Struggle, 120–121
Illusion of Time, 171–172
Tolle, Eckhart, 41, 164, 177, 189
Traubel, Horace, 237
Truth or Dare test, 54, 55
Tzu, Lao, 74
*The Velveteen Rabbit* (Williams and
  Nicholson), 21–22
Vitale, Joe, 196–198
Volunteers in Service to America
  (VISTA), 23, 33, 176
Vulnerability, 154–156, 159

Want, defined, 168
Ward, Don, 72
*The Way to Love* (Mello), 168
Weil, Simone, 167
Wells. H. G., 31
Wheeler, Edith, 72
*A Whole New Mind*
  (Pink), 19, 97
Wie, Michelle, 186, 187, 190
Wilde, Oscar, 15, 41
Will, defined, 118
Williamson,
  Marianne, 37, 126, 130, 192
Willingness, 226–227
Willpower, defined, 118
Worthiness, defined, 73
Wright, Frank Lloyd, 235
Wright, Steven, 63

YES (your extraordinary self), 27, 30
Young, Margaret, 14